NORTH FROM GRANADA

In 1982, two unlikely companions, one an English jack-of-all-trades (the author) and the other an American doctor of psychoanalysis, set off to walk from Granada to Madrid.

Roy Nash's account of the journey is in no way meant to be a guide to other hikers. On the contrary, if anything, it is an indication of how not to go about things.

With out-of-date maps, wrong footwear and no forward planning they ended up in all sorts of trouble, including being arrested at gunpoint for wandering across a minefield into a secret military camp.

This frank and funny book describes their adventures and mis-adventures, their reflections and encounters en route (both real and imaginary) as well as impressions of the places they pass through.

In subsequent years their walks in Spain were better organised, but it is partly the naivety and innocence of this first trek that makes "North from Granada" so entertaining.

Born in London in 1937, **Roy Nash** left school at 16 to join the seven-man crew of a 74-foot yawl which set sail on a seven-year around-the-world scientific expedition. Stranded in Las Palmas, he managed to work his passage back to England aboard a British oil tanker as deckboy. Once ashore, twelve months older but none the wiser, he signed up as a trooper in the Royal Horse Guards. Three miserable years later, at the age of twenty, he discovered there was not much demand for an ex-sailor, ex-soldier skilled in the arts of deckscrubbing, horseriding and high quality spit and polishing, so he turned his hand to whatever paid maximum salary for minimum effort. This included working as a film extra, model, entertainer (singing and guitar), door-to-door salesman and night club bouncer.

In 1966, tired of the 'rat race,' Roy headed south to Spain and managed to buy a house in the little fishing village of La Herradura. Life there proved idyllic, with fine weather, good fishing, cheap living and a steady supply of young lady tourists. His account of these years will appear as *Home in Andalusia* (Oleander, 2003). But despite all this, there was nothing he liked more than to set off, knapsack on back, to explore more remote parts of the country.

Roy now spends most of the year in Sussex with his wife and son, and returns to Spain whenever possible. He has been married three times and has five sons.

NORTH from GRANADA

Roy Nash

The Oleander Press

The Oleander Press
16 Orchard Street
Cambridge CB1 1JT
England

© 2002 Roy Nash and The Oleander Press

ISBN 0-906672-46-5 Hbk
ISBN 0-906672-47-3 Pbk

A CIP catalogue record for this book is available from the British Library.

Typeset in Great Britain and printed and bound in India

CONTENTS

List of Illustrations

Foreword

It is rumoured that if it weren't for dogs an Englishman would never go for a walk. This, of course, is untrue. We are a nation of walkers. The Ramblers Association of Great Britain has 135,000 members and a recent I.C.M. survey revealed that 77% of the population walk for pleasure at least once a month and 62% favour walking as their main source of exercise. Whatever the weather, especially at weekends, groups of woolly-hatted backpackers stride forth to take advantage of the 150,000 miles of footpaths, bridleways and byways rigorously maintained and preserved for their use.

Things are very different in Spain. Although exploring the countryside is now becoming more popular, during our three-week hike from Granada to Madrid in 1982, Bob and I came across no other recreational walker. The majority of Spaniards we met did not walk unless they had to, and today, of the 50 million visitors that arrive each year, only a handful venture far from the coast.

This is a great shame for, as one of the most unspoiled countries in Europe, Spain offers scope for just about any outdoor activity. Its varied geography ranges from near-desert in eastern Andalusia to green countryside in Galicia and from the snow-capped mountains of the Pyrenees and Sierra Nevada to the baking-hot plains of La Mancha.

A hundred years ago, a book was published called *España Agreste*. The opening chapter reads: "Among European countries Spain stands unique in the range of her natural and physical features. In no other land can there be found, within a similar area, such extremes of scene and climate." We found this to be true.

Crossing this southern part of Spain proved more difficult than we had imagined. We found the first week up in the cool mountain region relatively straightforward (apart from becoming lost!), but the sweltering hot, flat meseta we encountered later on completely exhausted us. It was lucky that we had decided on the month of April to attempt this trek, for starting out a few months later might have made it impossible. Those living in the little villages we passed through could not understand why anyone should choose to travel on foot when they had the wherewithal to travel by train or bus, and I frequently overheard the word 'loco' (mad) spoken behind our backs.

"Walking?" they would ask, staring at us with an astonished expression. "Walking to Madrid? But why?"

We did not find it easy to give a satisfying answer and I must admit that at times we, too, questioned our motive for this venture.

Their lack of comprehension led to some awkward moments. The only walkers these people met were goatherds who roamed the hills with their little band of bell-tinkling, farting goats – and then only because it was necessary. So we soon came to realise why the sight of two scruffy, sweaty strangers hobbling into little hamlets must have caused some concern, if not alarm, and understood why, on occasion, we were treated with a certain amount of wariness. The impression we sometimes gave did not help matters either when it came to finding accommodation for the night. Although we did our best to smarten up before entering anywhere, some hostal owners must have had their doubts about our ability to pay. I quickly learned that it was better to demonstrate solvency by presenting a large denomination note at the bar before asking for a room.

Camilo José Cela tells in *Journey to the Alcarria* how his unkempt appearance led to his being turned away from an inn. The woman there looks him up and down and sends him off 'with his tail between his legs'.

Nevertheless, the problems we encountered through not being always welcomed with open arms were more than compensated by the feeling that perhaps, in some places, we were the first foreigners to visit. The absence of tourists was amply demonstrated by the interest aroused at the sight of my red hairy legs. It was clear that local folk were not accustomed to seeing men wearing shorts.

But, although we had our ups and downs – literally as well as emotionally – I would not have missed the adventure for anything.

* * *

A few years ago I walked the 750-kilometre Spanish section of the Pilgrims' Way, from the Pyrenees in the north-east of Spain across to Santiago de Compostela in the north-west – an experience of considerable historical, cultural and religious interest. The chances of going astray were minimal, for I had been given a detailed guide-book. Besides, yellow markers by the side of the trail pointed the way. In fact, I had no need of either, for I could simply follow the pilgrims in front of me. No call for my large, cumbersome maps or my little plastic compass. No grumpy companion. No wondering what I would find over the next hill or whether there would be anywhere to stay when I finally arrived somewhere. And later, in the evenings, when I joined a group of noisy, excited people from all over the world, the beer did not taste nearly as good.

It was never quite the same.

Acknowledgements

I should like to thank the travel writer and editor Philip Ward for the tremendous help and advice he has given me in preparing this book. I am also indebted to my son, Oliver, whose mastery of the computer has been invaluable, my wife, Zenda, who has helped me see this project through from beginning to end, and my good Spanish friend, Dr. Luis Aranda, whose kindness and invaluable suggestions have made my task easier.

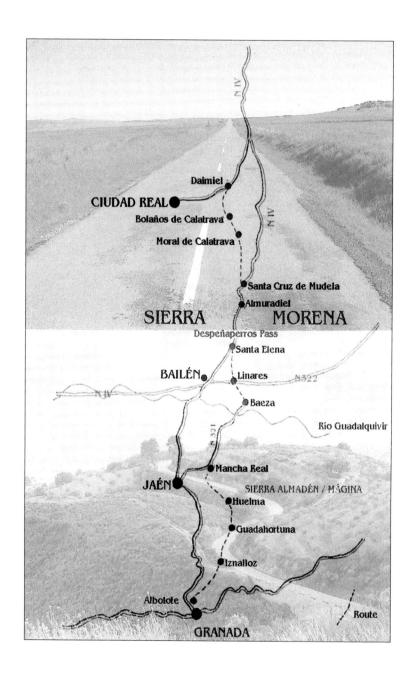

Daimiel

CIUDAD REAL

Bolaños de Calatrava

Moral de Calatrava

Santa Cruz de Mudela

Almuradiel

SIERRA   MORENA

Despeñaperros Pass

Santa Elena

BAILÉN   Linares

N322

Baeza

Rio Guadalquivir

Mancha Real

JAÉN   SIERRA ALMADÉN / MÁGINA

Huelma

Guadahortuna

Iznalloz

Albolote   Route

GRANADA

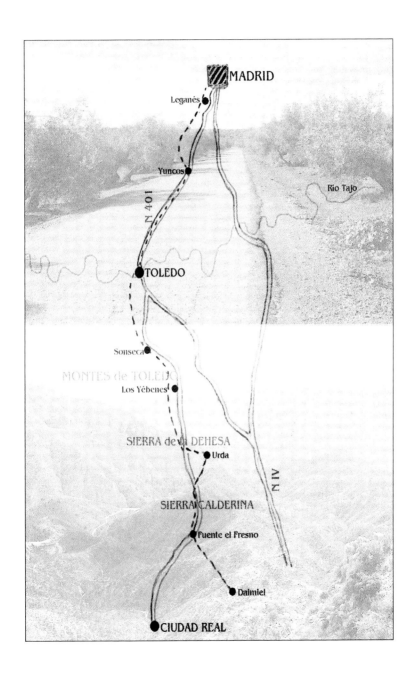

1

I found him looking so forlorn,
A fellow traveller in distress;
With head in hand and shoulders hunched,
Sitting, carpet-slipper-less.

In early June the sun bursts like a flame from behind the sierras to the east of Granada at seven a.m. and by seven-thirty, having first greeted the towering pink watchtowers of the Alhambra, moves its rays slowly along the camino de Ronda.

As it burns away the early morning mist, prompting cats to stretch and dogs to scratch, the warm sunlight arrives at a halfway point where busy bars and restaurants bustle with competitive activity. Some have been open all night with coffee cups at the ready, lined up along the counter with shiny spoons and sugar packets at their side, waiting impatiently. In their midst, like some fat hen guarding her chicks, sits an ugly, grey concrete structure of solid appearance, stretching for some thirty metres. The building stands aloof, confident in the knowledge that without its presence these neighbours would not survive – for this is the mighty bus station.

The large, hangar-like construction behind is full of buses in rows with engines constantly running, filling the air with suffocating diesel fumes. Through the purple haze shapes can be seen hurrying to and fro with handkerchiefs pressed tightly to their faces. Leaving this gas chamber presents no problem. Merely pass through the adjoining room, out again into the welcome fresh air and hurry away to the waiting coffee. Buying a ticket, however, is a different matter. Queues are unheard of in Spain. The room with the chequered floor, known as the reception area, has in it a small, glass-partitioned

Granada – guitar-maker

section, around which a collection of people gather like bees round a honeypot. Questions asked in any language other than pure Andaluz Spanish are totally ignored by the inscrutable officials at the desk, who give a blank stare, accompanied by a shrug of the shoulders, in reply to queries not immediately understood. A clearly written destination, followed by the exact fare slid through the hole in the glass, will sometimes work, but time spent at the counter must be short, for the ominous rumblings from those waiting behind can be unnerving.

On this particular day in June I arrived on the 11.20 a.m. train from Madrid and, as there was plenty of time to kill before my bus was due to leave, made my way across town towards the Alhambra. Leading up to the arched Puerta de las Granadas is a steep, curved street lined with mini-markets, tobacconists, confectioners and, best of all, little studios where guitars are made and sold. Whenever I have the chance, I visit this part of the city and climb the Cuesta de Gomerez to visit these fascinating little workshops. Inside, rows of beautiful hand-made instruments line the walls while craftsmen stand working, leaning over benches laden with tools. Sometimes, if you are lucky, an 'aficionado' or two may be heard trying out an instrument of his choice. The music is nearly always flamenco.

Back down again then, across the Plaza Nueva, and into the narrow calle de Elvira, where, squeezing my way past parked vehicles, I arrive at number twelve to stop for a chat with my antique-dealing friend, José Santiago. Sometimes I manage to find something to buy in his cluttered, chaotic shop that I can sell for a profit back in England. Turning west at the Iglesia del Sagrado Corazón, I cross the Gran Vía de Colón and continue on through the now deserted streets towards the depot, from where a bus will take me to a town called Almuñécar which lies almost seventy kilometres directly south. My eventual destination is La Herradura, a small village eight kilometres along the coast towards Málaga.

Laurie Lee ended up in Almuñécar at the end of his walk through Spain. The Civil War was about to start when he arrived there and, as he did not want to incriminate anyone who may have shown Republican sympathies, in his book *As I Walked Out One Midsummer Morning* he changed the name of the town to El Castillo.

I reached the terminus at around 4 p.m., and had my first encounter with Dr. Robert Smith, my future comrade in pain, suffering and pleasure. At this hour of the day it was siesta time for most. The dry, hot streets were quiet, with few pedestrians and little traffic. Shops would not re-open until later, when the temperature had dropped a little. The bars and restaurants near the bus station were still busy, of course, with many customers still eating 'comida'(lunch). The sun had moved further to the west by now, bringing the bus station's exterior stone benches into shade, while the opposite side of the road now received the full blast of scorching heat. These seats held a colourful assortment of characters, nearly all wearing the customary chequered carpet slippers and smoking the inevitable cigarette. One person, however, stood out from the others. Firstly, he was not smoking or wearing the usual footwear but, more notice-ably, appeared middle-aged and fit.

Now in 1981 this was at once both a distinguishing feature and, at the same time, a contradiction in Southern Spain. Both sexes start to develop middle-age spread in their late twenties or thirties. In the village where I lived a husband is expected to demonstrate his virility by fathering a child within the first year of marriage and, if this does not happen, must expect jibes and leg-pulling from his workmates. Young señoritas with beautiful, graceful teenage figures become señoras at an early age and consequently often mother two or three children before the age of twenty, losing their shape in the process. The responsibility of now being the head of a family soon changes the young man's way of life. Watching football on TV takes over from actively playing the game, and being overfed by mothers, mothers-in-law and new wife soon expands his waistline.

This unslippered, non-smoking, fit-looking person seated there appeared to be waiting for my approach and, as I

Bob at bus station

passed, looked up dejectedly and asked, with an American accent, if I spoke English. When he learned that I not only spoke his language but also Spanish, he brightened and asked if I would help him get to a place called Calahonda. He explained that his efforts had got him nowhere. After a bout of pushing and shoving in the reception area, he had eventually reached the hole in the glass and in his best phrase-book Spanish had pronounced the name Calahonda slowly and distinctly. In reply, he had received the usual poker-faced response, accompanied by a heavy dose of shrugging. Then, having clearly written down his destination, he had again fought his way back to the counter and handed over the piece of paper. It was no good. He had been unable to understand the fare demanded or instructions regarding the bus. Could I please help a desperate man? I left him waiting outside while I, being an old hand at this sort of thing, went inside. I returned a short while later with the tickets, but nursing bruised hip-bones, for although my six foot three inch height and long arms helped, short rotund ladies have sharp elbows. We both needed the same bus, which would be leaving in forty-five minutes, so I suggested that we pass the time by partaking of a glass of something in a nearby bar.

For the next forty-five minutes we sat perched on bar stools enjoying very welcome ice-cold beers. With each swallow Bob, as he wished to be called, became more talkative and told me more about himself. He had flown from Berlin to Madrid, then taken the night train to Granada, intending to continue on to Calahonda. This is when his troubles began. He had been waiting most of the day for some sort of assistance and was beginning to despair. He added that, while working in Germany, he had met someone who owned a property in Calahonda. This man had invited him to visit. Such a happy-go-lucky lifestyle, along with the fine weather, sounded good. Bob's fifteen years in Germany, working as a teacher at various universities, was a thing of the past. He wanted a change and felt ready for anything that came along. Maybe Spain would be the answer. I liked the look of him. For a man of fifty he appeared to be in very good physical condition, and I told him so. We sat chatting and drinking for a while longer, then got up and coughed our way through to the waiting bus.

The red and white bus left on time, as most buses do in Spain, and headed out of Granada, first along the N323 Motril road for ten kilometres, then taking a right turn into the Valle de Lecrín.

It was at this mournful spot, in 1492, that Boabdil is supposed to have paused to take one last look at his beloved Granada. He had finally, after many years of bloody conflict, surrendered the city to the Christians and, as he stood there lamenting and sighing, his mother Fatima remarked, 'You do well, my son, to weep as a woman for the loss of what you could not defend as a man.' A hotel now marks the site of this Moor's Last Sigh ('El Último Suspiro del Moro') and that name provided Salman Rushdie with the title for his celebrated novel.

Whenever I look down this, mainly straight, road which stretches for some thirty-five kilometres, with the forbidding sierras silhouetted against the clear blue sky in the distance, my heart always gives a little jump, bringing an excited feeling to my stomach, for I know that 'my' village is not far away.

The flat landscape ahead is full of colour at this time of the year, with yellow gorse, purple, sweet-smelling lavender dotted here and there and splashes of red poppy all sewn into a background of scarlet earth and light green fields. The sight makes my head whirl. It's the yellow-brick road leading to my Land of Oz, where a wizard is waiting in his emerald castle to perform his magic. At this hour the sun was still high enough to be shining in our eyes and, at the same time, glistening on the snow which capped the Sierra Nevada mountain range behind us. It would soon be beginning its westerly descent, sinking slowly beneath the Sierra de Almijara in front of us and casting a shadow over the stunning landscape. After a while the road started to climb up to the high point near Herrero and from this peak there was a magnificent view down to the blue Mediterranean some fifteen hundred metres below. Sometimes, if the air is clear enough, the Atlas Mountains of Morocco can be seen on the horizon. Whenever I could, I would stop and marvel at the scenery. Up here the vastness and stillness seemed to combine to create a hushed calm that could actually be heard: a 'sound of silence'.

To the east, atop the Sierra Nevada, is Mulhacén which stands at 3,481 metres – the highest location in the mountain range. Gerald Brenan, in *South from Granada*, claims to have climbed up 3000 metres to a site near there in order to spend the night beside a tarn – where legend asserted that a beautiful woman, with an insatiable lust to sleep with men, lies in wait. He lay shivering the night away – alone. From this vantage point he could see the whole coast of Africa from the Strait of Gibraltar to Oran.

Then down, down, ever down the narrow road, flanked on one side by sheer rock and on the other by a precipitous drop into a deep gorge; twisting, turning, tunnelling its helter-skelter way past the burnt-out stubs of trees where annual fires have destroyed the pine forest; down for a thousand metres to eventually arrive at the more fertile, cultivated areas around the villages of Jete and Otívar. The bus has become quieter now. The easy-going banter has stopped and the knuckles of

Road from Granada to Almuñécar

passengers show white as their hands hold tightly on to the seat in front. It is not for the faint-hearted to sit at the front or back of this bus for it has to poke its nose or swing its rear end over the edge of the ravine in order to navigate the tight corners. After a few more bends the road becomes straighter and the descent more gradual while the landscape turns much greener, with the Río Verde watering adjacent fields. This river shrinks to a mere trickle in the summer but in the spring, when snows melt on the Sierra Nevada, it can become a torrent, sweeping over everything in its path. Coastal villages in this region have built high-walled viaducts to channel these raging waters into the sea, but the village of La Rábita, whose defences were not strong enough, suffered a disaster when, after the annual meltdown, these cascading floods swept many houses into the sea.

We are now not far from the coast and pass through the very profitable area growing chirimoya, avocado and mango. These recently introduced tropical fruits fetch a good price on the world market and are rapidly replacing the more traditional olive and almond trees which once used to set the hills alight with their lovely pink and white blossom. Ah, well, that's progress, I suppose.

The temperate weather has led to this stretch of coastline being called 'Costa Tropical' and, unbelievably, a recent development of nearby apartment blocks and houses has been given the name 'Costa Banana'!

When I arrived in these parts in 1966, fields of sugar cane were a common sight but now they have all but disappeared, and a sad-looking processing factory stands derelict in Almuñécar. The Moors introduced sugar cane to this part of Spain in the tenth century along with oranges, lemons, melons, figs and bananas. Pomegranates, too, were brought over from Africa and can still be found growing wild along river beds. The Spanish name for this fruit is 'granada'. At one time it was more popular, providing refreshing liquid to the thirsty traveller. A ripe pomegranate can be rather messy to eat, being full of pips, but I learned from the locals that the best way was to make a small hole in the hard, outer skin, then squeeze and direct the sweet, pink nectar straight into the thirsty mouth. Delicious!

Long before the Moors arrived, the Romans had made use of the plentiful supply of water by building magnificent aqueducts to irrigate their olive groves, vineyards and cornfields. Many of these ancient water-courses are still in use. This whole area is steeped in history and remains virtually unchanged. A recent excavation in Almuñécar unearthed a site which showed that, fifteen hundred years ago, the 'boquerón' fish was salted and soaked in much the same way as it is today. Ghosts of the past cling to the present, with nature itself dictating any changes to be made. But change will come. Already, further along the coast towards Almería, the dreaded plastic has arrived, and instead of green fields, the dazzling glare of shiny plastic assaults the eye. This method of growing is known as 'plasticultura' and crops such as peppers, cucumbers, tomatoes, courgettes, watermelons and even flowers are force-grown this way and shipped in refrigerated containers to many parts of the world. Produce that reaches the market earlier will fetch a better price. This, along with the various chemicals and pesticides being introduced has, in the last twenty years, changed the method of agriculture practised for centuries.

The bus arrived at Almuñécar one and a half hours after leaving Granada, with both driver and passengers needing a short break. Bob and I headed for the nearest bar to make our farewells, but before he went on his way I gave him my address and invited him to visit me in La Herradura if he had a chance.

A week later he knocked at my door. At that time I lived in a little house situated just back from the seashore, in a perfect position. From my flat roof I could check the condition of the sea each morning and make plans. White tops meant no fishing that day, for they warned of rough weather ahead, but on calm days I could usually be found out in my beloved wooden dinghy, trying my luck. It was better to be prudent when putting out to sea. The prevailing wind came from the west and was known as 'poniente'(coming from the point of the setting sun). A 'levante' (rising sun) meant that it blew from the other direction, east. From time to time, red sand wafted across from Africa and this current of air went by the name of 'sirocco'.

On October 19, 1562, a fleet of galleons en route for Málaga, under the command of Don Juan de Mendoza, sought shelter from a fierce 'levante' by anchoring at the eastern side of the bay. Suddenly, the unpredictable, treacherous wind changed direction and the ensuing terrible storm brought about a shipwreck that claimed the lives of between three and four thousand persons. Most of these poor souls were rowers, chained below deck. Many bodies were washed ashore on a nearby beach, which, to this day, is still known as La Playa de los Muertos – Dead Men's Beach. This disaster is mentioned in *Don Quixote* and Cervantes' reference to La Herradura is proudly on display outside the parish church of Don José.

The kilometre-long stretch of stony shoreline has a lot to answer for, for there I met two of my wives, Catherine at one end and Zenda at the other. They must have been 'white tops' days!

Bob stayed for a week. He told me that Calahonda had not suited him but that he had found the Spanish weather and way of life tempting him to think seriously about spending more time in this part of the world. We both agreed that, although nowhere is perfect, this country had plenty to offer.

When I first arrived in 1966, La Herradura or 'The Horseshoe' was one of many small fishing villages dotted along the Mediterranean coastline, but in the 1970s it began to develop into a weekend retreat for Granadinos. Instead of sugar cane, apartment blocks started to sprout up and local fishermen found it more profitable to turn builders. It was sad to see their brightly painted boats, once so meticulously cared for, now left to rot on the beach. Before long, the tide of change swept along the coast, especially near the airport at Málaga where the land was flatter and therefore easier to build on. Hotels, restaurants, banks, estate agents, discos or anything else that would persuade holidaymakers to part with their money, were creeping, like a white fungus, over much of the land near the beaches. Almost overnight, farmers who sold their property became peseta millionaires, while others, a little wiser, became part-owners in some new enterprise. Today, with a new Marina del Este built just over the point, a smarter, richer set is moving in and the atmosphere has changed completely.

The Franco Government welcomed this new source of revenue from tourism and did all it could to encourage investment. Planning permission could easily be obtained, which resulted in ugly, cheaply-built blocks of flats and estates of small houses popping up everywhere, with everything selling quickly to eager Northern Europeans who wanted to own their little place in the sun. Who could blame them?

I suppose that I was one of these escapists myself although, fortunately for me, La Herradura was situated in the province of Granada. This was a more mountainous area which had not been exploited in the same way as the adjacent province of Málaga, where places like Torremolinos, Marbella, Fuengirola and Torre del Mar had already changed the landscape beyond recognition. The Mediterranean coastline became a new Yukon of the gold rush days, with investors flocking down from all parts of the world to seek, and often find, their fortunes.

The problem, as I saw it, was that this explosion of change brought prosperity to some but misery to others. With the large influx of foreigners came a new life-style for which the local people were totally unprepared. Stringent rules had previously been applied by the church when it came to safeguarding peoples' morals. For example, boxing matches were not shown on newsreels because it meant displaying too much of the male body and if a 'still' of the event was published in the newspaper the following day, a vest had to be added to the boxer by a 'retocador' (retoucher). These artists were also ordered to use their skill to diminish the size of women's breasts if the censoring authorities thought them to be too large. Any sort of sexual titillation was frowned upon. When I first came to these parts bikinis could not be worn on the beach and too short 'shorts' were outlawed. Taking a chance with the customs, I would sometimes smuggle a copy of *Playboy* into the country as a present for my Spanish friends. I could have offered no better gift.

However, with the arrival of the 'swinging '60s', things started to change. This era, which had been blossoming in Northern Europe for quite some time, spread rapidly south to Spain like a plague, causing much heartbreak. The modern all-night discos with pop-music and bright lights before long seduced the local young men and women into joining the 'hippie', fun-loving set now living in their midst and, in order not to appear 'old fashioned', they fell into this new mode of behaviour themselves. It did not take much encouragement for them to join in the common practice of 'sleeping around'. The newly-introduced birth pill was unavailable in Catholic Spain and so unwanted pregnancies with – later – unmarried motherhood, started to shock local communities.

The state of affairs stunned the families of these unfortunate girls for the strict, traditional customs of the older generation, who had been used to very little contact between the sexes, had suddenly been abandoned.

However, where I lived this was not the case. La Herradura was a very small village and distant enough from the airport at Málaga to escape the exploitation suffered by the places farther west. Only about a dozen or so foreigners lived nearby at that time and everyone knew each other's business. There were eyes everywhere and not too many secrets. I had been warned by a good Spanish friend that to offer to date a local village girl appeared tantamount to a proposal. Shotguns would be reached for and loaded. If a girl were to associate with a foreigner and be persuaded to enter his house, everyone would think the worst. She would become a tainted woman with no hope of finding a local lad to marry her. The village population consisted mainly of two large families; to upset one meant falling out with the relatives. Any wrongdoing would make future life in the neighbourhood most unpleasant, if not downright dangerous. I therefore took no chances, although I felt tempted, for some of the young señoritas were stunningly beautiful. However, enough young ladies of other nationalities passed through to keep me satisfied. In fact, I had it made. Here was I, a fine, fit fellow who knew his way around, spoke the language and owned his own house. What girl could resist me? It was my modesty that they found most endearing!

At the end of the '60s and into the '70s the number of foreigners increased dramatically with the sudden appearance of a multitude of young Americans who set up residence in the region, all professing a sudden urge to learn the Spanish language or research the country's history and culture. A war in Vietnam had led to men of a certain age being drafted into the American armed forces and sent to fight in a struggle to combat communism, which was said to be spreading throughout South East Asia. Those who escaped this call-up were sons of well-heeled parents who thought it safer to send their heirs out of America for the war's duration. Quite a few, it seems, came to Spain, where living was inexpensive. American citizens, at that time, had no problem living in Spain for Franco had received plenty of financial help from the United States after the crippling result of the Spanish Civil War. This assistance had helped kick-start his ailing economy and in return (for there was a motive to the generosity) he later allowed nuclear bases to be installed.

I used to wind these young Americans up. "Draft dodging?" I would ask.

"No man, you got me wrong!" they would reply, defiantly. "I'm here to study."

In the mid '70s, however, at the end of the Vietnam War, they quickly disappeared.

This colourful gang of long-haired hippies, with their faded blue jeans, coloured shirts and guitars, moved into and around my little village. Many took to 'crafting', that is making leather sandals, beaded bags or studded belts, ostensibly to sell. This did not happen very often, though, as they considered their handiwork to be worth more than most were willing to pay. They sold amongst themselves, however, in order to justify their labour. One original crafter made glasses from old bottles. He would pour oil up to a certain required level in the bottle, then plunge a red hot poker inside, causing the glass to crack off the top. The rim of the newly-formed glass would then be smoothed with wire wool and sand. The result was satisfying and the glasses, some made from Coca Cola bottles, others from anis containers with their pimpled sides, and the most common, brown or green wine bottles, kept in constant demand. 'Specials' or glasses made from the bottle of your choice, like the square whisky shape, for example, posed no problem.

The image these Americans liked to create was that of an impoverished 'beach bum', but every so often they would weaken and suddenly, from somewhere, find the money to buy something like a motor bike!

A steady supply of young, pretty girls with good complexions, perfect teeth and long legs, arrived at intervals to visit their brothers and I became involved with quite a few of them. These young women amused me with their use of the word 'neat'. It was used for any occasion. I remember the fabulous Alhambra, in Granada, which must have had every adjective possible used to describe its beauty, was considered 'neat'. Another time, after sharing a siesta and a passionate love-making session with one of these little beauties, I remember the episode being summed up by her as being 'neat'.

Nevertheless, in the 1980s it suited my tastes perfectly. Weather permitting, I would fish for sea bream or sometimes grey mullet, while if the winds blew up I went exploring back into the hills. Bob was not much of a sailor but he, too, liked hiking and proved a good walker. We spent many pleasant hours rambling together in the hot sunshine, developing a thirst which we quenched later in a nearby place of refreshment. Bars, however, are dangerous places to enter when thirsty, especially with tasty tapas served with each drink. After each round our future plans became more grandiose.

Which of us originated the idea of walking to Madrid I cannot recall, but the subject arose and set us both thinking.

"Why," I declared, quoting Don Quixote, "there are opportunities, brother Sancho, of putting our hands into what are called adventures up to our elbows."

We took a map of Spain and drew a straight line from my village to Madrid and, since it was a small map, the line did not look too long. The distance we calculated to be about five hundred kilometres, so for two fine, fit fellows like ourselves, full of confidence, we reckoned that by travelling at five kilometres an hour for eight hours a day, the journey would take us about two weeks. I had read somewhere that Roman legionnaires could march forty kilometres a day wearing armour and helmet, carrying sword, dagger, lance, shield, plus thirty kilos of equipment, while shod in nothing but leather sandals. Why, with a light rucksack on our back and proper shoes, that distance would prove no problem. Only that day we had been to Almuñécar and back, covering

16 kilometres: a mere stroll. The fact that the Romans were the masters at building dead straight roads and fording every river in sight was not taken into account. We shook hands on the whole project and ordered another beer. We had been in the bar for quite a while and were in the sort of state where anything seemed possible.

And the idea did not go away. Bob returned to Berlin while I stayed put. We kept in touch and planned to meet the next year in the spring, when the weather would not be too hot and the delights of the countryside would be at their best.

We met in Paris the following year and travelled south together, arriving back at my house in the third week of April. There, we tried to decide on the sort of equipment we needed to take with us. I had not much to choose from for my possessions were few. An easy-going, carefree existence was all I had ever wanted and I had tried to adopt the philosophy that 'a rich man is he who needs little, while a man who needs much will forever be poor'. Living in a good climate certainly made it easier to adopt the simple life. For one thing, unlike in Northern Europe, heating proved no problem. Keeping cool seemed more essential. Typical village houses were built with small, shuttered windows designed to stop the heat from entering. Most places, though, had fireplaces for in the winter after sunset, temperatures dropped and we lit fires. It was traditional to wait until the flames had died down and then put a kind of iron trivet into the glowing embers and, atop this contrivance, place a large frying-pan half filled with freshly pressed olive oil. After a while, chorizo, bright green and red peppers, juicy onions and garlic and whatever else lay at hand would be cut into pieces and tossed into this bubbling liquid. With the cooking came mouth-watering aromas, which led to a large glass of the mountain wine, the vino terreno, being drunk to assuage the growing appetite. Soon, with fork in one hand and a large slice of bread in the other, the forking and 'dunking' would begin. And no dishes to wash afterwards.

Fresh food from the local market cost little. Sometimes, when conditions were right, and my catch good, the local restaurant would take my surplus fish and offer me free meals in exchange. Yes, as the song goes, living was easy and I had no complaints. Perhaps it had become too easy. Bob reckoned that a man occasionally needs a challenge. This trek north would be ours.

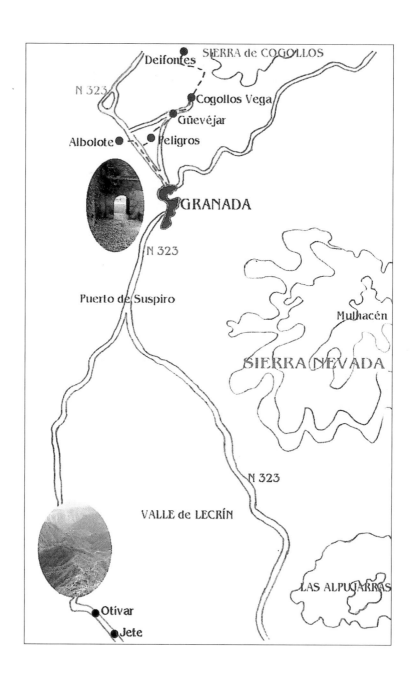

SIERRA de COGOLLOS

Deifontes

N 323

Cogollos Vega

Güevéjar

Albolote

Peligros

GRANADA

N 323

Puerto de Suspiro

Mulhacén

SIERRA NEVADA

N 323

VALLE de LECRÍN

LAS ALPUJARRAS

Otívar

Jete

2

Oh, to go a-wandering,
With a knapsack on my back

We set off on Saturday, April 24.

My small back-pack held a shirt, a spare pair of socks and underpants, trousers, my old seaman's sweater and a book (Thomas Hardy's *Tess of the D'Urbervilles*). I also included, along with a leather pouch containing my toilet gear, a small plastic compass and six large military maps. In *Gatherings from Spain*, under 'Hints to Travellers', Richard Ford writes, 'The chief object will be to combine in as small a space as possible the greatest quantity of portable comfort, taking care to select the really essential; for there is no worse mistake than lumbering oneself with things that are never wanted'. Although his recommendations were meant for horse-riders, I knew his advice made sense for hikers too.

The maps were on a scale of 1:200,000, published in 1971. It needed all six to cover the area from the Mediterranean to Madrid but we discovered later that, although full of detail, we could not rely upon them. I spoke to an ex-soldier from my village who had served his time as a conscript in the chart-making division of the army and he informed me that, instead of walking the tracks shown, he would simply ask in the nearest bar if they still existed. If the majority there thought that they did, then he would simply include them on his map. No walking for him. Unfortunately, these small 'caminos' or 'carriles' are rapidly being ploughed and planted out of existence. Mules are being replaced by Land Rovers and new roads are criss-crossing Spain to accommodate the growing number of vehicles. Walking and riding are becoming a thing of the past, and the same is true of footpaths.

Asking – if anyone could be found to ask – was often the only way, but we reckoned that if the sun was on our backs we should be heading in roughly the right direction: north.

Bob's equipment proved slightly more sophisticated than mine. He had a smart-looking rucksack with a contraption built into its frame which could be cleverly unfolded to make a seat. He never used it. This carrier held clothing similar to mine but, to my astonishment, he had included five thick, heavy books relating to philosophy or analysis. However, he had also wisely included a change of footwear to supplement his old trainers. My wisdom failed in this department, for I had only a pair of 'cowboy-style' boots which zipped up at the sides and had thin soles made of a sort of sponge rubber known as crêpe and, as the terrain was rough and stony in places, my poor feet really suffered.

Gerald Brenan, a practised walker who lived in the Alpujarras for periods between 1920 and 1934, carried his belongings in an 'alforja' – a type of saddle-bag – slung loosely over his shoulder, maintaining that it prevented the

Alforja – a type of saddle bag

sweat problem caused by a container worn on the back. I fancied it must have been cut from the magic carpet for he once reckoned to have covered a distance of sixty miles in one day by walking from Granada to his house in Yegen. Phew! Penelope Chetwode, wife of Sir John Betjeman, also crammed her belongings into 'alforjas' when she journeyed on horseback among the sierras to the north of Granada. In *Two Middle-Aged Ladies in Andalucia* she describes hers as very smart with beautiful embroidery.

We should have preferred to walk to Madrid by starting out from the coast but, as the stretch from Almuñécar to Granada, with nowhere to stay en route, amounted to seventy steep kilometres, we decided that even Roman legionnaires, without their equipment, would have found that a struggle. We opted, instead, to walk to Almuñécar, take the bus from there to Granada, and stay the night somewhere nearby.

So ten dreary kilometres north from our old friend the bus station, on past the bull-ring and prison, we arrived at our first stop: Albolote. This busy little town is now an industrial suburb of Granada. The Moors gave it the name 'Albulut' due to the profusion of oak trees growing there in those far-off days. In this part of Spain the Moors held out against the Christians until the end of the 15th century and Boabdil is well remembered. In many parts of Granada, bars and restaurants bear his name, especially in the vicinity of the Alhambra, while in Albolote there is a street called 'Boabdil el Chico' and a bar is named after him, next door to the animal clinic 'Beethoven'.

Moving on to more recent times, an event took place in the mid-nineteenth century which woke up this then sleepy town. In the summer of 1854 the local inhabitants were surprised to hear that the large, white house in the Plaza Real, the Casa Blanca, had been sold to strangers from Málaga. They looked even more startled when decorators started work and expensive furniture was carried inside. Later, when the place was ready, liveried carriages drew up in front and two gypsy-like characters, accompanied by a retinue of servants, took possession. The woman, named Catalina, with her man-friend or husband (the truth has never been established), dressed in the latest fashion and wore fine jewellery. They later discovered that she was indeed a Romany who, in her youth, had worked in a circus. She had married a dock worker, Pedro Durán, who had died soon after the marriage, and then she had taken up with this man of the moment, Manuel López, another Romany, a jack-of-all-trades and master (so reputation has it) of shoe-making, with the occasional bout of banditry thrown in for good measure. Speculation ran high. Where did their never-ending supply of money come from?

The truth of the matter is that the fountain of wealth came via their pretty daughter Pepita, who had met a rich foreigner, an Englishman named Lionel Sackville-West, who had seen her dancing in Paris. They had met in 1852. He was a diplomat, an aristocrat who had fallen head-over-heels in love with her at first sight. They became lovers and lived together, from time to time, for the next twenty years, with Pepita bearing him five children. The second of these became the mother of the novelist and poet Victoria Sackville-West. This relationship was not uncommon in Spain at that time: it was quite normal for a man of means to keep a mistress.

When Pepita eventually came to Albolote in 1855 to visit her already installed parents, the whole town enjoyed spectacles never before seen: parties nearly every night with wine flowing and delicious food constantly at hand. The whole town was invited to these events and the locals were full of admiration for this Estrella de Andalucía, this 'Star of Andalusia', her stage name. In fact, everyone was completely bowled over by these newcomers, who were treated like royalty and seemed to consider themselves as such. They even had their own plush, red armchairs carried into church when they attended mass. The constant flow of funds from Pepita to her parents permitted them to completely indulge themselves in Albolote, where they could do no wrong. It did not last, however, and after a few years Pepita and her entourage moved to a new, bigger house with more land. This new abode, the Buena Vista, lay on the Jaén road some kilometres from Granada. The sumptuous furnishings were transferred from the Casa Blanca, no longer enjoying days of glory, and the house soon stood naked in the Plaza Real, before being eventually pulled down.

We arrived at Albolote at dusk, so we booked into the first place we came to, which turned out to be an hostal used by lorry drivers. The small, airless rooms were very basic and cheap, having no windows or hot water. It was noisy and, being a light sleeper, I tossed and turned that night. Or maybe my aching feet caused my discomfort for, before going down to the restaurant to eat, I had removed my boots and socks only to find my soles covered with large, white blisters. Bob's feet were in a similar state. Here we are, we joked, two fine fellows of legionnaire mettle crippled after a few kilometres with only another four hundred and ninety to go!

Perhaps, I pondered, we should have again taken heed of Richard Ford. He wrote, "No one should ever dream of making a pedestrian tour in Spain", and "Walking is the manner by which beasts travel … No Spaniard ever walks for pleasure, and none ever perform a journey on foot except trampers and beggars." Although this was written one hundred and fifty years ago, we learned that many people's opinion of walkers in this country had not changed. This was understandable, for, in many areas, those that had no car or mule had no option but to travel on foot. A Spanish friend of mine put it this way: "Walking," he said, "is a pleasure only when you can afford to ride if you prefer."

23

3

With aching legs and sunburned nose,
Cowboy boots and blistered toes …

Lying in my hard, too-short bed the next morning, I slowly and carefully bent my toes forward and felt the blisters crinkle. Ouch! After dressing and gingerly pulling on and zipping up my cowboy boots I shuffled down the stairs, holding tightly on to the rail. Bob, who joined me after a while, was walking as though trying hard not to break a carpet of eggs underfoot. We munched our way through 'desayuno' (breakfast) of tostada and drank our coffee without speaking. We were thinking of those hundreds of kilometres to come and the tough day ahead. After paying our bill and retrieving Bob's American passport from the desk, we shouldered our packs and, stepping carefully, set off.

The footpath shown on our military map strayed off a little to the right of the straight line we had drawn. It passed through two villages that each, so we had been led to believe, had somewhere to stay. These were Güevéjar and Cogollos Vega – about ten and fifteen kilometres away respectively, and either one of those would do for today, we thought, considering the state of our feet. It was 8 a.m. and the sun was rising, gradually changing the sky from dark purple behind Granada to a greenish shade of blue in the north. The heavy lorries which had been parked outside had nearly all rumbled on their way but the sound of traffic on the nearby N323 could be heard thundering along. Standing on the steps outside our hostal, we looked again towards the enticing, craggy outline of the Sierra de Cogollos and could not wait to get up there to escape all this noise and pollution. We took our final deep breath of foul air and hobbled off. Dodging the speeding motorists, we crossed over to the other side of the highway and followed a small, new-looking road for a few kilometres as far as Peligros where a cluster of ugly, recently-built houses stood. A plump woman, holding two fat children by the hand, had been watching our painful progress with interest. She started to look quite worried as we approached, but stood her ground.

"If you please, señora," I asked her, "Could you indicate the small road that leads to Güevéjar?"

"For Güevéjar" she replied, staring down at my hairy legs sticking out from my shorts, "you must take the Jaén bus and change at El Chaparral."

"No", I said. "We don't want the bus. We are walking."

"Walking to Güevéjar?" She stood open-mouthed. It must have been seven kilometres.

The two small children had been eyeing Bob closely. He had been performing what appeared to be a sort of dance by hopping from one foot to the other in an effort to relieve the pressure on his blisters. One child, thinking perhaps that it was some kind of flamenco step, joined in this spectacle by doing a sort of skip, while raising his chubby arms above his head and crying "Olé!" in a squeaky voice. The other little darling bided his time then suddenly kicked out at Bob, who glared and moved farther away. The woman said that she had never heard of such a path and sounded as though she never wanted to. She waddled hurriedly off, dragging her children behind.

By following the edge of the nearby field we eventually found a rough track leading north and stumbled along it doing our best to avoid the sharper stones underfoot. A few neglected olive trees stood here and there like wind-swept scarecrows and it looked as though the overgrown, untidy fields were about to be used for building. After two hours of clambering up this rocky road we arrived at the village of Güevéjar only to discover that there was nowhere to stay. We experienced the short-lived pleasure of taking the weight off our poor feet in a nearby bar, soothed our

Cogollos Vega

parched throats with a couple of beers and then reluctantly set off again for the next place, Cogollos Vega, where we had been assured that we could certainly find a fonda. For those long five kilometres our feet shrieked protest at every step. We stopped at the first bar we came to and ordered two more drinks. The last ones had sweated out of us.

"If you please, where is the fonda?" I asked the barman.

"Fonda? There is no fonda here," he replied as he watched our faces fall along with our shoulders. "Go on past the Institute, to Deifontes," he continued. "It is only twelve kilometres, but the road is not too good. What car have you?"

I explained that we were on foot. No car. He looked at us both in astonishment for a moment, then walked away.

If we had not been so concerned with the effort of placing one foot in front of the other during this next twelve-kilometre stretch, we might perhaps have taken more notice of its beauty. The views were spectacular with the Sierra Harana on our right, the river Cubillas on the left and the smoky blue haze above Granada down behind us. In fact, although our feet did hurt it was impossible not to be aware of the landscape. As I looked about me, I wondered if this might have been where Washington Irving stood as he made his final exit from Granada in 1829. He writes in *Tales of the Alhambra*, "at some little distance to the north of Granada, the road gradually ascends the hills". The main highway to Madrid, passing through Jaén, wends its way through the sierras rather than over them and does not offer much of a view down to Granada. Irving goes on to say: "Towards sunset I came to where the road wound into the mountains and here I paused to take a last look at Granada. The hill on which I stood commanded a view of the city, the vega and the surrounding mountains. It was at an opposite point of the compass from 'La cuesta de las lágrimas' (the hill of tears)". This related to the incline south of the city where Boabdil sighed his famous sigh.

The sun was well up by now and, to add to my troubles, began to burn the backs of my legs, especially in the crease where the knee bends. Bob wore long trousers so did not experience my problem but he felt sore from the rubbing of his books on his sweat-soaked back (we were beginning to think that Gerald Brenan was right about shoulder bags) and kept stopping to move them around in his pack, trying to cushion the edges with some article of clothing. We knew that we should have to be careful with the sun beating down on our exposed skin. I had my spare shirt draped over my shoulders while Bob, using his other shirt for the book padding, had to make do with a sock around his neck. Luckily, it was clean. We determined to buy hats as soon as possible.

We struggled onwards and upwards, past the Institute, a large, modern-looking building that, we learned, can accommodate and teach five hundred pupils at a time up to university level. It was, by now, siesta time for most sensible folk and getting hotter by the minute. The road had been warming up, too, which did not help the state of our blisters but, after passing the Institute, we turned off onto a small track which, according to the map, led to Deifontes. It took us another three hours' hard walking to cover the twelve kilometres, and we felt quite disappointed at not keeping up with the legionnaires' marching rate. We put this down to their wearing sandals, preventing the problem of hot, sweaty feet. With tight cowboy boots and thick socks, my skin kept soft. By now, it felt as though I had blisters on my blisters and Bob, in his trainers, was faring little better.

I had been told of a variety of wildlife up here in these Sierras, including eagles and vultures, but as our eyes were directed downwards most of the time, trying to avoid treading on any protruding rocks, we had to give bird-watching a miss. The town appeared suddenly just over the brow of a hill and, once there, we limped into the nearest bar, took off our packs and slumped into seats. I winced as the hard, cold surface came into contact with my hot, sunburned legs. The bar was empty but we did not care. It felt good to be out of the sun and sitting. After a while a pretty young girl came over and asked if she could help. She had been eyeing us with a certain amount of caution and, as I had come to expect by now, seemed particularly interested in my shorts. Could she be trying to suppress a smile? We were both very thirsty and desperately needed something to soothe our sore, dry throats.

In a dry, croaking voice I asked for two beers and, as I watched the delectable amber liquid filling the glass, reflected on how the taste of a drink can vary according to when and where it is supped. On a cold day in England, for example, there is nothing better than to sit around a log fire with a not-too-cold beer. The drink needs to be served at room temperature, or thereabouts. Lagers, on the other hand, should be kept cold, but are regarded by the old tipplers as being a foreign, non-traditional, yuppie drink. It was Washington Irving who said, "they who drink beer will think beer." On our way to Madrid, we certainly did both.

One place where I really appreciated a cold beer was in Australia. I was lured there by an Australian girl I had met in

La Herradura. (Yes, the same beach!) The Commonwealth Employment Bureau, a government department that found work for 'New Australians', as they dubbed us, had sent me, along with five others – two Frenchmen, a German, a Pole and another Englishman, from Liverpool – to a wheat testing station in New South Wales, which went by the name of Narrabri. No self-respecting Australian would wish to work in this hot, dusty, fly-ridden area where they used the scarce water only for drinking. Once a week we were all picked up by Land Rover and driven to the nearest town, fifty miles distant, where after six sweltering days in the hot sun, they let us loose at the local bar. The feel of that first ice-cold beer sliding down my throat I leave to your imagination.

At the end of the wheat testing season we all put our hard-earned money together, bought an old Volkswagen camper and went in search of our fortunes by opal digging in a place called Goober Peady. The result was that we returned to Sydney with nothing. We had been forced to sell the camper to cover the cost of our train tickets.

When our beers arrived I held mine in my hot, sweaty hands for a moment or two just to feel its coldness. Bob, I noticed, had foregone this pleasure for his empty glass was almost immediately back on the table. When the girl returned with replacement drinks I asked her where we could find the hostal in town. She hesitated for a moment and then replied that she did not know but would ask her mother, who came over to our table a few moments later looking as though she had just been roused from a siesta. She told us, sleepy-eyed, that the hostal had recently closed down. There was nowhere to stay in Deifontes.

We said nothing, but just sat there quietly. What the woman read in our faces at that moment I shall never know, but she hurried away to the kitchen, where it sounded as though she was having an argument with the pots and pans. I felt angry and probably looked it, perhaps even menacing. Bob was staring vacantly at his glass.

"What do you think?" I asked him quietly. He did not answer.

"This is the second time we've been let down," I said despondently. "Can we really carry on like this? They don't know what's happening in the next place a few kilometres down the road. How can we find out if there's anywhere to stay? It's not the walking. We can take that. It's not knowing what we will find when we arrive. Besides," I added, "my toot-sies are killing me."

"So are mine," replied Bob. He thought for a while without speaking. "Look at it this way, Roy. We knew it was not going to be easy. If we'd wanted a trip where we could plan ahead we could have chosen a recognised trail with guide-books detailing the route, the scenery, the hotels and everything else, but we didn't want that, did we? It was the unknown that attracted us, wasn't it? The uncertainty was the challenge."

He looked in my direction and managed a half-smile. "Where's your sense of adventure?" "Ask my feet," I answered.

The good woman returned with a sizzling plate of hot, spicy chorizo and some bread. She must have thought that we needed it, for we had not asked for anything. After washing the delicious food down with some more beer we began to feel a little better. We paid, thanked our hosts who bade us, "Go with God," and ventured outside again. At 6 p.m. it felt a shade cooler.

At the far end of Deifontes we joined a small road which ran by the side of the río Cubillas and there saw a sign that read: 'Iznalloz – 8 kms'. We followed the way it was pointing for another half an hour and then stood, open-mouthed, looking at another pointer that told us that Iznalloz was 9 kilometres away. After a prolonged bout of swearing from Bob, we continued on for another three hours.

I now felt pretty peeved, too. On the way I said to Bob, "If we are let down again, the adventure, or challenge or whatever you want to call it, must be seriously reviewed." He said nothing. There was a limit to his optimistic reasoning.

Iznalloz

To our relief, we learned about somewhere to stay at Iznalloz. A small bar called Los Arcos had rooms above. Following instructions, we passed through the town, down a curving hill, over a bridge and saw the place on our left. We collapsed through the swing doors at 10 p.m. A few domino players sat at a table and some drinkers lined up at the bar counter. As we entered they all stopped what they were doing and looked curiously in our direction. They had not seen or heard a vehicle pull up outside and were intrigued to observe two red-faced, sweaty cripples of foreign appearance enter as if from nowhere. The man behind the bar counter looked at us questioningly by simply raising his eyebrows.

"Two beers," I ordered.

"Where are you from?" he asked, while pouring.

Everyone in the bar waited breathlessly for an answer. If I had said that we had just landed from outer space I don't think any of them would have been more surprised than to hear me say,

"We have just walked from Albolote."

There might have been just a hint of pride in my voice. It all fell very quiet – which was most unusual for a Spanish bar.

"Why?" asked a short, unshaven individual on my right. He was looking up at me with a wrinkled brow. I was not expecting this response to my boast and stiffened slightly. Bob's attention was focused more upon the glass of forthcoming beer than on anything else, but he could sense the suspense all around us.

"What does Shorty want?" he asked me.

"He wants to know why we have walked from Albolote," I said, quietly. Bob sipped his beer and looked pensive. They were all waiting for some logical explanation. The little man spoke again.

"You could have taken the Jaén bus that stops not four kilometres from here and just walked the four," he said.

"Yes," I declared. "I know that but you see...." The clientele were standing stock still, as if someone had waved a magic wand and turned them all into statues. "You see ... Well, we are sporty!"

Everyone appeared very happy at this triumphant explanation.

"Aha!" they cried. "Of course, sporty foreigners!" and went back to their talking, drinking and dominoes. The room was instantly very noisy. Everything had returned to normal.

"What did you tell them?" asked Bob. "It seems to have done the trick."

"I said that we had walked the forty-odd kilometres because we are sporty," I explained.

"Oh, did you?" exclaimed Bob. "Now spell it out for me, will you? I need more reason than that. Baseball is sporty enough for me."

Up in my room, I looked longingly at the bed, but knew that to lie down now would be fatal and would probably result in my not stirring again until morning. Somehow, with much willpower, I collected Bob and we returned to the bar for something to eat. It was a near silent meal for we felt too exhausted to talk much. Afterwards, we dragged ourselves back upstairs and finally lay down to rest our weary bodies. No reading that night for me.

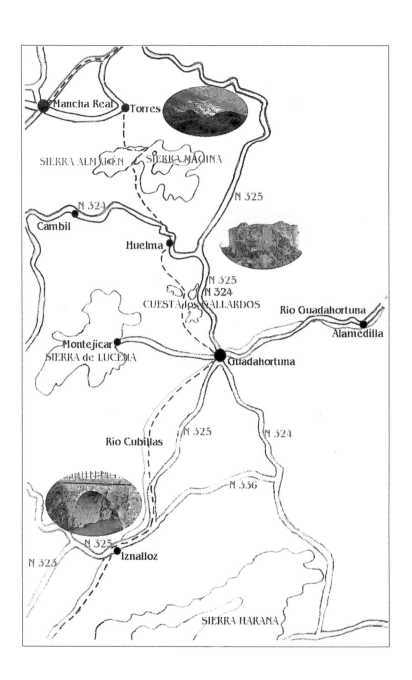

Mancha Real
Torres
SIERRA ALMADEN
SIERRA MÁGINA
N 325
N 324
Cambil
Huelma
N 325
N 324
CUESTA los GALLARDOS
Río Guadahortuna
Alamedilla
Montejicar
SIERRA de LUCENA
Guadahortuna
Río Cubillas
N 325
N 324
N 336
N 325
N 325
Iznalloz
SIERRA HARANA

4

We travelled along,
But not for long,
Side by side.

I awoke feeling stiff in all my joints and gingerly tested various parts of my body. The blisters still hurt but I expected that. I felt them and they seemed to have hardened a little but the sunburn on the backs of my legs felt sensitive to the touch. In a strange, masochistic way it distracted attention away from my sore feet. Two pains must be better than one, I thought, for discomfort divides and thus, dilutes. The test would come when I pulled on the tight boots and tried walking. I had another hour to go before the pre-arranged meeting with Bob in the bar downstairs so I lay back on the bed and contemplated another potential problem.

For the past three weeks tension had been mounting between Argentina and Britain concerning the ownership of a group of islands which lay 300 miles to the east of the Argentinian coast, known as the Falkland Islands to the British and Las Malvinas to the Spanish. The Argentinians had been claiming sovereignty over them since the early 19th century and, as the matter had not been solved diplomatically, they had recently launched a military invasion by putting 10,000 troops ashore. They had overcome a small British garrison of marines stationed there and seized possession. This act had very much upset us British and led our Prime Minister, Margaret Thatcher, to issue threats to Lt. General Leopoldo Galtieri, the Argentine President, ordering him to remove his soldiers at once – or else! She had then held a referendum, which showed that most Falkland Islanders wanted to remain British subjects. This did not

35

impress the General who took no notice of our lady or the wishes of the islanders. On the day that we arrived at Iznalloz a task force had set sail from England to retake the islands, while Mrs. Thatcher declared a war zone of 200 miles around the Falklands. This was considered to be a declaration of war.

Spanish sympathies lay entirely with the Argentinians, for many had relatives who had fled there during the Civil War. They almost considered Argentina part of Spain. The Spanish media made the British out to be the bully boys of the piece and reckoned that their Argentinian comrades had merely recovered what was rightly theirs. The British had better watch their step or Gibraltar would be next in line to be occupied. This small, rocky peninsula had always been a thorn in their side. The Spanish thought it belonged to Spain and wanted it back.

Whatever the politics, I was here in Spain at a time when to be British was bad news. For the whole of our trip we showed only Bob's American passport. It would have made things much more difficult, especially when it came to finding accommodation, if I had declared my nationality, especially when, on May 2, a British submarine sank an Argentinian warship, the *General Belgrano*.

In the bar some of the characters we had seen the night before were coughing and spluttering on their cigarettes while drinking coffee and brandy. A little alcohol and a dose of nicotine seemed necessary before they could start the day. Once again, we immediately became the centre of attraction. Our short, shrivelled friend explained to his wide-eyed neighbour that we were sporty people from America. His companion was listening but, as he watched us limp painfully to the door, must have had his doubts about our 'sportiness'. It seemed likely that the bar-owner had been showing off Bob's passport, for we passed out through the swing doors to the cry of "Buen viaje, americanos!"

Outside, the sun was just beginning to show itself over the Sierra Harana and the birds, which had spent the night quietly roosting in the riverside trees and bushes, suddenly, as if being switched on like a musical box, started to sing their little hearts out. We saw not a cloud in the sky and it looked like being another hot day. The television weather forecast had predicted such the night before: we tried to take note every evening.

I remembered an occasion once when a visitor staying with me asked some local fishermen, sitting crouched on the beach mending their nets, what they thought the weather was going to be like that day. One of them glanced up and said that before long the wind would come from the west, bringing cloud. My friend joined me later in a bar and proudly told me the news.

"It's amazing, you know," he said, "how these fellows can forecast the weather. One look at the sky is all it takes."

It seemed a pity to disillusion him, but he had to know the truth of the matter.

"They just watch television like everyone else," I said.

Having decided that it was going to be a little warm that day, we thought that it might be a good idea to try to buy hats and sun cream, so we crossed the Cubillas by a 1st century Roman bridge, and climbed the hill to the centre of town. Bob was fascinated by the bridge.

"Wow, Roy!" he exclaimed. "It's been there since the time of Jesus! Just think of all those sandals that must have passed over it!"

Iznalloz was bigger than Deifontes or Cogollos Vega combined. The remains of a Moorish castle stood at the highest point and a huge, red-bricked 16th century parish church stood out in the middle of a cluster of white houses. At the corner of a little cobbled square we found a shop that seemed to sell just about everything, including hats of various design. I came across, and purchased a jar of sticky substance called 'crema Julia', which had a label stuck to it, proclaiming that it cured all ills from coughs (if rubbed on the chest) to dog bites. The shop had nothing specifically for sunburn. Nobody would be mad enough to leave their skin exposed to the sun for any length of time, it seems. Only mad dogs and Engli-oops! I mean Americans. I rubbed some of this paste onto the backs of my legs, much to the amusement of the shopkeeper's wife and children who had come to watch, with my shorts, once again, providing plenty of amusement. The giggling no longer embarrassed me. Let them have their fun, I thought, and realised that I would be running the gauntlet just about everywhere I went in Spain and must risk being laughed at. There was no risk involved. I *was* laughed at.

We left Iznalloz on the N325. It had a smooth and, as yet, fairly cool surface, on which we set out as confidently as our aches and pains would allow, resplendent in our newly acquired headgear. Bob had purchased a straw hat with a black band while I had one made of white cloth. After yesterday, we said, everything must get better for nothing could be quite as bad. It was then back again down the slope, over the little Roman bridge (getting quite used to our comings and goings), and straight ahead for Guadahortuna.

According to the map, the río Cubillas seemed to be heading in the same direction as the road we were on, so we clambered down the steep bank to a little riverside track.

Roman bridge at Iznalloz

Río Cubillas

Although we were a little reluctant to leave the flat asphalt surface and face a stony path again, we had made up our minds to stay on footpaths wherever possible.

My pace was faster than Bob's and before long I ended up being some way ahead of him. It wasn't that I walked particularly fast, just that Bob was so slow. He ambled, lost in thought, and could not be hurried, except perhaps for the last stretch that ended up in a bar. As I strolled along I thought back on what my companion had said the day before about our reasons for attempting this walk, and agreed with his summing up. For him it was probably the old pioneering spirit showing through, 'Wagon Trail West' and all that. Off into the Unknown. Not *quite* the unknown, of course, but many of the places we passed through were unfamiliar to the non-Spanish. While at the shop I had asked the man there if many foreigners had visited the town. Oh, yes, he replied, only last year they had seen a Frenchman who had come to look at the remains of the Arab castle.

We were now heading towards a much smaller place than Iznalloz. It was not mentioned in guide books, but for us it had the two necessities: it was on the way north and had somewhere to stay. The proprietor of Los Arcos had confirmed this last fact by telling us that his sister Carmen lived there and ran a sort of bar-cum-dance hall in which, he assured us, she had spare rooms for travellers. Sometimes, he said, dancers, who may have had one too many, stayed overnight themselves. It sounded from his description to be a bit noisy but lay the right distance away – 25 kilometres – and small and unsophisticated enough to appeal: a place where the traditional life-style had not changed too much. I knew that anywhere back from the sea, even just a few kilometres inland, would be very different from the hustle and bustle experienced at the tarted-up tourist resorts on the coast. The cost of living was bound to be much lower too.

As Guadahortuna offered nothing to attract tourists, we continued on our way quite happy in the belief that perhaps we would be the first. Although the muscles in my legs and blisters on the feet were not completely ignored, I managed to take more notice of the surroundings than I had the previous day. Olive trees stretched in thousands as far as the eye could see. With tall irises poking their heads above the green-brown grass, accompanied by the purple hue of Spanish gladioli, it was pretty enough walking beside the river, but the humble poppy really set things alight. These common, short-lived flowers just could not be ignored, for they took the limelight from everything else around. Their blazing carpet of bright red caught the eye and, although plenty of other colours proliferated too, it was this common bloom, growing anywhere and everywhere, massed, like a gathering army about to charge, that really stole the scene. Along with the sweet-smelling yellow broom, the fragrant scent of lavender, rosemary and oregano assaulted our nostrils. It is the aroma of these herbs that I associate most with Southern Spain. A little tip for sweaty walkers – and it's impossible not to be sweaty when walking uphill, pack on back, in the hot sunshine – is to rub some crushed lavender under the armpits, chest, face, hair or anywhere in fact, before entering a bar or hostal. People there will not move away from you quite so quickly. It acts like a roll-on deodorant. Put some in the pockets, too. They say that a young girl, on the night of her marriage, would be rubbed all over with this fragrant herb before joining her new husband in bed. It saved taking a bath, I suppose. Gerald Brenan observed in *South from Granada* that, although clothes were kept very clean, bodies were not often bathed.

When Richard Ford journeyed in Spain more than one hundred and fifty years ago, he noted in *Gatherings from Spain*, 'At the same time it must be remembered that this fluid (water) is applied with greater prodigality in washing their inside than their outside'. The Romans and later, the Moors were known for their building and use of baths but after the conquest of Granada, Ferdinand and Isabella abolished them. They encouraged only the use of holy water. Fire, not water, was the element of purification. Monks of the time considered dirt as a test of moral purity and true faith and consequently wore the same, unchanged woollen frock year in and year out.

In earlier times still, Isabella, the favourite daughter of Philip II, made a solemn vow never to change her shift until Ostend was taken. The siege lasted three years, three months and thirteen days! It is recorded that, by then, the garment had acquired a 'tawny colour'.

As we sauntered along side by side, we discussed our newly acquired headgear. Bob reckoned that his straw hat had the edge on mine.

"It lets the air pass through," he maintained.

"Ah yes," I said, "but can you wash it when it gets all sweaty and dirty? You know they say that wearing a hat all the time makes a person go bald."

Bob thought about this for a moment then replied, " If you're wearing a hat all the time – who would know?" He had an answer for everything.

I gradually pulled away from him as we established our regular walking pace. It was better that way. We became involved with our own thoughts and preferred no interruption. From time to time I would look back to see how far behind he had fallen and eventually stop at some shady spot to wait for him. Sometimes we walked all day saying hardly a word to each other. We had no need to chat. We knew that we were treading the same path, sharing similar feelings of expectation, frustration and relief. The sharp, pointed stones of a rough track dug into Bob's feet as well as mine and if the hot sun beat down on me, I knew that it was roasting him as well. I was not alone in this madness. At the end of the day we would unwind and make light of it all. Sitting back with a full stomach and an empty bottle of wine on the table put things in a different perspective. At the same time, while out on the road, I felt glad to know that another person was nearby if help were needed, for some of the areas we passed through, especially up in the high sierras, were so isolated that to be incapacitated in any way would probably have meant the end of the road. We agreed that it would have been quite foolhardy to try this trip alone.

So we trudged onwards, moving farther away from the road with every step. It now lay a few kilometres to our right so, by now, we were more or less committed to keeping to the riverside trail. My hat proved to be good at keeping the sun off my neck but the 'crema Julia', although it seemed to have alleviated the smarting, attracted all sorts of flying insects. I constantly had to switch them with a sprig of rosemary to keep them off the backs of my legs.

En route we saw not a soul. I kept my eyes open for any sign of wildlife, for there was supposed to be quite a variety in these sierras – including ibex and the cat-like lynx. We saw nothing, however, for the lynx is nocturnal and my shiny, new hat would have been spotted a mile off by other wary creatures. Apart from this, I used to burst into song from time to time and, as my voice seemed to echo resonantly around the hills, probably disturbed anything within earshot. The animals we did come across, though, were those we would rather have avoided. Farmhouses, or 'cortijos' have dogs in residence. These large, fierce brutes are left to guard the property while its owners are away, and know their job well. We soon learned to collect a few stones and a stick when approaching these dwellings for it helped to keep the snarling beasts at bay. Throughout the walk we found them a constant menace.

After a while we saw a group of houses in the distance but, as we approached, the few people that we had seen moving about suddenly seemed to vanish and we ended up entering what looked like a ghost town. We found nobody to ask directions and, what was worse, not a bar in sight. We remembered that the Iznalloz man had said that the hostal was at the far end of town so we made our way through to the other side, sensing all the while that eyes were peering out at us from behind shutters. To our relief, Carmen's brother was right. There it stood: the Hostal los Montes, which had rooms in an adjoining barn-like construction, where the dances were held, but none programmed for that night, fortunately. The friendly, rather plump woman who greeted us was indeed Carmen and she showed delight at our having stayed at her brother's hostal in Iznalloz the night before.

"He is a disgrace to the family," she said, "he and his investments!"

If I had not been so tired I should have liked to learn more about this broker brother but we needed food, drink and our rooms. As we turned to go to a table, Carmen asked, "Are you from the circus?" Apparently a circus was coming to Guadahortuna. We had noticed a poster stuck on the side of a house. I assured her we were in no way connected to this forthcoming event. My answer seemed to bring a look of disappointment to her face, but her two young children, clinging to her skirt and staring at us shyly, did not seem at all convinced. Why else should I be wearing cut-down trousers and a funny hat? It was about 4 p.m. – siesta time. Everywhere had fallen very quiet. We had covered twenty-five kilometres and felt sorely tired. Good Carmen fed and watered (well, not quite 'watered') us, after which we padded to our rooms where I deposited my stiff socks, sweaty shirt, underpants and now grimy hat into a sinkful of cold water.

Hardly any of these hostales provided hot water, while many offered nothing in the room at all beyond a bed, a chair and some sort of simple cupboard. As I had brought two of everything in my pack, I decided to wash one and wear one. Bob and I had discussed the matter before starting out and had agreed that clean socks, in particular, were essential to comfortable walking. As the most important part of our anatomy our feet must always be kept happy. So we dutifully gave them, along with our socks, a wash and brush up at each stop, with a massage thrown in too, if they had behaved themselves. If our washing had not dried by the following morning, we would simply hang the damp items outside our pack to let them dry in the sun as we travelled along. That was the theory, at any rate. Without sun, then we should have to think again.

On this occasion I took *Tess of the D'Urbervilles* to bed with me after I had completed this little chore, but I'm afraid that I was of not much use to her for I fell asleep almost immediately. It seemed that I had only just shut my eyes when I heard Bob banging on the door, shouting for me to wake up and meet him down at the bar. I saw that I had slept like a log for two hours. I forced my aching body to rouse itself, put on clean clothing, including long trousers this time, and went creakingly through to meet my partner who sat in his usual place: at the bar, beer in hand. By this time some other customers had sat at a table with dominoes in front of them, and I could see that they were keeping one eye on their game and the other on Bob. When I joined him they forgot the dominoes completely and stared intently in our direction.

"One of these guys keeps asking something," said Bob. "He doesn't seem to get it that I don't get it."

"Good evening, señores," I greeted them, swivelling around on my stool. "I am afraid that my friend does not understand the language. Can I assist you?"

"Is it true that you are from America?" asked one of them.

Bob's passport again. No confidentiality here. I replied that we were indeed from America.

"Are you here to watch the circus?" asked the one who seemed to be the oldest of the four. I noticed that he was wearing carpet slippers of the Granada bus station variety. Before I could reply another of the players said,

"A lady is eaten by a crocodile."

"And the following night," continued his excited neighbour, "is again eaten, but this time by a giant octopus."

"Her name is Zavrina," chimed in the one who had not yet contributed anything, "and she will be dressed in nothing but a bathing costume."

They sat looking at us defiantly as though expecting contradiction.

"Wow!" I exclaimed. "That sounds like a real circus!"

"A real circus, indeed!" they all echoed.

I translated to Bob who wanted me to explain how Zavrina could be eaten twice on two consecutive days.

"Let's go and look around town," I said wearily.

Other bars in town we had missed on our walk through, as they were shut for siesta. Outwardly, these hardly differed from the houses on either side. Bob wanted to pay them a visit, for it was one of his firm resolutions to try all the local bars at each place we stayed overnight. It was a rather ambitious resolve for, although in small towns like this there was no problem, larger places, like Toledo, with well over a hundred drinking establishments, would prove difficult. Knowing Bob's thirst, though, I say difficult, not impossible. Guadahortuna, we discovered, was situated at the junction of four roads and on the boundary between the provinces of Granada and Jaén. Our N325 met up with the N324 and a smaller road, passing through, stretched from Alamedilla in the east to Montejícar in the west. This latter village is situated in the Sierra de Lucena and from there the river Guadahortuna makes its debut, running through Guadahortuna itself and kidnapping, on its way, our old friend and companion the river Cubillas. Eventually, further east, it drains into the huge lake-cum-reservoir, the Embalse del Negratín.

Surprised to find no other hotels or hostales at such an important road junction, we came across only four other bars, which were dutifully inspected for beer and tapas quality. Each of these places seemed to fill with people during our visit. Most of them, we realised, were folk we had seen before and it became obvious that they were following us around. Brightly coloured placards advertised the arrival of the circus and, sure enough, there were pictures of the buxom, scantily-clad Zavrina standing in a large container of water, being crunched by a huge crocodile on the Wednesday, while on Thursday she was shown wrestling with the tentacles of a giant octopus. In each lurid pose she had the look of utmost horror on her face. These aquatic creatures, we decided, had been chosen so that the voluptuous Zavrina could show off her charms in a scanty costume. It was tempting to stay and see just how charming she really was.

Bob, who wore a tight-fitting 'T'-shirt, possessed muscled, broad shoulders and bulging biceps which he had developed by working out three times a week in a gymnasium. His good physique drew plenty of attention and I constantly had to deny that he was an acrobat, strong man or anything else to do with the circus.

"He must work very hard," commented one young man.

I acknowledged that he did work hard.

"What is his work?" the young man asked.

Now, for me to say that Bob was an analyst, a doctor of psychology, I knew would lead to unimagined complications so I merely nodded.

The young man would not give up. "Does he work on the building?" he further questioned.

I understood that, in Spain, if a person looked fit and muscly, it suggested that he probably practised some sort of manual labour like farming, fishing, roadbuilding or construction work. In these parts more respect was shown to someone who looked unfit and unmuscled, for it labelled them as being what we would call a white-collar worker. A pot belly and unweathered, pasty complexion indicated office work of some sort. An official perhaps? These were the types to be wary of. I remember once, in Almuñécar, a newly-arrived Swedish couple opened a gymnasium. My Spanish friends were intrigued.

"What do you do there?" they asked.

"You lift weights above your head and pull on things," I answered.

"How much will they pay for you to do such things?" one enquired.

On learning that no financial reward was paid for such acts but, on the contrary, it was expected that the pusher and puller must pay, they laughed and scratched their heads in bewilderment. The gymnasium closed after a month.

Back at the hostal, Carmen presented us with a meal of fried green peppers, egg and chips with salad, bread and wine, which we thoroughly enjoyed. We chatted for a while over coffee, cognac and cigar (we knew how to live!) and then retired. I was greeted by a congealed mess in my sink; I rinsed it out and hung it by the window to dry. I felt exhausted so, having apologised to Tess once again for neglecting her, I clambered wearily into bed.

5

I'm lonesome since I crossed the hill
And o'er moor and valley.
Such heavy thoughts my heart do fill
For the girl I left behind me.

The next morning, Tuesday April 27, I was woken up by the sound of a cockerel crowing very loudly just outside the window. As the sun rose the bird was obeying its nature. In Bob's room, next to mine, through the thin walls I could hear him cursing and then slamming his window shut. My watch had stopped.

"What's the time, Bob?" I shouted through the wall.

"Too early," he answered. Then a few moments later: "It's six o'clock, man. That goddam bird! We might as well make an early start."

I reached across to the coat-hanger on which I had hung my wet laundry and found that it was still damp. Downstairs in the empty bar Bob looked irritable.

"That goddam bird!" he said again. "If we'd been staying tonight I would have asked the señora for a chicken dinner." He jabbed his finger angrily towards the back yard. "That chicken!"

We spread our map out on a table and waited for the usual breakfast of coffee and toast. It was brought over by a pretty young woman who resembled Carmen but looked quite a bit younger, in her late teens, I reckoned. She had the same soft plumpness about her that was not at all unattractive. The girl greeted us with a "Buenos días, señores," accompanied by a dimpled smile revealing a row of small, fine teeth. Her eyebrows rose a little when she spotted my bare legs and she muttered something that sounded like "Caramba!" The map, covering the whole table top, caught her attention and she asked where we were going, then, to our surprise, sat down beside us. Her abundant, thick black hair was tied behind her head and, as she leaned forward to inspect the map more closely, I could see that she was wearing no brassière under her black dress. Straightening up and putting her hands behind her neck she pushed her large, soft breasts, with their hard nipples, outwards, and I could see that under her armpits grew a mass of dark, curly hair. She then stared boldly at us both, one after the other, with her large, brown eyes. We stared back, speechless, forgetting the coffee and toast. It was my turn to think, if not utter, "Caramba!"

She repeated her question.

"Where are you heading for, americanos?"

I noticed that one of her breasts lay resting on the town of Baeza and I felt like answering, "Towards your left nipple," but instead replied,

"We were thinking perhaps that Huelma might be our destination for today. Do you know the place?"

"Huelma! Oh, yes!" she said. "A very pretty walk of some fifteen kilometres. I have made the journey many times with my father."

She traced on the map a route that followed the river Cubillas. Starting opposite the hostal, her proposed trail ran across country for a while, passed between two hills shown as Los Gallardos, and later joined a small road that led into Huelma. This avoided the main road – the N324 – completely. No problem with overnight accommodation, she guaranteed, having stayed there herself a short while ago. As she had been pointing the way with her soft, slightly podgy little fingers, my mind had been wandering and I found it difficult to concentrate. She kept glancing up at me with those big, liquid eyes and must have known the effect she was having. Bob's hand had been on the map almost touching her brown arm, I noticed. Was she just flirting with us? After all, we surmised later, this was a dance hall and there were many brothels in Spain. We never discovered the truth. In fact, we didn't even know the young lady's name. Perhaps she was simply

Carmen's sister. Whoever, or whatever she was, her magnetic appeal kept our attention long enough for the breakfast to get cold. As she left our table to walk back towards the kitchen her large buttocks swung from side to side in the most seductive manner and I contemplated discussing with Bob the possibility of spending another night in Guadahortuna.

The night before I had asked for, and was given by Carmen, some safety pins and so, this morning, armed with these invaluable items, we awarded our packs decorations of honour in the shape of damp socks, underpants and shirts. Thus bedecked and looking very untidy we took our leave of the Hostal los Montes with all its temptations, crossed the road and set off along a faint track. In the distance I could see the high sierra that the young siren had pointed out to us. It was hard to miss, for it rose to a height of 1400 metres and we had been instructed to pass by the left side of it, heading north. We judged the distance to be about eight kilometres, or two hours, away. The weather prospect looked good with not a cloud in the sky and a slight breeze blowing. Perfect walking and drying conditions, we agreed.

For the first hour we said nothing to each other but I guessed what was going through Bob's mind. He looked wistful.

"What do you think, Bob?" I asked.

"About what, man?" he returned.

"You know about what," I retorted. "I can read your thoughts!"

He smiled. "Yeah, I guess it doesn't take much working out," he agreed. "Maybe we should have stayed another night."

"I was thinking the same thing," I said with a sigh. "We could always turn round."

"She would have kept you warm on a cold winter's night, for sure," put in Bob, adding in his no-nonsense manner: "What an arse and tits she had on her! She was like a ripe plum ready to be plucked!"

So, in this rude manner we continued on our way, discussing all the while what might have been back at Los

Olive trees covering the hillside

Montes. We were now in the province of Jaén, with the province of Granada behind us. This completely landlocked part of Andalucía is best known for its abundant olive trees, which cover the hillsides and punctuate the horizon in every direction. It is the world's leading producer of olives and olive oil and the area stretches north to the Sierra Morena, with the famous Despeñaperros Pass – which we later came to know well, west to the river Guadajoz and east to the Sierra de Segura. Running through the centre of this province is the river Guadalquivir which rises high in the Sierra de Cazorla, runs into and replenishes the Tranco reservoir, then turns west and continues in this direction until, finally, 600 kms further on, it ends its long, winding journey by flowing into the Atlantic at Sanlúcar in the Gulf of Cádiz. On its way this mighty river, the second longest in Spain, after the Ebro, irrigates a fertile valley of vineyards and wheatfields. At the same time, it provides an environment supporting a tremendous variety of animal life and fauna. Several wildlife parks can be found dotted along its route. We were still quite a distance from this flat river area and could see from the map that there were a couple of sierras to climb over before reaching it.

Marching along side by side (I controlled my pace to stay with Bob) we continued our discussion concerning the women we had known. Bob had been married many years before but things had not worked out. He never told me the reason why. At this time I was married, with a wife and two young sons back in England. Catherine, their mother, was the first of the women I had met on the notorious La Herradura beach. We had lived in my little house in the village and, as was customary in Spain, were delivered of a son at a hospital in Granada within the first year of marriage. Catherine never really took to the way of life that I enjoyed so much. It was not everybody's cup of tea, I know. A month's holiday is one thing but to adapt to a completely different culture without speaking the language and then, before long, have a young child to look after as well, must have been difficult for her. In the end, when our son was of school age, we returned to England and lived in Spain only during the holidays. I remember that when I lived there I used to feel sorry for the poor holidaymakers who regretfully had to return to their own countries, and they often confessed to me how much they envied my good fortune in being able to stay as long as I liked.

Bob and I had already spent quite some time together so we knew practically all there was to know about each other's past lives and loves and didn't pull any punches when it came to tales of sexual indulgence and romantic encounters. We listened patiently to each other's stories while waiting our turn to confess or exaggerate conquests involving the opposite sex. Talk about male chauvinism! There was plenty of time for us to be contemplative and I sometimes found myself remembering episodes from bygone days best forgotten. But, with a good friend acting as a father confessor, we purged our minds. Bob admitted to me that he had told me things about himself that he had never thought to admit to anyone. At the end of the day, especially after a couple of beers, we talked openly on any topic.

As we made our way towards Huelma we eventually exhausted the subject of what might have been back at Los Montes and I assumed my normal stride, moving slowly ahead of Bob. We had been walking for two hours now during mounting temperatures. The hot sun had all but dried our dangling washing and my hat, which I had been wearing though still wet, had become bone dry. We started to skirt the high sierra to our right and, as instructed, headed for the gap between the other two hills. All was going well, though our path had faded out completely and it looked as though not many people had come this way lately. But that did not bother us, for with the landmarks shown on the map, along with the girl's instructions, we felt we could hardly go astray. This time our assumption proved correct, for after another three hours' pleasant walking we could see buildings in the distance. I stopped and waited for Bob to catch up and we then smartened ourselves up by stuffing our now dry laundry away back into our packs. As we approached the outskirts of the village we came across a large, deep stone trough into which sparkling water poured from a metal tube jutting out from a rock. We were sorely tempted to plunge straight in but contented ourselves by holding our hot, sweaty heads under this cascade of cool, clear liquid and then drinking greedily. A short, stout woman, who had a large, filled jug at her side, had been standing a short distance away while all this was going on, watching our antics.

I greeted her with a "hola!" and Bob nodded politely. To our astonishment the woman replied, "hola, americanos!"

I am pretty sure that she had been waiting there looking out for us to arrive, for the next thing she did, without our saying a word, was to offer to lead us to the hostal. Knightly Bob, gallant as ever, insisted on carrying her container of water. At first, she did not seem too keen on the idea, but, after a sort of tugging match, she finally consented to let him. We could hardly have missed the inn for it was situated just a short distance down the road and, as we came closer, I saw that it wasn't just a humble lodging-house, but more of a smart hotel with a restaurant attached.

On Friday, December 1, 1961, Penelope Chetwode arrived in Huelma astride her horse ' the Marquesa'. She had set out on November 5 from Illora, 25 kilometres to the west of Granada, and ridden east, then north to Úbeda. We could see from the map that, between the villages of Domingo Pérez and Torre-Cardela, she must have crossed the trail we had walked out of Iznalloz. She writes that it was here in this town that she discovered an excellent café which is described as being the 'Fortnum and Mason of Huelma'. It could well have been this very place we were now approaching.

Outside this impressive-looking establishment, a little gathering of people regarded our arrival with uninhibited curiosity. Their eyes, especially the women's, seemed torn between my shorts and Bob, still carrying the water. As I had now come to expect, my sunburned, hairy legs seemed to trigger a widening of ladies' eyes and, at the same time, the cupping of hands over their mouths to stifle laughter. So, there they stood: a small reception committee to meet us, it appeared. One of the old men in the crowd removed his hat! We assumed that news of two mad Americans heading their way on foot had been relayed to Huelma from Guadahortuna and this little group was there to welcome us. Questions came thick and fast. Did we not find the Spanish countryside beautiful? Did we have wives? How many children? Why were American women so thin? (They had been watching *Dallas* on television.) Was it not difficult for them to bear children with such small hips? The reason for our walking seemed to mystify them most. The 'sportiness' explanation did not convince but, in the end, had to be accepted. I said that journeying on foot gave us a chance to observe the beauty of their country more closely.

"But you can see it quite well from the bus," pointed out one helpful character.

"Ah, yes!" said the man at his side, "but there is nothing 'sporty' about sitting your bum on a bus seat and, besides, it costs nothing to walk."

Now herein perhaps lies the most logical reason for the Spanish to understand our trek to Madrid on foot. We simply could not afford to travel any other way. I had learned in earlier times that rural Spanish folk could justify walking on two counts. One is that the person is mad and the other, more common reason, is that he or she is penniless and has not the wherewithal to buy a bus or train ticket. To arrive at a hostal, fonda, or pensión on foot will suggest to the owner of the establishment (as long as he considers you sane) that you have no money and, in such a state, will not be able to meet his bill. A bedraggled appearance, inevitable after a hard day's walking, will add to the impoverished look. With this in mind I forthwith always made a point of buying a drink or something at the bar and, in doing so, opened my wallet to show that I had money. Perhaps I would present a peseta note of large denomination and, only after this demonstration of solvency, would I ask if there was accommodation available. To ask for rooms before performing this little act would often result in a shake of the head by the proprietor.

"No rooms," he or she would say. "We are full."

The place might be completely empty but they did not want scruffy, destitute tramps like us staying there. It was understandable. They just were not used to ramblers. We were not in England now.

It seemed that here at Huelma, though, the knowledge of our ability to pay had preceded us via Guadahortuna. We entered the hotel and found more folk apparently expecting us. As we approached the bar the man behind the counter placed two beers in front of us without our saying a word. News, it seemed, certainly had travelled fast. So, not to disappoint anyone, and to live up to their expectations, we drank three each in quick succession. Eyes were watching our every move and after this demonstration of our ability to drink, I almost expected them to break out into a round of applause.

Rooms were not a problem. They showed us to two comfortable rooms upstairs (with bedside lights, I noticed) where we deposited our packs and had a quick brush up before returning downstairs. Despite our hunger, the bustling crowd determined to question us further and gathered around again as soon as we re-entered the room.

Suddenly, they were pushed aside by a chubby, bespectacled young man wearing a tight-fitting white jacket and blue chequered trousers, who had an authoritative air about him. The crowd fell silent. I stared at him. He was the spitting image of Billy Bunter!

"Good morning," he said to us in English. (It was 4 p.m.) He then turned to the admiring onlookers and reprimanded them firmly.

"Can you not leave these gentlemen alone? Can you not see that they are tired from their exercise and no doubt in need of nourishment? Give them peace!"

They looked at each other and then down at their feet like naughty, scolded schoolchildren.

He returned his attention to us and asked us if we would like to eat. His accent was good but he lacked grammar. It came out as: "You eat?" with the Arab sign of the hand held, with pinched fingers, to the mouth. Bob seized his chance to talk to someone and assured him that we would, indeed, like to eat. In a very dignified manner the corpulent one led us to the restaurant, showed us to a table and then, like a magician bringing a rabbit out from a hat, proudly presented a menu written in English. The whole episode only lacked a "Hey, presto!"

In the other room, the crowd slowly dispersed. Billy Bunter had stolen the scene. Added to that, siesta time approached. Out of the corner of my eye I could see our young man hovering nearby, white napkin folded over his arm, waiting to take our order. Everything about him reminded me so much of the Fat Owl of the Remove – the greedy fat boy of Greyfriars – that I shouldn't have been surprised if he had suddenly shouted out that we were "beasts!" or "rotters!"

The English menu was littered with mistakes, of course, but we pretended not to notice. He would have been most upset, I am sure. The tapas served with our drinks at the bar had been very good – always a good sign when it comes to the restaurant. One of the dishes read 'fish and chips', so I ordered a mixed fish with the chips – in English. The word 'mixed' left him stumped but the word 'different' worked.

Bob, probably remembering our early morning call, ordered chicken and chips. These orders were written down with a flourish by our chubby cherub who asked Bob if he wanted the chicken well done. Bob was a little taken aback.

"Well done chicken?" he asked, looking at me.

"As you think best," I said to our Billy. "I have full confidence in your decision."

The chicken was perfect. Throughout the meal the attentive waiter kept on returning to our table to practise his English.

"Is good?" he would ask with a beaming smile. He wanted to know the names of the fish in English, although many of them did not live in our seas.

Though eager to please, his constant interruptions to our meal became a little annoying after a while. He informed us that he had learned his English at a school in Granada but had returned to Huelma, where his family lived, and worked for his uncle who owned the hotel. He wanted to improve his English, he said, and spoke it whenever the opportunity presented itself.

Moorish castle at Huelma

It seems that we were mistaken in thinking that Huelma did not receive many visitors, for it was famous for a large, Moorish castle standing high above the town complete with several intact towers. From here, narrow, whitewashed alleyways retaining the original Moorish street patterns led down to the Renaissance sandstone church of La Inmaculada. This castle was viewed in all its glory by the lady riding 'the Marquesa' as she quit Huelma. It was seen 'standing out against a backcloth of the deep blue Sierra de Mágina'.

By the time we had eaten our good, but frequently disturbed, meal, taken a siesta and dutifully seen to our socks and things, it was getting dark and too late to visit these attractions but we felt we should inspect the bars. We discovered four or five, each of which gave good helpings of tapas with the drinks, so we had no need of another meal that day. Feeling pleasantly tired, we then returned to our rooms and, this time, I took advantage of the bedside light to read a little.

6

Standing there to strict attention,
Like soldiers on parade,
The rows of olive trees await
Their morning accolade.

There was no early morning call the following day by a noisy feathered friend, so we met at our usual time of eight o'clock. Instead of a buxom, black-eyed beauty to greet us and serve breakfast we had to make do with the just as buxom Billy. He looked very spick and span in his waiter's uniform at such an early hour and brightened the day for us with a beaming smile and a "Good morning, Misters". We showed him our map and asked his advice regarding our next port of call. He studied the map intently with many "mms" and "ahs" before finally suggesting a place called Torres which looked to be about thirty kilometres distant and not far from our straight line. It looked a good choice. Little did we know! The track shown on the map appeared to stray off from the N 324 after a few kilometres, climb steeply over the Sierra Almadén and then drop sharply down to this village of Torres. I suppose, in retrospect, I should have been suspicious of a thousand-metre descent shown as one short line but the map had been more or less correct up till now so we had no reason to doubt its accuracy. Mr. Bunter (once again we never learned his real name) told us that he had never actually walked the track but had been to Torres many times in the past. We could see from his waist-line, however, that walking was not something he practised very often. Torres, he said, was much smaller than Huelma, with only a few thousand inhabitants, while here in Huelma there were three times that number.

Accommodation would prove no problem, he assured us, for he knew of a small fonda in the village square. It sounded better all the time. After a satisfying breakfast, we pinned on our washing, bade our fond farewells, in English, to our smiling friend and then strode off down the N 324 in the direction of Cambil.

We had been told that we should find the trail off to the right after about four kilometres. The road started to climb uphill almost immediately and we saw it twisting and turning through a landscape covered by a vast expanse of olive trees standing in orderly, precise lines. These remarkable growths have been around for some six thousand years. A tree can live for six hundred years and bear fruit for most of that time. At this time of the year we saw no olives on the branches, only little buds that would soon burst into flower, with the fruit itself being harvested in the winter. In this particular area the only type of olive grown is a variety called 'picual', highly valued because its low acidity results in the oil produced being 'Extra Virgin.' I stopped for a moment and weighed up the situation. Why not cut out a few of these bends in the road? 'The shortest distance between two points …' and all that. The idea sounded fine to Bob and so, with the aid of my little compass, we directed our walk in a calculated line, straight into the labyrinth of trees. After no more than five minutes, however, we became hopelessly and completely lost! The point of the compass wavered all over the place for the broken, reddish earth underfoot made me lurch from side to side and to hold the apparatus steady proved impossible. I found that if I stood still and took a reading it was just as difficult to follow the line because of the damned trees. We had to weave this way and that to get round them.

On we blundered, pushing our way through the branches growing so close to each other that the shadows they cast seemed to intermingle and were of no use in trying to work out a direction. History tells us that when Caesar's legions assaulted Seville, their horses could barely make it through the closely growing trees that ringed the city. I know how they must have felt. After an hour of staggering around hither and thither over the rough, stony earth when we should have arrived back on the road long before, we had to admit that we had a problem. We tried climbing to the top of a tree but, once there, all we could see was more of the same, each topped with a mass of grey, green leaves. At a rough estimate, there are thought to be two hundred and fifty million olive trees growing in Spain and, by now, it felt as though we had made the acquaintance of most of them. What to do? I could see that Bob was becoming angrier and more frustrated. In bygone times olive branches were a sign of peace and I considered breaking one off and offering it to him but I don't think it would have helped matters.

"Well, man," he said. "So much for your damn short cuts! Where's all that sailor stuff I've heard so much about? You and your compass!"

I nearly said, 'Give me a star to guide by,' but that would have added fuel to the fire, so I held my tongue. What could I say? He was right in that I had boasted of my seamanship, having been a sailor, and I suppose I should have been able to find my way out of this maze. We clambered around for a while longer until Bob exploded.

"Shit, man! We're getting nowhere! What's the use of wearing ourselves out like this? We're going round in circles!"

"What else do you suggest, Bob?" I asked. "That we just lie down and die?"

"It may come to that," replied Bob, pensively.

Eventually, after more cursing and torment, we came across a small white-painted house, which stood out glaringly amid the dark foliage and red earth. As we approached it, the manic barkings of a large, skinny dog which was fortunately attached to a strong-looking cord, brought a shrivelled, weather-beaten looking old man on to the terrace. If ever a character fitted his surroundings it was he. His gnarled, crooked appearance blended perfectly with the trees and if he had sat in the branches of one, it would have been impossible to spot him. His grey-brown clothing and leathery, brown skin formed perfect camouflage.

The man watched our approach with what looked like uncertainty on his parchment-like face, although it was not easy to read much with all those wrinkles. We had closed in on the house as much as the dog leash would allow, when one of the cracks in his face opened and a creaky, high-pitched voice asked what we wanted. Though tempted to ask him if he knew where we could find an olive tree, I restrained myself and explained our predicament. We then went through a sort of little pantomime, as he pointed the way to the long-lost road and I took a further compass bearing in that direction. Bob, who had been watching this little act with sighs of exasperation needed only to say, "Another fine mess you've got me into, Stanley!" to complete the picture. After accepting a very welcome drink of water from our guide, we set off again on a new course and, to Bob's surprise and my relief, we joined the elusive road just a few kilometres from where we had left it.

It was, by now, almost midday and the sun was high in the clear, blue sky. We should have been half-way up the Sierra Almadén by now, I thought, instead of wasting three hours adrift in those trying olive trees. One hour later, after twisting and turning our way up the road (no more short cuts!) we found the track leading off to the right. It looked very steep and we prepared ourselves for a tough few hours ahead. It was not easy. Not only was the path very loose underfoot, which caused us to slip and slide all over the place, but the earlier episode had taken more out of us than I realised. Both Bob's ankles and mine had suffered badly on the uneven, stony earth of the olive fields and my soft-sided cowboy boots and Bob's trainers had not provided much support to our ankles. So, puffing, panting and hobbling lamely along like a couple of old invalids, we must have looked a fine pair as we slowly crept our way up and up.

The trees, thinning out by now, were being replaced by large, craggy rocks. It made a pleasant change to return to more open territory and, once again, enjoy the sight and smell of wild flowers. Up here in this terrain we were hoping to catch sight of some resident wild life, for this was the habitat of large birds of prey such as the Spanish imperial eagle. Keeping our eyes peeled, we came across plenty of starlings, finches and cheeky magpies, but had no luck with larger birds. Over four hundred different types of bird inhabit these sierras, and some of them can be found only locally. Lately, bird watching, or 'twitching', as I think it is called, has started to become popular and I wonder what the locals think of these characters wandering about with binoculars and cameras slung over their shoulders. They must wonder why anyone should wish to seek out birds without carrying a gun.

As we neared the summit, we saw, growing between the boulders, clusters of parched-looking fir trees offering welcome shade, so we sat down carefully beneath the first ones we came to. I say 'carefully' because to sit anywhere out in the wild countryside (particularly when wearing shorts) can be dangerous. Firstly, take the ants. Size doesn't seem to matter when it comes to the amount of irritation caused by these little devils. Secondly, scorpions live and lurk under the rocks, waiting for the unwary sitter. Although not so common, snakes live here, too, one kind being poisonous though most are quite harmless. As it's not easy to tell the difference, I recommend leaving them all well alone. Even without all these creatures, sitting under fir trees can sometimes lead to the sharp-pointed pine needles sticking into various tender parts of the anatomy.

As we sat, we took in the wonderful view. To our right rose Sierra Mágina which, we had been given to understand, had a lake at its centre. One day, we promised ourselves, we would explore this area further and visit this crater-capped Sierra. Other mountain ranges could be seen in the distance, while below the terrain was studded with tight ranks of olive trees. Up here, at a height of over two thousand metres, the clear, pine-scented mountain air, mixed with assorted aromatic herbs, made the head spin. Our euphoria was short-lived. After a little rest we continued on our way, heading north, and now that we had reached the summit, expected to find the path running down to Torres at any moment. We found Torres all right – looking up at us from a thousand metres below! There I stood, compass in hand, at the edge of a precipice looking down upon it! We stood dumbfounded. The first thing I did was to look at Bob, who was starting to fume. I sensed that a "me and my damned compass" was coming on, so I got in first.

"Thar she blows!" I cried, in my best Captain Ahab voice, pointing straight down. Bob was not amused. He glowered.

I cupped my hand over my mouth and tried again. "Torres, ahoy!" I shouted downwards. Bob's shoulders hunched and his fists clenched, so I considered it wise to step back a few paces. If looks could have killed, I would have been buried there on top of that Sierra. He spoke quietly.

"It might be easier all round if we just jumped."

Our situation was not at all funny, though. The sun had disappeared behind the mountain ranges over to the west and the shadows up here were lengthening. Before long it would be dark and the temperature would start to fall dramatically, and I had learned from experience how bitterly cold it can become at this altitude. With no torch it would have been foolhardy to move around in the blackness for there were sheer, thousand-metre drops nearby. But, we realised, to sit and wait for daylight, without warm clothing, would be no picnic, either. What to do? We discussed various options but could not come up with any that made sense. The thought of going back down the steep track with no light tempted us less than staying put. Bob had some matches and suggested lighting a fire to keep us warm until morning. This seemed the best idea that we could come up with, although we both realised that we needed a good night's rest to continue our walk the following day. We felt terribly tired: it had taken us six hard, hot hours to clamber up the twelve (although later we calculated it to be more like twenty) kilometres to the top of Sierra Almadén. This was after our little escapade amongst the olive trees. We felt despairing. We felt despondent. We felt shattered. I could continue but I think you get the picture.

Suddenly, in the half-light, we heard a ghostly cry and, turning round, saw a strange, phantom-like apparition coming towards us from out of the trees. We blinked in amazement. The figure approaching us, with a long, loping stride, was that of a young boy wearing a ragged, loose fitting cloak and the strange sound we had heard, we now realised, had been the bleating of a goat. Was this a mirage? It couldn't be. It wouldn't be seen by both of us at the same time. We stood open-mouthed as he removed his shabby, wide-brimmed hat and greeted us with a "Buenas tardes, señores." He was a handsome, slim, fit-looking youth, probably in his early teens, with blond hair, fair complexion and very light blue eyes. A band of goats followed him, making their goat-like sounds and farting away for all they were worth. The good-looking scarecrow asked if he could help us. I replied that he certainly could if he could show us a way to get down to Torres without a parachute. He grinned. We had missed the road leading down to Torres some way back, he informed us. Follow him. Off we set, as he seemingly glided over the irregular, bumpy ground while we, poor souls, stumbled along behind. He led us back the way we had come for a while, then off into the undergrowth to another faint trail, which led to a stony-surfaced, unmade road which, our guide said, descended down to the village. How could we show our gratitude? With profuse thanks I offered him a few hundred pesetas which, at first, he refused to accept, but I pressed them on him. I knew that we would never have found a way to Torres without his help.

These goat people can be found wandering all over Spain – mainly in the mountainous, uncultivated parts. They live a very lonely life with only goats for company and those I have encountered, while walking the hills behind La Herradura, have all been tall, loose-limbed, healthy-looking individuals with little or no conversation. Gerald Brenan refers to their strikingly good looks and goes on to say that many of these shy young men are snapped up by village girls, who find their beauty irresistible. Their goats are their wealth. The milk is very rich and the cheese made from it delicious, but dangerous for foreigners to eat or drink unless processed. A couple of friends of mine developed a serious ailment oddly called Malta Fever from eating unprocessed goat's cheese. One of them, a Norwegian, died from the illness and is buried in the local cemetery of La Herradura. The other, a South African, remains still very unwell. Camilo José Cela, while journeying in the Alcarria, was aware of this fever when offered a glass of goat's milk, but was so hungry and thirsty that he took a chance anyway. He writes, 'the horn of hunger gores deepest of all.' There is no danger from cooked meat, however, and a favourite dish of mine is that of young kid or 'cabrito', casseroled with garlic and made into a dish known as 'choto ajillo'.

In many remote villages up in these sierras much inter-marriage unavoidably takes place, resulting in disabled and mentally retarded offspring. The story goes that these wandering goatherds are, from time to time, invited into the house and led to bed by some of the mountain women in order to introduce new lineage. I made the mistake of relating this tale to Bob.

"A drop of American blood," he generously offered, "is here for the asking."

Our spirits had been raised at being shown the road down to Torres but after an hour of curving to the left and then to the right, not being able to see a thing in the darkness, we began to wonder when this nightmare of a day would ever end. To walk down a slope puts a different strain on the joints from when you are ascending and the knees, in particular, soon begin to protest very strongly.

At last, lights glowed ahead and we breathed a sigh of thankfulness as we entered Torres. We followed a long, empty, narrow street, flanked by high rock on one side and tall buildings on the other, to a small square which had a walled-in lime tree growing at its centre. Two elderly men sitting on the wall stared at us. I asked one of them where we might find the fonda and he pointed with his stick to a building opposite. He was speechless. Two or three others came out from a nearby bar to gawk. We had not noticed the bar or we would have checked there first, as was our usual custom. The house indicated had a large letter 'F' painted

Entrance to Torres

Lime trees in Torres

over the entrance. I knocked and the door was half-opened by a young girl who peered out at us with frightened eyes. My request for rooms was met by a shake of the head. I thought that perhaps she had not understood so tried again, explaining that we were foreign tourists, travelling on foot and urgently needing somewhere to stay for the night. Again she shook her head. By this time five or six other onlookers had arrived. One of them spoke.

"She is alone in the house, señores. Her parents are away."

"But," I said, with a hint of desperation in my voice, "what can we do? We have crossed over the Sierra Almadén from Huelma on foot and are very tired. Is there nowhere to stay for the night here in Torres?"

I had not kept to my golden rule of showing money at the local bar. The little crowd started muttering, looking from one to the other and I noticed that in the background there stood a couple of Guardia Civil policemen looking on. I walked over to one of them and explained our problem. He slowly looked me up and down and I realised that, with our dishevelled, dirty appearance and washing still hanging down outside our packs, our scruffy look would not impress him too much.

"There is somewhere to stay at Mancha Real," he said, curtly.

"How far is that?" I asked.

"Twelve kilometres," he answered.

I turned towards Bob who had understood most of what had been going on. The girl's shake of the head was obvious and the twelve kilometres he had worked out. It was nine o'clock in the evening, pitch black away from the lights, becoming cold, and we were tired, hungry and thirsty.

"Can you drive us to Mancha Real?" I asked the man with the gun and shiny hat. He didn't waste words.

"No," was his answer.

In retrospect, I thought it strange that he did not ask for our passports or some means of identification, but perhaps he did not want the paperwork that would result. He just wanted us out of Torres. One of the bemused crowd asked if we desired transport. It was the local taxi driver asking the question and, as we had more or less given up, we piled into his taxi and drove off into the darkness to Mancha Real. It had been a long, long day.

As the Guardia had told us, the distance from Torres to Mancha Real was twelve kilometres. It took half an hour's drive along a very twisty road to cover this stretch and we saw nothing en route through the murkiness outside but, next morning, we discovered that we had not missed much, for the whole area was covered with our old friends – olive trees. What else? By the time we arrived at the hostal we had almost fallen asleep. It proved to be a good place. The food tasted delicious and we found the rooms comfortable and cheap. Mind you, in our condition, any sort of a meal would have seemed wonderful and I should not have noticed if the bed had been full of rocks. The others there in the bar showed curiosity, of course, but we had no desire to answer questions. I ached all over and could see that Bob, like myself, could hardly keep his eyes open. After greedily scoffing our meals we both hobbled off to bed.

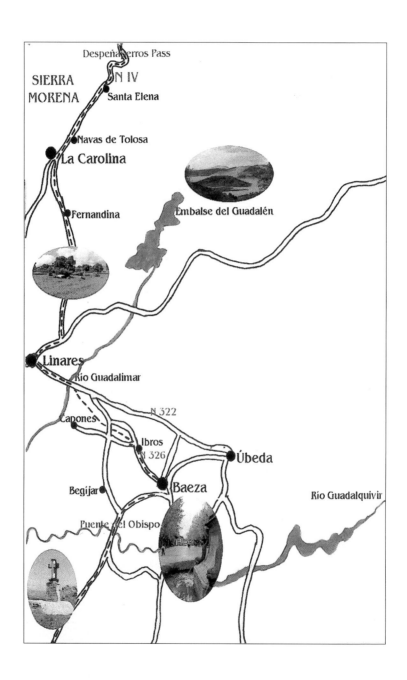

Despeñaperros Pass

SIERRA
MORENA

N IV

Santa Elena

Navas de Tolosa

La Carolina

Fernandina

Embalse del Guadalén

Linares

Río Guadalimar

N 322

Capones

Ibros

N 326

Úbeda

Begíjar

Baeza

Río Guadalquivir

Puente del Obispo

7

Not giving a thought to where I'm going,
And less from where I came ...

I found it difficult to move any part of my body the next morning. Just about every muscle had stiffened during the night and I lay there like the Tin Man from *The Wizard of Oz*, feeling that I needed a spot of oil applied to my joints before I could operate properly. But not only my physical person had suffered from the previous day's events. My spirit had also been damaged by the affair at Torres. Bob, who I found sitting slumped miserably at a table in the bar, coffee in hand, summed it all up. His pride had been hurt, too.

"Well, Roy," he sighed. "We can't boast about walking from Granada to Madrid now, can we?"

The truth was that we both felt guilty at having taken the taxi. It was as if we had failed in some way.

The map showed Mancha Real no nearer to our next intended destination, Baeza, than Torres. If anything, it was farther away, we declared! Were we just trying to kid ourselves? Perhaps. We thought it better to change the subject.

"It was a miracle that the young lad found us like that, up there in the wilderness, don't you think, Bob?" I asked. The scientist did not believe in miracles.

"That boy didn't just stumble upon us," he said. "He must have been silently shadowing us."

"A pretty hard thing to do, with all those goats along," I argued. "All that farting and tinkling of bells."

Once Bob had made a statement, he didn't argue the point. He was probably right, though, about the goat-boy following us. Distractions are few for these lonely wanderers. The sighting of two weird foreign-looking characters slipping and sliding their way up the Sierra Almadén would have intrigued any onlooker. Whatever the explanation, it was a good job that he had appeared when he did. There might be bleached bones up there to this day otherwise!

It looked as though we would be forced to stay on the N 321 all the way to our next stop. Bob could see me searching for another way to reach Baeza without using the road, and interrupted,

"Let's forget the trails today, eh, Roy? We had enough of those yesterday and look where it got us. Remember those damned olive trees?"

As it happened, we hadn't much choice. Our map showed that, south of Baeza, there was the wide river Guadalquivir to cross and the only way to do this was by means of a road bridge called the Puente del Obispo – the Bishop's Bridge.

"And you can keep that damn compass of yours at the bottom of your bag," ordered Bob.

With olive trees in every direction, Mancha Real was, of course, primarily involved with the production of olive oil, but we discovered other interests as well, including the manufacture of farming machinery, furniture and building materials. Originally it was called La Manchuela de Jaén but, after gaining independence from the jurisdiction of Jaén in 1557, it eventually, in 1653, received its present name in commemoration of a visit by King Philip IV.

We did not stay to look around for we resented the knowledge that the town had been thrust upon us against our will. It was rather like a forced marriage, we having been the unwilling party, and we wanted no further intimacy with it. I know that it wasn't the poor old town's fault but, in a way, we held it responsible for the unplanned diversion. We felt cheated. How dare this upstart of a town interfere with our plans? We did not want to come here! As we left we saw nothing much to impress us. It all looked shabby and uninteresting and, noticing our disdain, Mancha Real hung its head in shame at our departure. It looked guilty for being there at all.

After carrying on downhill for about half an hour we came to level territory which, we could see, stretched ahead of us for some twenty-five kilometres. There would be no sierras to climb today. We needed a day like this, we told ourselves, in order to recover from the traumas of the day before. Little traffic disturbed us and, before long, I fell into my 'guardsman's pace', and, once again, gradually pulled away from Bob, who soon trailed behind.

This 'pace' had been shaped many years before during my three miserable years as a trooper in the Royal Horse Guards, an experience that had a great effect on my later life. During the first few months of training, known as square-bashing, I and my fellow 'squaddies' learned to march in step with the aid of a contraption called a 'pace stick', which was opened to the required length of tread and measured against the soldier's step. Failing to keep in step resulted in a whack over the shins. This required length of stride has stayed with me ever since. I had joined the Household Cavalry, the regiment being formed by the Royal Horse Guards and the Life Guards, at the age of seventeen. The previous year I had spent at sea. My first twelve months were spent at Combemere Barracks, Windsor, where, along with the 'pace', I learned the useful arts of spit and polish, riding, grooming and looking after a horse, and, at the same time, how to obey any order given, instantly, without question. It took me a while to accept the last part but eventually I succumbed and became a little robot like the others. Then I left for Knightsbridge Barracks in London. This ugly yellow-brick building had been used to house soldiers since the Crimean War. The barrackroom I shared with about twenty others had one cold tap, which we all used for washing, shaving and drinking. This room had no heating but, as it was situated directly above the stables, the heat given off by the steaming horses below (along with the smell) managed to keep the temperature, in winter, just above freezing. None of this really mattered at the time. Such privations probably did me some good and I quickly learned to look after myself and keep my possessions in order. It was not all bad. I found it hardest of all to accept coming into contact with, and seeing examples of, inherited privilege. The officer class had their own comfortable quarters, a personal slave (called a batman) who had to clean and polish all their equipment, military and personal; and a groom, who had to look after their horse and saddlery. These 'toffs', for want of a better word, would be helped into their newly-pressed uniform (with all the spit-and-polished leather accessories) by their batman and then helped on to their likewise well-presented horse by their groom. The resplendent officer would then inspect us poor devils who had to stand bolt-upright to attention, looking straight ahead. The inspection was rarely completed without some chargeable offence being discovered – like a button not being upright or the plume on the helmet not hanging to the officer's satisfaction. The resulting punishment could be anything from whitewashing coal to cutting the grass outside the Officers' Mess with a knife.

I must admit that I did not make a perfect soldier. Luckily, while in London, I became involved with the sport of wrestling – the style known as 'catch-as-catch-can'. I took the whole thing seriously and, although I say so myself, became one of the top light-heavyweight contenders in the country. Whenever I had the chance I practised hard at the Central Y.M.C.A. or at a club called Ashdown, where pent-up anger and frustration built up in me while at the barracks could be released against some unfortunate opponent. I was a bad loser. Winning, at all costs, was my aim. Thanks to a request from an important British coach, the army reluctantly released me from duties during the last part of my military service so that I might train. I spent many afternoons jogging around the Serpentine in Hyde Park or wrestling at various gymnasia. Another reason for my success at wrestling was the fact that I did not really care whether I injured myself. A broken bone or pulled muscle meant being plastered or bandaged for a while, but that was all part of my three years' loss of liberty. I continued my sport for a short while after my discharge from the army, but I never felt the same, doing it in my own time. With the anger and frustration gone I took fewer chances with regard to injury. The final straw came when I fractured my ankle during a competition. A bad break, in which the ankle-bone broke out of its socket – a

Potts fracture – resulted in my leg's being encased in a plaster cast for six months and then spending another three with a cane. My wrestling days were over.

After finishing my miserable guardsman episode I returned to the East End of London, where I had been born and brought up (apart from a five-year evacuee period during the war). The local Labour Exchange did not seem to have much to offer a young man of twenty skilled only in wrestling, spit and polishing and horse-riding. I had plenty of hang-ups then, too. Bob would have found me an interesting case.

These are the sorts of thoughts that pass through the mind on a straight, not very interesting, road leading towards Baeza. At ten o'clock, the sun still hung low in the clear sky, shining directly on to our backs. I was glad of the Julia cream. The night before I had applied some of this wonder ointment to my blistered feet and found that it had done them the world of good. My toothpaste had nearly all gone and I wondered …?

After four hours' steady marching I waited for Bob to catch up. At a turning off to the left, a road sign indicated the way to a town called Mengíbar. We sat, in what little shade there was, by the side of a concrete monument marking the spot where Antonio Chinchilla, aged 50, and his son Manuel, aged 20, had been assassinated on 27 July 1936. During our trek we came across many other such markers, all honouring those killed by the 'rojos,' or reds (Communists). There was no sign of anything commemorating the Republicans, of course. For ten minutes we rested and refreshed ourselves by eating a couple of oranges, for fruit and water was all the sustenance we normally carried with us. Before setting out we had resolved that stopping to eat at a roadside bar (if one could be found), might prove dangerous, for we were aware of our weakness when it came to 'one for the road'. Anyway, a walk is much harder to continue on a full stomach. To be sure, we felt hungry and thirsty at times and looked forward to eventually arriving somewhere and tucking into a good meal. As Bob used to say, 'anticipation is half the pleasure'. We surely had our share of anticipating.

Civil War monument

The olive groves had, by now, given way to vineyards and, as we continued further, we crossed a little river – the Río de Torres – where the fields looked as though they were laid out for wheat. Over to the left we could see a large lake with a variety of birds either on it or circling over it. (It was, in fact, shown as the 'large lake' or 'laguna grande' on the map). At this time of the year an assortment of wildlife can be seen in this area, especially the winged variety. Those migrating north from Africa and others coming south to breed here make these wetlands fascinating for bird watchers. The resident birds include larks, martins, thrushes and warblers, but the arrival of ducks, plovers and mallards attracts the raptors. Kites, harriers and eagles from the nearby sierras appear in search of prey. Farther to the west, in the Doñana National Park, flamingoes can be seen.

At a crossroads we saw a signpost pointing south-east, revealing that our old friend Torres was 25 kms in that direction, while another, indicating back the way we had come, read: 'Mancha Real, 26 kms'. We felt a little happier to know for certain now that the taxi ride had not, in any way, cut the kilometres. Just a detour, we agreed. And so, after crossing over the river Guadalquivir by means of the long, many-arched Bishop's Bridge, and passing under a railway line, we started to go up a slight hill on our last stretch to Baeza. The small railway station we passed went by the name of 'estación de Begíjar' which made sense for there was a small town called Begíjar not far away. The track ran from Granada to Madrid but this station was the nearest to Baeza, and I wondered why it had not been built a little nearer to this large town, for the line appeared to run through the middle of nowhere. Later, I discovered that the railway followed the path of the river and that, in bygone days, it was the main trading route through to Sevilla, Córdoba and on to the Atlantic. The line was not constructed for people but more for the transportation of crops and goods grown and manufactured in this area and then sent on to other parts of Spain. Also, of course, it was much easier to lay a railway line on a flat surface, as found by a river. The track gauge adopted was slightly wider than that prevailing in the rest of Europe. Ostensibly, they chose the greater width to support larger and heavier trains but another reason, it is thought, could have been to prevent the movement of troops and armaments into Spain from other countries.

Although we had encountered no real problems that day, we still felt exhausted. The rigours of the previous day still troubled us and we had covered over thirty kilometres in very hot conditions. Up in the mountains it had been a little cooler but here, in the flat, marshy plain, we found no respite from the sweltering, shimmering heat.

Looking back down the road, I noticed that during the last, uphill part of the day, Bob had developed a limp. A van, heading towards Baeza, had stopped and offered him a lift into town and, at first, Bob had not quite understood, thinking that the man might be asking directions. The driver, realising this, performed a little miming act by pointing first to his spare seat and then towards Baeza. Bob got the message but, to the kind motorist's surprise, shook his head. The incredulous van driver sat looking at him for a moment or two, then sped off, past us both, up the hill. Mad foreigners! He would have something to tell his mates in the bar that evening.

Later, Bob resolutely declared that he would accept no more lifts, come what may. The taxi episode would never be forgotten or forgiven.

"Sterling stuff!" I said to him.

"How's that again?" questioned Bob. These Americans!

So, with me at my guardsman's pace and Bob at his limp, we passed a little row of neat, white houses and entered Baeza. As we stood under a shady arch and looked around, my first impression of the place was one of orderliness, tranquillity and mediaeval beauty. I almost forgot aching muscles and sore feet as I stood looking about me. In front of us I saw a large oblong plaza shaded around its edge by shady pavements, overhung by ornamented balconies belonging to the buildings above. Tables and chairs had been set out invitingly and, like a magnet, drew us towards them. Bob, limp or no limp, arrived first and immediately ordered a jug of beer. Although

Plaza, Baeza

his Spanish was almost non-existent, I noticed that he had soon mastered the art of ordering a drink. After polishing off this blissful jug of liquid, along with a plateful of delectable tapas, we followed the waiter's instructions to an attractive-looking hostal situated nearby. El Patio, as it was called, had everything we required. The rooms looked fine, the beds comfortable and it seemed inexpensive. After a quick wash and tidy-up we set off to explore this little gem named Baeza.

The exploration took us only as far as the nearest restaurant. We felt hungry and found a rather elegant-looking place overlooking the square. The prices may have been a little higher than those we had been used to, but we didn't care, for just to sit in comfort at a table covered with a white tablecloth laid with decent cutlery was worth the extra, we agreed. Later, with full stomachs, we leaned back in our soft chairs, with coffee and cognac set before us, smoking a cigar. The meal had been accompanied by two bottles of wine and we were on our third cognac. Everything looked rosy. The exhausting, thirty-odd kilometres we had covered that day became a 'mere stroll' to fine, fit fellows like us, while the suffocating, oven-like temperature we had been complaining about earlier had faded into having been 'just a little hot'.

"Hot!" I said, taking another sip of brandy. "You call that hot! Why, I remember one time in the Persian Gulf …"

Bob, also, brought to mind much hotter experiences he had suffered in the past. When I asked about his limp, he answered,

"Limp! Call that a limp! Why I remember the time …"

And so we reminisced and re-lived the past few days. At this moment, the bad times did not seem so bad and the earlier pains and frustrations we had undergone suddenly became amusing in retrospect, with Bob mimicking my expressions and tantrums and me waiting my turn. This ability we had to turn things around and make fun of our hardships became a great asset during the trip. At the end of the day, with a few drinks inside us, we loosened up. The motive for testing ourselves like this made sense. Bob, the analytical one, started to hold forth in his lecture-like manner,

Hostal El Patio, Baeza

"You see, Roy, a man needs a challenge in life from time to time. A dose of masochism won't do you any permanent harm. It's all a question of comparison. Why did that food and drink taste so good? I'll tell you. It's because we were so hungry and thirsty, that's why. Why does sitting or lying down, or simply taking the weight off your feet, give so much pleasure? Oh, you get the picture, don't you?" I tried hard.

We decided to put off our intended tour of Baeza until later. It was late, it was dark and, more to the point, crossing that flat expanse of the Guadalquivir basin while most sensible folk were taking their siesta, had taken it out of us. We felt totally whacked. I was thinking it but Bob said it first.

"How about a day's rest tomorrow?" he suggested, pointing out that we had not yet 'checked the place out'.

"A day's rest!" I exclaimed jokingly, in my aghast-like voice. "Where do you think you are? On holiday?" He could tell that I was not serious. "I was about to say the same thing myself," I confessed. "A recuperation day is called for."

I had noticed earlier that Bob's leg was troubling him. Hopefully, a slight pause in our trek would sort things out. And it would have been a pity to leave this town without making a tour. To clinch the matter absolutely, we learned from the waiter that the following day would be a public holiday, with much merrymaking.

"Just the ticket!" I exclaimed.

"What ticket?" asked Bob. These Americans!

8

Baeza, I've fallen under your spell.
You've captured my heart with the wonderful tale you
tell.
Of an age that's long forgotten ...

I awoke to the sound of banging drums, with two distinct sorts of beat. One came from somewhere outside my window and the other, I gradually realised, pounded away inside my head. As I lay there distinguishing one from the other, the resounding drumbeats were suddenly joined by blaring of trumpets and thunderous clashing of cymbals. I groaned and slid down beneath the bedclothes, trying to shelter from the noise. Never again, I vowed, for the umpteenth time, will I drink too much – or, at least, not mix my drinks. I needed coffee, urgently.

Downstairs in the breakfast room I found a miserable-looking Bob, head in hands. A half-empty jug of water and a mug of coffee were on the table beside him. We said nothing until I had finished my second cup.

"Fancy a beer, Bob?" I asked, cruelly. He groaned.

The cheerful proprietor could see our problem and was most sympathetic. I felt like asking him if he could do something about the loud music floating in from outside – but I knew that it would be a waste of time. After a gloomy breakfast we both went back to our rooms. Baeza would have to wait a while. At midday we met up again and, feeling slightly better, ventured outside. The brilliant, glaring brightness was accentuated by the white walls of the nearby houses and a golden hue radiated from some of the other, larger buildings around us. Our hats helped with the overhead radiance from the sun but there seemed to be a dazzling beam coming up from the cobbles under my feet. I had to look somewhere. Lucky Bob wore spectacles which adapted themselves to become sunglasses in a strong light ('umbramatic', I think they were called) whereas I, poor fellow, had nothing with which to shield my sensitive eyes.

"Sunglasses, sunglasses, my kingdom for some sunglasses," I muttered.

Bob looked in my direction with professional interest. Had I finally cracked? After all, it had been very hot yesterday.

As I squintingly groped my way slowly towards the plaza, it was impossible not to take in the splendour of our surroundings. Though not quite in the mood to examine very closely the honey-coloured, elaborately carved, sandstone structures we passed on the way, I enjoyed the mediaeval feel to the place which permeated everything and simply could not be disregarded, even by me in my state. I would make a closer inspection later, I promised myself. The boisterous din could not be switched off, so we decided that we might as well join it, and by following the sound, strolled back to the square we had discovered the previous day. Once there, we saw people milling about everywhere and little stands laden with food and drink were dotted about the plaza, each surrounded by an assortment of merrymakers. Each emplacement had been adorned with banners advertising a certain political party and playing its own brand of music. The result may have been pretty chaotic, but it seemed to go unnoticed by the throng. It all looked very rowdy to us, in our delicate state, but at least the trees cast shade around the edge of the square, so Bob and I gritted our teeth and headed towards the melée. As we pushed and shoved our way through the bodies I suddenly realised that the date was May 1: Labour Day! This explained all the politics.

The busiest and liveliest group appeared to be crowded around the Communist stall which, we soon found out, served the cheapest drinks and choicest tapas. We concluded that Baeza either had a lot of Communists or, as with us, loyalty to a particular party was governed by the quality and price of what was on offer. My firm resolve about drink, I'm afraid, did not last long for I soon discovered a very tasty mountain wine. My favourite. A few glasses of that inside me and I started to feel much better. Sitting there, in the shade, with a glass in one hand and a slice of tortilla in the other, I reflected on how much things had changed since the death of Franco in 1975. There would have been no Labour Day festivities then, although May 3 was, and still is, celebrated as the Day of the Cross – la Cruz de Mayo. This date was devised by the church to take the place of May 1, with all its pagan associations.

When I first came to Spain, in the late '60s, I quickly learned that political opinions were best kept hidden. If the thought of living in a fascist country really upset you, then you had better move on or stay away. All foreigners were scrutinised very closely and it was most unwise to become involved in political discussion – especially in public places. Bars would empty at a rapid rate if the word 'fascista' or 'comunista' was used in conversation. The 'draft dodgers' from America were the worst culprits. I suppose they knew no better.

"Hey, man," they might innocently ask, in a crowded bar. "How's things out here? What's it like under the fascists?"

Nervous glances would be directed towards the speaker, glasses quickly emptied and hasty exits made. Except, maybe, for one or two smarter dressed types who had been listening attentively rather than talking. They would look on with interest. Franco's so-called 'secret police' (I say 'secret' with a smile for, down in my village, everyone knew their identity) were, at the same time, on the look-out for users and dealers in drugs. Marijuana or 'hash,' as it was then called, was readily available and, as it was only a short ferry trip from Málaga to Morocco, could be purchased there with no problem. Growing the stuff in Spain was not difficult either, and many did, but to be found in possession of 'hash' or any other drug was regarded by the authorities as a very serious offence. I will quote a letter that I, and other British residents, received from the British Ambassador:

"THE GAME IS NOT WORTH THE CANDLE.
This is an open letter to British visitors to Spain. It just has one thing to say. Stay off the hash. Don't smuggle it in, don't peddle it, don't carry it for others. And keep away from hash parties – when the law arrives, you will find it difficult to convince them that you were just looking on.

At home in England the penalties are mild. Here in Spain they are extremely severe. Don't think that as a first offender you are going to get away with a small fine or a suspended sentence: what in fact you will get is 6 years and a day. And you are unlikely to get bail on a narcotics charge. You may wait many weeks in prison for trial. The game is simply not worth the candle. We have too many young British people in gaol here already: please don't join them."

I still have a copy of this letter. It was absolutely true. Unwise, stupid friends of mine, who perhaps thought it all a bit of an exaggeration, disappeared from the scene almost overnight. While serving their six years in prison, many young people committed suicide. It is said that boredom drove them to it.

In my village the local police knew all there was to know about foreigners living locally. I was not into drugs, and they knew it. I was what was known as a 'day' person who enjoyed the daylight hours and went to bed at night. With a good physique and healthy, sun-tanned appearance this was pretty obvious. My only drug was sex – and the police did not count that as something to be punished. The 'night' folk, however, were watched more closely. They slept during the day and ventured out when the sun went down. Like vampires or owls. Some bars in Almuñécar stayed open all night, and these are where these paler-complexioned, frailer-looking types met. Occasionally, by chance, the 'day' and 'night' people would cross paths and discover that they had both lived locally for years without meeting one another. With my reputation then, I was most surprised to have the

Guardia pay a visit one evening and ask, politely, if they could search my house. A few friends of mine were there at the time, drinking and playing music. After a look around the officers thanked me, saluted and went away. It was then that one of my guests declared, with relief in his voice, that we had been lucky. He dug down into the earth of a plant-pot by his side and produced a small glass container with hash inside. He had buried it there when he heard the police at the door. I threw him and his jar out of the house and never spoke to him again. In fact, our paths didn't cross again for he kept well out of my way.

Here at the fiesta in Baeza, there was no hash, I felt sure. Just plenty of wine. By now, we had joined in the celebrations with gusto by moving around and giving our support to all the political parties in turn. Bob seemed convinced that a young woman was making eyes at him.

"She's giving me the come-on, man," he maintained. I looked. She couldn't have been more than sixteen years old.

"Leave her alone," I warned. "She spells danger." It was true, though, that the girl was staring at him with unabashed interest.

"Gee, I wish I could speak the language," he said. "Ask her if she'd like to come up to my room and give my leg a massage. Do you think her family needs a bit of new blood? We can't be related, tell her." He sulked at my refusal to act as a go-between.

We stayed there in the square for a few hours more, attracting quite a bit of interest from the crowd, but not the open-mouthed inquisitiveness that we had come across in the smaller villages. As I stood chatting, I noticed that Bob had wormed his way over to the girl and was doing his best to communicate with her. He was waving his arms about all over the place in an effort to make her understand, while she was watching him with a mixture of amusement and flirtatiousness on her pretty face. I hoped that he was not inviting her up to his room with all that sign language, for those watching his antics might be able to understand his gestures as well. At about 3 p.m. the crowd started to disperse. For most, it was time to eat and siesta. We were so full of tapas that we had no appetite for any more food but considered that it might be a good idea to follow the example of the others and head back to the hostal for a little rest. As we left the festivities, Bob cast a longing glance back at his sweetheart who waved goodbye.

"Man, she had hot pants for me. I'm sure of it," he sighed.

"Her father probably has something for you, too," I warned.

We didn't rest for long, determined to see more of Baeza when it was cooler and the streets more shaded. It did not take long to understand why this town had begun to attract tourists for it possessed a seductive charm all of its own. It had a population of 15,000 compared with Granada's 250,000, and we could quite easily walk around it in one day. But the compact, impressive beauty of the place provided an unforgettable experience. The lyric poet, Antonio Machado, who worked as a teacher in Baeza between 1912 and 1919, summed it up by writing 'I shall dream of you when I cannot see you'. The town's proximity to the river Guadalquivir made it important to the Moors, Romans and later, the Christians, and it reached a pinnacle of consequence and prosperity in the 16th century, when adopted by the rich merchants who traded in the area. These merchants built the impressive yellow sandstone buildings, a magnificent university, various plazas (some with fountains), a stunning town hall, a granary that looked more like a palace, an elegant corn exchange, an extraordinary abattoir with an enormous coat-of-arms over the doorway, and many other outstanding structures including the renovation of the 13th century cathedral built on the site of a former mosque. These, and many more, architectural treasures are still there in all their glory waiting to be viewed by the discerning visitor. It seems that these renaissance 'yuppies' spared no expense in making Baeza the 'in' place of its time. Everyone, it seems, wanted to impress his neighbour by displaying conspicuous wealth gained from the textile industry and agriculture in the 16th and 17th centuries. Something exciting and exotic in the air has made it one of my favourite cities.

By the time of our walk, Baeza had not become too 'touristy' and, on that particular day we came across no other foreigners. Since then, they have begun to arrive in greater numbers with each passing year. The narrow, wonderfully tiled streets are impressive enough but, from the edges of Baeza, the view over the surrounding countryside is quite breathtaking. We congratulated ourselves on having chosen such an admirable spot to enjoy a day's rest, and felt that it had done us the world of good.

Later that evening we again joined the re-assembled crowd in the plaza. Bob, failing to find his girl-friend, consoled himself in a liquid way for a while, but we both knew that the next day would bring another challenge, so we decided on a good night's sleep. We found another cheap restaurant, enjoyed a decent meal and returned to the hostal.

9

We bear the burden and the heat
Of the long day, and wish 'twere done

Next day we somewhat reluctantly bade farewell to Baeza's mediaeval charms (and more modern, female ones as far as Bob was concerned) and turned our faces towards our next port of call – Linares, which lay in a north-easterly direction. Our map showed that, to reach it, we should have to walk over a flat, marshy delta very similar to the last stretch between Mancha Real and Baeza. The morning air hung very still and, as the brilliant sun began to show itself, we knew we were in for another session of being baked. We had to cross another river, a tributary of the Guadalquivir called the Guadalimar, and to achieve this we had three possibilities, according to the map, without straying too far from our straight line. The simplest method was to stick to the N 322 which ran from Baeza to Linares but, as I have pointed out before, we wanted to avoid roads as much as possible. Who wants it to be simple, anyway? We then noticed a very small road further south that ran to a tiny place called Torrubia and from there we could see a railway line passing over to the other side of the river. Using this, I calculated, would save us at least five kilometres, so I put the suggestion to Bob, who sighed wearily. It was the Laurel and Hardy scenario once again – he being the fat one.

"My experience of railway bridges that cross over rivers," he said, sarcastically, "is that they are usually quite elevated."

"So?" I retorted. "So we might have to do a bit of climbing. So what? Think of the five, hot kilometres we'll save."

Bob thought for a moment. "Do you happen to possess a time-table, by any chance, Roy? Just imagine, for a moment, the two of us stuck in the middle of a single-track railway bridge, high up, with a river 200 ft. below and a locomotive steaming towards us."

"Oh, where's your sense of adventure now?" I asked.

"Still in one piece," he replied. "And I want it, and me, to stay that way."

I shall never know whether we could have used the railway track to cross that river for we decided to play it safe and use the road. However, looking once more at the map, we discovered another route which cut out the N 322 for most of the way. A minor road, the N326, led from Baeza to the village of Ibros and from there we spotted a footpath pointing towards Linares, joining the road just before the bridge. The first part appeared to be downhill, for Baeza was at 800 metres and this Ibros was located 200 metres below. We could then continue our descent from there to the marshy plain and, as we knew from experience, have fifteen, sweltering kilometres in oven-like heat to look forward to before starting to climb uphill again. The day's rest at Baeza had refreshed us a little but had not cured Bob's pulled muscle in his leg for, after the first few kilometres, I noticed him limping again. I stayed with him for a while but his continual mutterings about the girl he'd left behind him (as the song goes) eventually got on my nerves and I walked ahead, leaving him to limp and mutter on his own. At Ibros, eight kilometres down the way, I waited for him to catch up. While I stood there, the usual crowd of starers came to inspect my shorts and laundry, then saw with astonishment that another foreigner appeared, hobbling up the road to join me. On the outskirts of the village we passed a school where children were playing. They all immediately rushed over to stare at us and, to their delight, we put on a little show for their benefit by holding our hats in one hand and dancing a little jig as best we could. This triggered a fit of screaming and laughing. Bob did the best he could with his bad leg, but seemed to be looking more intently at the two young female teachers standing behind the students. He told me afterwards that he was on the look-out for signs of too much in-breeding, in case his services might have been required. I should never have mentioned those goatherds.

A little farther down the road, we heard the rare sound of a vehicle coming up behind us and moved over to let it pass. To our surprise, the dark-green Land Rover stopped. There were two Guardias Civiles inside. One of them got out and approached us. Quite a big man for a Spaniard, he looked very smart in his dark-green uniform with its customary shiny, three-cornered hat, knee-length leather boots and other accessories. At his side, fixed to the belt, hung a pistol in its shiny holster. It brought back dreaded memories of my guardsman days for everything looked so spit-and-polished. The Guardia was very polite. Saluting smartly, and wishing us "Buenos días," he asked for our papers. We obliged by fishing out our passports and handing them over. He gave Bob's to the man inside the Land Rover then looked at mine with interest. He appeared surprised.

"You are not American," he stated rather than asked. "I was given to understand that you were both Americans."

We had presented only Bob's passport at the hostales because of the Argentinian troubles, hoping that the authorities would assume we were both American. It seemed that they were keeping track of us.

"You stayed last night in Baeza, at the hostal El Patio."

Once again, a statement of fact. I nodded. He seemed to know all about us. What was this all about? Had we not paid our bill? Had I committed some offence by displaying my bare knees? Did he consider me to be some sort of pervert, dressed like this? Then a dreadful thought came to mind! What had that young thing in the plaza at Baeza made of Bob's sign language? Had she told her father? Perhaps he was a Guardia? While all this was going on, the other man inside the Land Rover, who had been scrutinising Bob's passport, came over and whispered something in my interrogator's ear. They both looked first at Bob (who was taking the opportunity to sit on the ground and rest his leg) and then back at me.

"Your American friend is a doctor?"

Now, Bob was a doctor of sorts. He held a doctorate in psychoanalysis and his passport had him down as Doctor Robert Smith. I knew that the Spanish people had a profound respect for doctors or anybody else who had some sort of title before their name and referred to them as 'Don'. I seized my chance.

"My friend is an eminent American doctor, yes," I said, trying to put a hint of annoyance in my voice. Why are you asking all these questions?"

I turned to the bewildered Bob and said to him, in English, hoping that the Guardia did not understand,

"I've told them that you are an eminent American doctor. Stand up and try to look eminent."

He struggled up from his sitting position and stood straight, pulling his shoulders back. The socks, vest and underpants dangling around outside his pack did not help his attempt at eminence, but the faces of the Guardia now began to look uncertain. They looked at each other, then at Bob again, and finally, once more, back at me. I glanced with overt impatience at my broken watch but couldn't peek at Bob for more than a second without sensing that I was going to break into laughter. He was trying to appear distinguished but just gave the impression of being a little drunk and I was forced to hide the grin on my face. After taking down the necessary details in a little black book, the Guardia returned our passports – a little grudgingly, I thought, – then saluted and drove off back towards Ibros. They knew that they could find us again whenever they wanted. We, at least, now had something to talk about. Why were they so interested in our movements? I never found out, but I had not forgotten the Falklands War. It could have been something to do with that, for I knew that my American disguise had been blown.

Although I did not know it at the time, I had even more reason to hide my Britishness, for the date happened to be May 2 – the day on which the Argentinian cruiser, the General Belgrano, was sunk by a British submarine, resulting in the deaths of many sailors. This really put the cat amongst the pigeons. Spanish television portrayed the British as the villains of the piece and to admit British nationality, here in Spain, would have caused all sorts of hassle. In the past I had always found both the police and the Guardia Civil to be fair-minded to those who live within the law. Officialdom in any country can be helpful or obstructive depending on how it is treated. As Bob and I continued our passage down the hill we discussed the earlier episode with the officers. I told him how impressed they had been by his credentials. That was a mistake.

"I thought so," he said, gleefully. "I saved your bacon yet again, Roy. Where would you be without me? Behind bars, no doubt." I hit back.

"I wouldn't be surprised if one of those guys wasn't the father of that young innocent piece of skirt you made a fool of yourself with, back in Baeza."

"So, what if he was?" argued Dr. Bob, limping faster to keep up with me. "A doctor for a son-in-law would have been a feather in his shiny cap, you know."

By walking faster still I managed to pull away from ' Don Bob' as he now started to call himself. The title had gone to his head. It brought to mind a young man, down in La Herradura, called Donald who made the most of his name by becoming known to the locals as 'Don Ald', and conse-quently enjoyed the utmost respect.

After a while, I became concerned. According to the map, the little road that we were on led eventually to a village called Capones which seemed to be stuck all on its own out in the middle of nowhere, so I was pleased to find the track, off to the right, that led towards the bridge and then on to Linares. My pleasure did not last long. The path, on a sharp descent, we soon discovered to be very rough and stony. All the rocks underfoot seemed to have been deliberately sharp-ened with their points facing upwards and it didn't take long for these painful obstacles to start sticking into the bottoms of my feet, for the thin crêpe soles of my cowboy boots offered little protection. I tried to step on the less-pointed bits, but there were not many to be found. As well as this, loose, smaller pebbles lay all over the ground, making the surface very slippery. I looked back at the doctor who had, somehow, managed to find a long, stout stick to use as a staff and I could see that it gave him a useful 'third leg'. I wanted one, too, but, after a fruitless search, gave up looking. To keep my balance, I held my arms out to my sides, which resulted in loud aeroplane noises coming from my compañero behind.

Two hours and eight hard, painful, slipping and sliding kilometres later we met up with the little road but, by then, I had joined Bob in limping. I knew my feet to be in a sorry state. Back on level ground again it was easier to walk, but the damage had already been already done. So we hobbled along together: this was becoming a habit. It had changed from hot to very hot. The sun stood directly overhead and the heat seemed to be even greater than that of the Guadalquivir basin. Bob reckoned the temperature under-foot hot enough to fry eggs and I worried that this furnace might just melt the soles of my boots, for they kept clinging to the road. I must keep moving, I thought, or I could just stick fast! No traffic, no breeze and no shelter in sight.

I remembered a few lines of Alexander Pope and sang them,

'Where e'er you walk, cool gales shall fan the glade.
Trees, where you sit, shall crowd into a shade'.

Bob, not amused, instructed me to 'belt up.'

We ate our oranges and drank some water sitting by the side of the road, out in the full blast of the sun. As I sat there, I noticed some large birds circling overhead. Vultures, I wondered? Perhaps just waiting. On this marsh-land a wide selection of duck, stork and other aquatic crea-tures can be seen, either wading or swimming. The whole region, north and south of Baeza, is a bird paradise. In the hills behind my village of La Herradura I often used to watch the various birds of prey circle high in the sky and then dive, like a rocket, down towards something they had spotted far below.

Another bird I used to sit and watch, in the cool of the evening, was the little swift, swooping in and out of the shadows, almost touching the ground in its search for insects. Swifts live in a vicious, never-ending circle, needing constantly to eat in order to replace the energy spent in their incessant flying. During their lifespan, it has been calculated, these small birds fly, in distance, from the earth to the moon and back, five times! Another feathered friend of mine has always been the much-maligned, humble seagull. Not everyone's favourite, I know, but the cry of the gull brings back memories of my sea-going days.

'As friendly as stars to steersmen in mid-seas
And remote as midnight darling stars
As nigh the hand as windflowers in the wood
But inaccessible as Dido's phantom.'

That's the gull, in words written by the granddaughter of Pepita.

Apart from the birdlife that abounds in these parts, plenty of other wildlife can be found up in the nearby hills, including the mountain goat, or ibex. To observe these animals, I have found it best to keep very still and wait, especially at dusk or early in the morning. They can be spotted only if they move: their camouflage in the rocky hills is perfect. Then there are wild boar (best avoided, especially if they have young with them), two types of deer, a long-tailed rodent-like little animal called the genet, rabbits and hares, and, rarely seen, the lynx.

However, we did not have much opportunity to study any of these creatures. There could have been herds of ibex and deer galloping all over the place or wild cats pouncing on genets a few paces from us, for all we knew. We trudged steadily onwards with shoulders slumped and hats pulled firmly over our downward-looking heads. Our gaze inclined more to the long lines of ants which busied themselves carrying loads hither and thither. Occasionally we came across lizards which scuttled away if we trod too close. A giant type

Lizard

of lizard in Southern Spain resembles an iguana. I saw one, once, from the flat roof of my house. It must have been at least a metre and a half in length. I couldn't believe my eyes! It looked up at me for a few moments and then waddled off. In this delta there are seventeen different sorts of amphibian and eight species of snake. Of the eight, three are poisonous. The triangular-headed Lataste's viper is the most dangerous, but also to be avoided are the false smooth snake and the Montpellier snake. Richard Ford noted, when he was in this country a century and a half ago, that a broth made from one of the harmless types was prescribed for certain ailments. Insects are not hard to come across. They find you. If you really want to inspect lots of different insects without much effort, I can recommend the application of some Julia cream to the skin.

Roasting in the heat, we continued on our weary way until, at last, our small road joined the N 322 which passed over the River Guadalimar. On the other side of this bridge we saw a station which stood beside a single-track line. Bob had been right in his assumption. It was probably just as well that we had not tried to walk it. The eight kilometres to go before reaching Linares in our sorry state seemed more like eighty. Our route lay mainly uphill and my poor bruised feet shrieked protest at every step. Passing traffic created a little waft of air as it passed, which felt good. Bob was right in his philosophy. Who could have imagined that something as simple as a passing vehicle could give so much pleasure? Eventually, at the top of the hill, we came to two long rows of houses, one on each side of the road. We struggled on, keeping to the shady side, for about another half-kilometre before finally finding a bar to stagger into and order a drink.

The place we entered might not have been elegant but it served the required potion, and that was all that we cared about. The fat lady behind the bar did not seem particularly overjoyed to see us and, instead of a charming smile, delivered a cold stare. A noticeable chill in the air seemed almost welcome.

Let me try and paint the picture. Imagine, for a moment, a scene from a typical cowboy film in which the activities of a Wild West saloon are suddenly interrupted by the entrance of a tall stranger (John Wayne?) who, pushing open the creaking swing-doors, lopes his way, spurs a-jingling, over to the bar and demands a shot of red-eye. The nervous bar-tender slides a glass of liquor along the counter. Tension in the air rises. The card-players cease their card-playing, the honky-tonk piano stops in mid-tune and all eyes fix upon the mysterious stranger. This will give some idea of how it felt when we first went into a local pub in these small places off the beaten track.

Linares could not be considered small, for it had a population of more than sixty thousand, but not many foreign visitors. Guide-books did not help this state of affairs for they described the town as ugly and industrial. This little bar at the edge of town had probably never entertained, or even heard of, car-less foreigners before and so, with our bedraggled, sweaty appearance and weather-beaten complexions we were probably taken for a couple of tramps and treated as such. In smaller villages the reception differed. The folk there did not care how we looked and often showed a bemused interest in our venture. The rude manner of this miserable woman was an example. Affronted, Bob suggested that I should let it be known that a Don was standing before her but, not wanting to complicate matters, I merely asked where we might find an hostal.

"Hostal?" she barked, looking not at me, but at the glass she was drying. "There is an hostal on the other side of town. They might give you rooms."

She emphasised the word "might" while continuing to polish away at the same dry glass. It did not sound too hopeful.

"We also have the Hotel Cervantes in the town centre," she continued, "but that is for business people."

She stressed "business" in a voice that suggested that it was not for our types. She now rubbed the glass harder than ever. Was she trying to make a genie appear, I wondered? It would dissolve soon, I thought.

Before leaving, we washed our hands and faces in a dirty little room at the back, packed away our, now dry, laundry and tidied ourselves up as best we could. I then went back and paid for the drinks with the largest denomination peseta note I had. I wanted her to realise that we had money for she might have telephoned ahead to let it be known that a couple of undesirable bums were on their way. As soon as we left, we heard the hubbub start again inside. Our ears started to burn. The row of low, white houses seemed to go on for ever. We continued on into the main, busier part of Linares, past the hotel that was not for the likes of us, and out the other side. After another kilometre or so we reached the run-down looking hostal, which made no problem about accommodation. We later discovered that we were the only residents. The rooms all faced the road, and suffered plenty of noise from passing traffic, but we did not care. We had found beds at last. As the time was eight p.m. and too early for restaurants to open, we decided to rest a while, meet later, and then return to town and find somewhere to eat. The

Hotel Cervantes, Linares

hostal provided no food. After dutifully completing laundry duties and washing and massaging my poor, sore, bruised feet, I lay my aching body down to rest. Oh, what a delight!

When I next opened my eyes I found myself in total darkness and tried to work out where I could be. My brain did not function properly. Very slowly, as though recovering from an anaesthetic, I came to my senses. Linares. Hostal. I had an empty feeling in my stomach. How long had I been asleep? With much effort, I raised myself and stumbled over to the window. Outside, in the street, nothing moved: no traffic and no lights from the buildings opposite. It was late. Too late, I reckoned, to try finding an open restaurant. Where was Bob? Unconscious, no doubt. He couldn't be in the adjoining room, I reasoned, or I would have heard his snoring, for he was a loud snorer. I considered my position but it did not take me long to work out my next move. Although I experienced pangs of hunger, fatigue conquered all. As soon as I lay down again my eyelids fell shut and I instantly returned to the Land of Nod.

10

Oh, Manolete! Why did you leave
The bed of laurels
You so richly deserved?

The next thing I heard was a loud thumping on the door of
my room: Bob, hammering away and sounding angry.

"Wake up, man!" he was shouting. "Do I have to break this
damn door down?"

"Why all the hurry?" I asked, still half asleep. "What time is
it anyway?"

"Time to eat!" he bellowed. "I'm starving!"

"See you downstairs in five minutes!" I called back.

We had both slept for over twelve hours and felt a little
guilty at not sticking to our customary practice of trying to
be ready for the road by eight a.m. However, to ease our con-
science, we agreed that the break in routine had been
unavoidable, for we had both been totally exhausted. After a
little discussion we decided that, as my feet and Bob's muscles needed more respite, we would convalesce here at
Linares for another day. But, we proclaimed, this sort of thing
could not continue. One day on and one day off had to be
ruled out. Madrid would never be reached at this rate. After
booking in for another night, we made our way sluggishly
back into the town centre. Once there, we scoffed a huge
breakfast of fried chorizo, eggs and tomatoes, followed by
sugar-coated churros (elongated doughnuts). The local olive
oil, used for frying, gives a delicious taste to everything. I
could feel strength slowly creep back into my body. It's marvellous what a good night's sleep and a full stomach can do
to restore a man's vigour. With all this newly-gained energy,
we set off to look around Linares. Bob had a few things he

wanted to do and I had some ideas of my own so we went our separate ways, arranging to meet up later in the afternoon at the celebrated Hotel Cervantes – just to lower its standard a little. Being on our own for a while, we thought, would do us no harm.

Although guide-books advise tourists to give Linares a miss, I found nothing wrong with it. There were lots of cheap, good bars and restaurants, and the people seemed friendly enough. Maybe it lacked architectural splendour or historical interest to attract the sightseer, but this added to its appeal, for there was not a tourist to be seen. I tracked down a sports shop that sold walking boots and asked if there were any of my size. The young assistant working there took one look at my size twelve feet, smiled and shook her head. Only in Madrid, she said, had I any chance of finding size forty-seven in footwear. She sympathised when I explained the problem with the thin soles of my present shoes and suggested that I could try putting an 'in-sole' at the bottom to improve the cushioning. I bought some and did as she had advised and, as I strode away from the shop, could immediately feel the benefit.

While exploring the town, I came across, in one of the small side streets, an unusually quiet bar where two men were hunched over a table, playing chess. I was not surprised, for I knew that world championship matches take place here annually when participants, including grandmasters, arrive from all parts of the globe to compete. Other men stood around watching the game and commenting amongst themselves after every move. The scene reminded me of the picture Cela paints in *Journey to the Alcarria,* in which the players are made most comfortable by the onlookers (Cela calls them 'toadies') who light cigarettes for them, call waiters and retrieve any pieces that fall to the floor. Roger Fry, who came to visit his friend Gerald Brenan, spent much of his time playing the game in Almería.

Chess has always been a favourite of mine and, at one time, became an obsession. I read somewhere, once, that chess is akin to life itself. Starting a game is like stepping forth into the

Chess, Linares

wide world with all its obstacles. Every move made on the chequered board can bring feelings of hope, sorrow, a deter-mination to fight on even when things are going badly, or sometimes, a realisation that all is lost, and then resignation. I found it to be a beautiful, romantic escape from reality, and played wherever I went, whenever I could. In Paris at the Cave de Boulé or Bar Polly Magoo, in Vienna the Café Museum, in New York on Washington Square and in Sydney at Central Park. The club to top them all, though, was the one in Hastings, England. In this seaside town there is a chess club that stays open every day of the year (except Christmas Day), and here I have passed many a happy afternoon and evening. At the time, I lived at St. Leonards-on-Sea, just west of Hastings. My wife, Catherine, would often need to telephone the club to let me know that my dinner was getting cold.

The game had a lot to answer for. While playing at another club in the south of England I faced across the board a Polish scientist named Dr. Bohdan Cwilong. Afterwards, we sat chatting and I learned that he was about to embark on a trip around the world on a seventy-four foot yawl, the *Princess Waimai*. Among other things, he wanted to discover more about the earth's magnetism. At the time, I was earning my keep by living-in and working at a riverside pub called the Bugle Inn, in the village of Hamble, Hampshire. It was right on the river Solent and most of the customers were trendy boating types. This Polish doctor had his yacht moored close by and the next day, after a restless night dreaming of adventure, I went aboard. Was there any chance of my joining the crew, was what I wanted to know. Dr. Cwilong already had a little group of participants, consisting of his wife, Marie, an Irishman and four Polish merchant seamen who had "jumped ship" from a Polish vessel which had docked at Southampton. However, there was room for one more, he declared. Welcome aboard! With plenty of media coverage, we set sail from England in November 1954. I was sixteen.

The month that we had chosen to cross the Bay of Biscay was not the best, weatherwise, we soon discovered, for as soon as we neared the end of the Channel and turned into the Bay of Biscay, we encountered terrible storms with mountainous seas. After being tossed about for a few days, the captain decided to sail 'with the wind' and head for Madeira, but a week later concluded that we had missed the island completely and headed south-east towards Africa, which is harder to miss. Somehow or other we arrived at Gran Canaria and anchored in Las Palmas harbour. How we had survived the terrible voyage, I shall never know. The crashing seas had opened up the decks of the yacht and for most of the trip it was only by taking turns at the hand bilge-pump, night and day, that we managed, somehow, to keep afloat.

While ashore, three of the Poles and I were arrested for not having the necessary papers or visas, and held captive by the Guardia Civil. I spent my seventeenth birthday and Christmas under custody. Eventually, the British Consul, discovering that I was a British subject and therefore his responsibility, managed to get me aboard an oil tanker, the *British Holly*. This vessel had docked at Las Palmas on its way back from the Cape Verde Islands, en route for the Persian

Gulf, and on this ship I worked my passage, as deckboy, back to England. The yacht was never heard of again and the fate of my three Polish shipmates, held with me in Las Palmas, is unknown, too. They had escaped from a communist country and the last thing they wanted was to be sent back to Poland, where they feared that a Stalinist reception committee might be waiting. But Spain was no safe haven for them either. This was 1954 and Franco wanted nothing to do with political refugees from communist Poland.

My experience did not change my feelings for the sea. I had been at the mercy of the mighty King Neptune and he had chosen to spare my life. Perhaps that is why the sea still fascinates me. Later I sailed all over the world as a merchant seaman.

So picture me now, contentedly playing chess in Linares. For some time I sat completely engrossed in the game. I forgot all my aches and pains and thoughts of the past or future; only my next move mattered. My concentration was broken by the sudden appearance of Don Bob. He did not stay long. Not being a chess enthusiast, and seeing that I looked in no mood for dialogue, he drank a coffee and left. The players assembled there did not appear to need an afternoon siesta, so play carried on into the evening and would probably have continued late into the night. I could easily have stayed but discovered that it was getting quite late, so reluctantly said goodbye to my fellow devotees and set off for the Cervantes.

I found Bob lounging in a very comfortable-looking armchair, beer in hand. As I walked towards him he looked pointedly at his watch. I apologised for my lateness and sat down next to him. The waiter brought over two more drinks.

"Cheers," I toasted Bob, raising my glass. "This is the life, eh? But not quite our usual style," I added, looking round the panelled, plush room.

"I don't know what drinks cost in this place," he said, "and I don't much care. It's good to join the other half once in a while."

We both felt good. He had spent a pleasant day. After changing money at the bank (where he had been presented with a town guide) he had bought a few items at the chemist and then sat, for a while, watching the girls go by – and there were plenty of beauties, he assured me. After that, aided by the handbook, he had visited the town museum where they had Roman artefacts (found locally) on display, then he had inspected an ornate façade of a building originally a hospital but now the Palace of Justice, and finally had gone to view the twelfth century parish church. He felt pleased with himself. The only boring part of the day, he complained, was watching the chess.

"How did you get on without my help with the language?" I asked.

"Who needs you?" he retorted. "And tell me, Roy. What did you see of the town?"

I had to admit that I had seen very little apart from knights, pawns, bishops and the like, but said that I had passed a delightful day, nevertheless.

With a name like Cervantes, I had expected the hotel to be decorated in a Don Quixote theme but, instead, the walls were plastered with photographs of bulls confronting flourished capes with matadors standing over them, swords poised. Above the reception desk hung a large picture of a beaming Ernest Hemingway standing beside a good-looking young matador named Antonio Ordóñez who, in the 1950s, was reckoned to be without equal. He was uncle to the equally famous present-day matador, Francisco Rivera Ordóñez.

Linares was well-known for its bullfights. The famous Manolete had been gored to death here in 1947. This legendary bullfighter had established himself as a purist and maestro of the art but, at the height of his popularity, decided that he had proved himself enough and just wanted to cut off his pigtails and call it a day. At the age of thirty, fame and fortune were his, and his attention turned more towards women and booze. A new torero appeared on the scene and started to win the fans' affection. His name was Miguel Dominguín. This handsome young man, brother-in-law to the aforementioned Antonio Ordóñez, was, at the time, linked to the film star Ava Gardner. Arguments broke

Ernest Hemingway with Antonio Ordóñez, Linares

out as to who was the better bullfighter and Manolete's
loyal supporters called upon him to prove himself once
more. He had no need to prove anything, but the word
'coward' goaded him to agree to one last season. Here in
Linares he faced a bull named Islero, which came from a
breed known as 'the bulls of death', so called because they
realised that the man holding the cape, and not the waving
cape itself, was the enemy. Manolete performed his magic in
the ring but, at the point of plunging the sword into the
neck of the bull (the most dangerous moment, for it exposes
the thigh) the exhausted Islero made one last desperate
thrust and stuck his horn deep inside Manolete's femoral
artery. The bull died there in the ring and Manolete a short
while later, in hospital. A public mourning followed throughout Spain. The nation felt guilty for hounding their hero to
his death, for clearly their stinging accusations had brought
about this disaster. Poor old Islero shared the blame and, out
of revenge, all his surviving relatives were slaughtered,
totally destroying the bloodline.

Andrés Segovia, the master of the classical guitar, was born in Linares in 1893. This famous musician lived for part of the year down south in La Herradura, where he owned a villa on a peninsula called Punta de la Mona (Monkey's Point) and could often be seen in the village or on the beach. I had the good fortune to hear him give a recital at the Alhambra in Granada, an unforgettable experience.

After a few more drinks we felt even more relaxed and decided to stay and eat at the hotel restaurant. As we sat eating and watching television we learned more about the Falklands War. It seemed that the British Prime Minister, Mrs Margaret Thatcher, had declared an area two hundred miles out from the Falklands to be a war zone and anything entering this zone, she threatened, would be attacked by the British task force assembled there. We then learned that this had led to the sinking of the *General Belgrano*. The depressing news soured what had been, until then, an enjoyable day, so we gloomily finished our meal and returned to the hostal. Before sleeping, I lay back on the bed, closed my eyes and mentally analysed the various chess positions and moves made earlier in the day.

11

Of a man with a knife
And trouble and strife
With dogs

My sleep that night was full of chess-related dreams, but
nonetheless I woke up feeling pretty good, and met Bob at
the appointed hour.

We decided to head for La Carolina, a small town of fifteen
thousand inhabitants, twenty-six kilometres to the north, at
a junction where the small road that we would be walking
met the N1V highway. The dreaded N1V! Although we had
pored over the map, with, at times, others leaning over our
shoulders making silly suggestions, there seemed to be no
way to cross the high sierras without keeping to this busy
road and using the Despeñaperros Pass. They served no
breakfast at the hostal so we started out on empty stomachs, but had been assured that there was a roadside
bar/restaurant just a few kilometres out of Linares, at
Linarejos. As we shouldered our packs and stepped out we
both remarked on how much better we felt. To ease the
guilt we sensed at taking a second, unplanned break in our
schedule the previous day, we thought up all sorts of feeble
excuses. I blamed Bob for not waking me and he reckoned
it to be my fault for not buying a new watch. Eventually we
decreed it to be the fault of the hostal owner. He should
have realised that we wanted to make an early start and
given us a call.

Bob showed no more sign of a limp and, since I now had
the marvellous new in-soles in my boots, we advanced merrily, almost with a spring in our step. We found the roadhouse

where it should have been so, after a good breakfast, we located, and turned off at, the little road heading north to La Carolina.

The landscape had changed: instead of the usual regiments of olive trees, ahead and around us lay rugged-looking, uncultivated fields studded with large boulders which looked as though they had been stacked there by some mischievous giant, ready to throw at some passer-by. The narrow, deserted, pot-holed road stretched in front of us in a long, straight line, inviting us to tread it and, with clear blue skies overhead and just the hint of a breeze, prospects looked good. I started to sing, "Follow the yellow brick road".

"Are you feeling all right, man?" asked Bob. "Too much use of the grey matter yesterday, with all that chess perhaps."

"Look," I said, waxing poetic, "the birds are singing, the sun is shining, but all I hear is your bloody whining!" I then

Rocky road out of Linares

danced a little hop and a skip and sang – "We're off to see the Wizard, the wonderful Wizard of Oz!"

"Let's see how much you feel like dancing by the end of the day!" replied Bob, the damp squib.

Together we made excellent progress and, two hours later, had covered ten kilometres. During all this time we had seen not a soul, so we were quite surprised suddenly to come across two colourful-looking characters sitting on a log in the shade of a tree, eating. The larger of the two wore a hat with a feather in it and was engrossed in digging sardines out of a can with a large, vicious-looking, curved-bladed knife. The other, skinny one was weasel-faced and had a shifty look about him. He tore at a large chunk of chorizo with his teeth. On their knees I could see wedges of what looked like mountain bread – that is, bread made without yeast. (It lasts a lot longer than the other sort.) They both had black hair, dark eyes and swarthy, weather-beaten complexions. I told Bob later that he had begun to look that way himself and might have been mistaken for their long lost brother. He was not amused. On the ground in front of these two characters lay a half-empty bottle of wine and wandering about nearby, trying to graze at the sparse, dry grass were half a dozen scraggy-looking horses and one mule. As we got nearer, the thin one with the chorizo stood up and called to us,

"Hola! Good day, señores. Where are you going?"

"Madrid," I answered.

"Madrid!" he exclaimed. "You are on the wrong road, Señores. There is no transport on this road. You must return to Linares. From there you can take the train or bus to Madrid."

The former sardine-eater slowly looked us up and down. He tossed his now empty sardine-can on to the ground, wiped his knife on a leaf, closed it and dropped it into his pocket. That little act made me feel better. I told the standing one that we did not want the bus or train, for we were walking to Madrid. His mouth dropped open, exhibiting a mixture of chewed chorizo and bread.

"Walking!" he cried, with wide eyes. "Walking to Madrid! But why?"

The other one looked at us even more closely now. I thought quickly.

"It is a promise I made to my mother before she died," I said. "It is a pilgrimage of sorts."

Señor Chorizo was silent for a moment.

"A promise, yes," he repeated, quietly. "To your mother. Yes, of course."

There was a rather unsure look in his eye now, and he stood there rubbing his chin, while his seated friend silently contemplated a likewise mute Bob. He then offered us some of their food and, when I refused, explaining that we had just eaten, held up the wine. I felt they might have been offended if we had turned this down as well, so Bob and I each took a swig from the bottle. The taste was that of 'vino de terreno,' or mountain wine. I handed the bottle back and, for a short time, nothing happened at all. Then, the seated one stood up, belched loudly and strolled casually across to join his friend. Bob loosened the bag from his shoulders, swung it to the ground and stood there, very still, hands on hips. There was tension all round and I could sense danger. If the bigger man had made any movement towards his knife pocket, I feared Bob would have acted first and thought later. Both of us had read *Gatherings from Spain* in which Richard Ford observes that 'where an unarmed Englishman closes his fist, a Spaniard opens his knife.' Bob had joked at the time that perhaps this did not apply to Americans. Little weazel-face would represent no problem, I thought, but I could not be sure. I had learned from my seagoing days that size is not always important when it comes to a tussle. After standing there like statues for a moment or two longer, the big one turned towards his partner, shrugged his shoulders and returned to his seat in the shade. Whatever it was, it was all over. I felt that perhaps it was my turn to ask questions.

"Are those your fine horses?" I asked the standing one. I could almost hear his brain ticking over. "Fine? Had I said, 'fine' horses?" There was no doubt of our madness now.

"Fine animals indeed!" he answered. "And excellent to ride!"

I could see what this was leading up to and before he could start telling me about his wonderful scrawny horses, I cut in with a sigh.

"It is most unfortunate that I have made the promise to walk. To sit astride a splendid horse like one of those would be a delightful method of travelling, but—" I sighed again and shook my head sadly. He thought for a moment. I had taken the wind from his sails.

"But your friend," he remarked, "he has made no such promise and, with the mule, you would not have to carry that heavy bag on your back."

It sounded almost tempting, but I lied, "Ah! But he made the same promise. He is my brother, you see."

Bob was dark with brown eyes and black hair while I was blond with blue eyes and fair hair. Weasel-Face had realised, by now, that we were not going to be easy customers. I asked him in which direction he was travelling. They were on their way to Seville, he told me, to a horse feria that was taking place there the following week. Seville was two hundred and fifty kilometres away, to the west, so I reckoned that they would have to get a move on to reach it in time, but they did not appear to be the sort that got a move on.

I would have liked to find out more about these two but I could see that Bob was becoming impatient. He kept looking at his watch and growling little obscenities. As we moved away it was 'buen viaje' all round and I think that they were as relieved to see us go as we were to depart. Words like 'Madrid' and 'promise' floated after us as we continued on down the road and the word 'brothers' was accompanied by a burst of laughter. Bob asked what had been going on back there.

"A couple of opportunists", I replied. "With us as the opportunity – but they obviously thought better of it."

"I thought for a while that we might have been in for a bit of action," he said.

"Maybe," I answered. "On the other hand, perhaps they thought we were out to rob them. Pinch their horses. I could see that the big one didn't like the look of you at all."

Without a shadow of a doubt they were Romanies, I told him. I had met plenty down in the south of Spain, especially around the Sacromonte part of Granada where they put on bogus flamenco shows for tourists. I say 'bogus' because their performance is purely a money-making affair, executed without any true feeling. Nearly all flamenco lovers agree that the commercialisation of the art has led to its deterioration. As with most forms of expression, the performer needs a sympathetic audience – one that can receive what is being transmitted. From my own experience in the folk-song world I know this to be true. It is not so easy to find the real stuff any more. 'Aficionados' of flamenco meet in out-of-the-way places, usually in rooms behind a bar, where tourists cannot easily find them. The intrusion of someone who does not understand the complicated flamenco rhythms, and tries to participate in the 'palma' or clapping sound of the hands, can completely ruin what might otherwise have been a delightful performance.

At a party given by a German friend of mine, down in the village of La Herradura, it was promised that authentic flamenco would be presented by Romanies from Granada. When they arrived, dressed in their colourful outfits, one of the group sidled over to me and whispered in my ear. It was a friend of mine from England! He warned me not to expose him. He looked every inch a Romany, with a deep suntan, tight trousers and a large, gold earring. Let it be said, though, that he is a great flamenco guitarist and teaches the art back in England.

When I first came to Spain, in pre-television days, flamenco singing was quite a common occurrence. It was known in the south as cante andaluz or cante hondo. Federico García Lorca loved this traditional music and it greatly influenced

115

his *Romances Gitanos.* In a local bar the hubbub of noise would suddenly cease at the shrill, heart-rending cry from somewhere amid the thick, blue cigarette haze. To someone not used to such sounds it might seem that murder was being committed but, on closer inspection, it would be seen that the note was coming from someone standing in a trance-like state, with eyes closed and brow wrinkled in concentration. The room would fall silent and those within would listen to the person sing. The content of the piece would not amount to much. For example, it might be something like, 'Today I watched the sunrise with my lover at my side. The day would be ours to share'. To read a sentence like that means nothing, I know, but to listen to notes being wrung from the heart and feel the tremendous emotion expressed, is something that has to be seen and heard, to be understood. The word 'hoy' (today) can be made to last fifteen seconds, with the delicate notes soaring upwards, sliding downwards, and all the while moving like a feather being tossed about in the wind. The music is unique to Spain and, as Richard Ford describes it, 'these ballad songs have formed the delight of the people, have tempered the despotism of their church and state, have sustained a nation's resistance against foreign aggression.'

Once, while sitting in a bar with my wife, I bemoaned the fact that the true art of flamenco had become a thing of the past. The man behind the counter, overhearing this, informed me that the elderly gentleman sitting next to us used to be a well-known singer in the village. My barstool neighbour drew himself up to his full height and cried indignantly, "Used to be?" and at once broke into song. He had never lost the art.

To call certain attitudes or acts 'flamenco' suggests that they are acting or living outside the normal way of doing things. This, of course, is true of Romany people. They have a bad reputation and are considered to be untrustworthy and likely to steal, given the chance. I personally have never had any cause to distrust them but many Spanish friends of mine give them a wide berth.

Romanies live all over the world and are looked upon in much the same way wherever they are. They are traditionally a nomadic people who work at jobs that allow them to lead an itinerant life-style – such as a bit of car- and scrap metal-dealing, occasional circus or amusement arcade employment, fortune-telling for the ladies, and in fact anything that does not tie them down.

It is thought that the Romany race originally came from India and reached Europe in the 15th century where the indigenous people, for some reason, imagined them to be from Egypt. Egyptians became ' 'gyptians' and so the word 'gypsy' developed. Because of their constant movement it has been difficult to estimate how many there are, but their numbers world-wide have been estimated at 2,000,000. Since their arrival in Europe they have had a hard time, and been banished, at one time or another, from just about every European country. Longfellow, in *The Spanish Student*, wrote,

'That the Egyptians and Chaldean strangers
Known by the name of Gypsies, shall henceforth
Be banished from the land, as vagabonds.'

In more recent times the Nazis eliminated as many as 400,000 of them. Whatever their faults may have been, without them we should have no Romani poetry, tales or flamenco music, and Spain, for me, would be diminished.

As we continued on towards La Carolina I told Bob what I knew of the Romany people. He listened with interest.

"What were you talking about to those guys back there?" he asked.

"I told them that we were walking to Madrid because of a promise we made to our mother," I answered.

"Our mother!" exclaimed the startled Bob.

"Yes," I explained, "I had to tell them that you were my brother or you might have had to buy a horse."

"You're winding me up!" he laughed, so I had to relate the whole story.

Fernandina

Before long we arrived at a little terrace of houses, fronted by trees. The map showed this to be Fernandina, a good spot to rest for a while and eat a few oranges, we agreed. Making our way to a shady spot beneath a tree, we became aware of two scruffy dogs lying sprawled out in the place where we intended to sit. Bob shouted at them and waved his arms about, which had the desired effect. They slunk off, looking sideways at us and showing the whites of their eyes. Just as we were starting on our oranges, the two dogs returned, accompanied by three others of similar appearance. They were now a pack and I knew that when this sort of dog banded together, they could be dangerous. They were thin, mangy-looking animals showing no sign of a tail-wag. All five of them just stood there, looking intently at us. Because we were sitting down, their heads were level with ours and I did not like the look of the things at all. Very slowly we got to our feet. The dogs did not move an inch. If one of them had attacked us, then I am sure that the others would have followed suit, while any sudden movement or hostile action on our part might have triggered an angry response, which could well have developed into something more serious. A bite from one of these fellows could have meant a dose of rabies, and the treatment required for this would have put an end to our trip. Cela tells of his encounters with dogs while journeying to the Alcarria. His response to meeting them seems to have been to give them a kick. He did this at Torija and then again, to a dog called Perlita, at Tendilla (where it led to his being refused a meal and ordered to clear off). Then again, George Borrow tells of an encounter with an immense dog which came bounding towards him with "eyes that glowed and fangs that grinned". The brave man stooped forward until his head almost touched his knees and looked the animal full in the eyes. He maintained that no fierce beast will attack a person who confronts it with "a firm and motionless countenance". I told this story to Bob later and he was intrigued by the eye contact technique, but fancied that a verse or two of one of my folk songs would have been enough.

As we backed away I noticed, out of the corner of my eye, some people standing at the door of one of the houses, watching. Were they expecting to see us torn to pieces? Were they the dog-owners? Had this sort of thing happened before? Perhaps that was the answer. They may have thought we were Romanies and did not want us hanging around. Whatever their thinking, they showed no signs of offering to help. We had encountered dogs before and usually a loud shout or a throwing movement with the arm proved enough to frighten them away, but with these five vicious-looking creatures, it might have been a different matter. It took quite a while before we stopped looking over our shoulders, and both of us carried a large stone in each hand until Fernandina lay well behind us.

Six kilometres farther on we came upon La Carolina, a town developed in the 18th century by order of Charles III, and at this point our small, quiet road joined the noisy N1V highway. Standing at the junction, we watched with dismay as lorries, buses, coaches and cars whizzed past. Once through the purple mountains in front of us, we knew that we should leave the province of Jaén and enter that of Ciudad Real; both of us felt a little sad at the thought of leaving Andalucía. For the best part of a week we had been journeying across this region, and it had provided many fond memories to take on our way.

Andalucía, the second largest of Spain's seventeen autonomous regions, has a population of seven million. It comprises eight provinces and we had traversed two of them: Granada and Jaén. The other six are Almería, Cádiz, Córdoba, Huelva, Málaga and Sevilla. It is the hottest of Spain's regions (as well we knew!) with an average temperature of 16.8 degrees Centigrade. The anticipation of climbing up into the cooler mountain air once again appealed to us after experiencing the stifling heat of the Guadalquivir basin, but getting there by walking on the N1V did not. This famous Despeñaperros Pass, with its tunnels, parapets and twisting road, is at a height of over one thousand metres. It was built as long ago as 1779, and, in those days was thought to be a marvel of engineering. Then, however, it was not so safe to use. Bandits made sure of that!

It was too early in the day to stay at La Carolina, so we had our first taste of highway walking by trudging miserably along the busy N1V for a further ten kilometres to a small place called Santa Elena. As we approached the roadside hostal we could see heavy lorries and vans parked outside. Inside drivers created the usual smoke and noise and barely gave us a second glance – even though I was in my shorts. The clientele seemed every bit as sweaty and scruffy as ourselves. We were back in civilisation.

We found the cheap accommodation very basic, providing small, cell-like rooms with paper-thin walls through which every sound could be heard from next door. I am usually a light sleeper and the sounds of bronchial coughing, loud snoring and the occasional loud fart would certainly have disturbed my sleep under normal circumstances, but we had covered thirty-six kilometres that day, and I could have slept through anything.

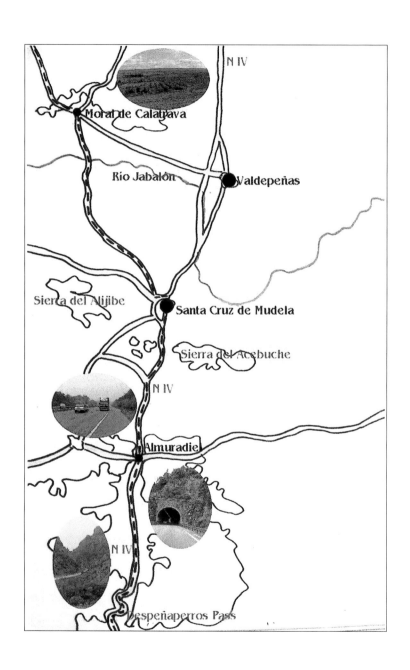

N IV

Moral de Calatrava

Rio Jabalón

Valdepeñas

Sierra del Alijibe

Santa Cruz de Mudela

Sierra del Acebuche

N IV

Almuradiel

N IV

Despeñaperros Pass

12

Around each bend we warily peered,
But 'twas not bandit gangs we feared.

Back on the N1V the next morning, we steeled ourselves for
a tough time ahead. Alongside the highway there was a slop-
ing strip, about a metre wide, on which we had to walk in a
clumsy, lopsided fashion, trying not to hold our breath whenever a heavy vehicle, spouting black diesel fumes, roared
past. We found nothing much to look at, other than the usual
assortment of motorway traffic and nothing much to look
forward to except more of the same. I saw that Bob was staring down at the ground, lost in thought.

"Can't get much worse than this, eh, Bob?" I shouted over
the noise.

"We need the occasional day like this, Roy," he called back
with a wry smile. "You didn't think that we'd be enjoying
ourselves all the time, did you?"

Enjoying ourselves all the time! I brought to mind the frus-
trating olive-trees episode, the shattering disappointment at
Torres, the excruciating pain of blisters on blisters, the tor-
turing, suffocating heat we experienced while crossing the
Guadalquivir basin – yes! We'd certainly been enjoying ourselves!

As we marched along, I remembered the times I had been
on this road, driving various 'old bangers' on my way to and
from my village in the south. The last time, I recalled, had
been with my old friend 'Whaletooth' Pete. Why was he nick-
named 'Whaletooth', you may be wondering? Well, let me
explain.

During the 18th and 19th centuries many different species
of whale were hunted and killed for their oil, bone and

'baleen' (the fringed plates through which whales sift their food). The oil was needed for lighting lamps and the bone and baleen used for shaping and supporting women's (and men's) corsets. Whaling fleets sailed early on north to Greenland but later, when the quarry became scarce in these waters, to the South Atlantic. While searching for these great mammals, sailors spent many long, dreary months at sea and, to while away the time, developed a skill for carving or engraving pieces of whalebone and whale's teeth. The art goes by the name of scrimshaw and, when an example of this work came on to the market, it fetched a high price and still does. A quick-thinking acquaintance of mine came up with the brainwave of putting a plain tooth into the hands of an experienced engraver and setting him to work. The newly scrimshawed tooth was then put into auction, netting him a tidy profit. He continued with this money-making scheme until it became virtually impossible to find any more plain whale's teeth to engrave, so he then hit upon another clever idea. Rubber moulds were made of several different examples of scrimshawed teeth, then a white resin concoction poured inside and, when the mixture had set hard, lo and behold! – an exact replica tipped out. With such a convincing result, few could distinguish the facsimile from the original.

For many years I had been making a bit of extra cash by dealing in antiques: the sort of work that could be taken up on my return to England, and discontinued when I decided to return to Spain. I specialised in buying pieces of sculpture in France and, hopefully, selling them in England. This clever associate of mine persuaded me to take some of his whale-tooth copies with me on my next trip to the Continent. They went like 'hot cakes' and, before long, I had a little group of entrepreneurs peddling these artefacts at various street markets in Paris. I met up with them in a certain bar once a week, when they would buy from me to replenish their stock. The plan worked well.

I met Pete busking with his guitar down in the Paris Métro. He had a hat placed on the ground in front of him, into which contributions could be tossed but, with competition from other musicians, it remained just about empty. We started chatting and I learned that he had been a student in California, and was now trying to bum his way around Europe. With his easy manner and infectious smile he seemed to be ideal material for my new enterprise. He admitted later that he thought me to be some kind of lunatic when I offered him a job selling plastic whale's teeth.

"Selling what?" he asked incredulously.

After I had given him more information he grinned and said, "Can't be any worse than what I'm up to down here. I'll give it a go."

Pete worked hard. It meant getting out of bed very early in the mornings in order to set up his little pitch at one of the many Paris street markets and, though he spoke no French, he managed to sell his wares by writing prices on his hand and pointing to the goods.

After six months or so I became bored with it all and told my little gang of salespeople that I'd be returning to Spain for a while and would be in touch at a later date. Pete, who had not only made a fair sum of money but had managed to save most of it, asked me if he could come too, because he wanted to see more of Europe. We filled up my old Citroën 2CV with a selection of reproduction artefacts and drove south together, selling at markets and shops on the way. With his share of the profit plus the money he had saved in Paris, Pete had enough capital to remain in the village of La Herradura for over a year. He loved the fine weather, and the laid-back life-style suited him down to the ground. He caused a few chuckles when he related his whaletooth experiences and, before long, became known locally as 'Whaletooth' Pete. During this period, one of my sons back in England was asked by his teacher at school what his father did for a living. My son replied, quite truthfully, that his father was a 'plastic whale-tooth salesman'. The bewildered teacher nodded and moved quickly on to the next pupil.

The walking became easier. With toughened leg muscles and hardened feet, my body seemed to move of its own accord. Without the distraction of aches or pains, we plodded awkwardly but steadily onwards, covering the kilometres at a rapid rate. Nothing much caught our attention or impeded our progress. All had changed, now we had no temptation to stop and admire fine views, for there were none, and the sweet birdsong of all our yesterdays had been replaced by the blaring of vehicle horns. Even the company of our old friends the ants and lizards came to an end, for they, it seemed, had more sense than to venture out onto this sort of territory. We tried to escape the monotony of it all by sinking deeper into our thoughts. I remembered the words to an old traditional Scottish folk song – 'Tramps and Hawkers':

'Oft times I've laughed unto myself when trudging on
   the road,
My toe-rags round my blistered feet, my face as brown
   's a toad;
Wi' lumps o' cake and tatie scones, wi' whangs o' braxie
   ham,
No' gi'en thocht tae where I'm gaun, and less frae
   where I've cam.'

We had little chance of meeting anyone else mad enough to be walking on this stretch of road, but felt a little apprehensive about the prospect of men in shiny hats ordering us off the motorway. We had no idea how the law stood when it came to the use of this road by pedestrians. Perhaps whoever wrote the regulations considered that no person in their right mind would ever wish to walk along the N1V and consequently, no such regulation had ever been made. We certainly had no problems. Why walk this busy, boring, polluted motorway? It would have been simple enough to have taken a bus or train to by-pass this stretch and continue on over the Despeñaperros Pass to a point where smaller, more interesting tracks started again. Had we some masochistic reason for our suffering? Perhaps, but we both knew, deep down, that without completing this difficult section, we

Despeñaperros Pass

would not, in retrospect, have felt the same sense of satisfaction. The sinful fiasco at Torres must not be exacerbated by our taking further rides. It might even have been, subconsciously, a desire to punish ourselves for this aforementioned shortcoming by enduring the next few days on this gruelling N1V. It felt a little like my three years spent in the Royal Horse Guards. It was great when it stopped and everything else appeared easier and better by comparison!

The road soon started to twist and turn its way upwards and we found that negotiating the tight curves was becoming dangerous. We felt safer facing the traffic but on sharp corners we couldn't see vehicles coming towards us and had to remove our packs and creep very slowly around the bend, keeping our backs as close to the cliff face as possible. Even then, some drivers, travelling fast, would cut in sharply and brush past us with inches to spare. This was bad enough, but when we reached the long, narrow tunnels things became even more uncomfortable. These ancient passages provided just enough space for two vehicles to pass each other, with no provision at either side for pedestrians. They were not anticipated. We waited until we saw nothing approaching and then ran as fast as we could through to the other side. If we had been unlucky enough to be caught sharing the space in the tunnel with two motorists, then we should probably have ended up as two smears on the wall!

This hazardous, daring escapade continued for quite a few kilometres as we made our way up the southern side of the Pass. At the summit we stopped at a bar/restaurant for a much-needed drink or two. Crossing sierras was not one of our strong points. The last time had been high up in the ill-fated Sierra Mágina, where we had become totally lost and luckily 'rescued' by a goatboy, but this present predicament we found more perilous by far. Had we been aware of these motorway dangers, we should probably have chosen a completely different route to Madrid, although a detour of this sierra would not have been easy. The mountain range stretches for 500 kilometres, from the mountains of Southern Portugal (the Sierras Aracena), through to the Sierra de Cazorla in the east and then

Narrow motorway tunnel

on to the steppe region of Albacete. It represents the eroded edge of the Meseta and, with a breadth of 65 kilometres, separates Andalucía from the rest of Spain. Although not terribly lofty (1323 metres at its highest point), the range is thickly forested and pretty much impenetrable. That is why it has always constituted such a wonderful natural barrier between Andalucía and the rest of Spain. During, and at the end of, the Spanish Civil War, the many caves up in the rugged peaks of these mountains provided splendid refuge for General Franco's enemies. Bandits used these same convenient hideaways in earlier times to rob travellers journeying to and from Andalucía. In the 19th century many romantic stories evolved around these 'Robin Hood-like' characters.

One of the most famous was José María Pelagio Hinojosa Cabacho, known popularly as 'El Tempranillo', the Early One. He originated from a small village near Córdoba, and at the age of thirteen is said to have killed a man for 'dishonouring' his mother. To escape arrest, he fled to the mountains and joined a gang of desperadoes that went by the name of 'Children of Écija'. A few years later José formed his own little band of brigands and set up headquarters in the cave of Los Órganos, which can still be seen from the road. He and his men charged a toll to those who used the pass and offered them his protection as they continued on their way. He declared that the King might rule in Spain but he ruled in the Sierras! Rather than argue the point, the King, in 1828, acknowledged his declaration and, in respect of his 'noble reputation', granted him a pardon from his wrongdoings. It seems that the wise ruler had adopted the – 'if you can't beat 'em, join 'em' philosophy. José died in 1833 and his tomb can be found in the village cemetery at Alameda, near Córdoba. His appearance remains a mystery: some describe him as being a tall, dashing, handsome figure, while others thought him to be short with bow legs. There is a reference to a bandit named José María who was around at the time of Richard Ford's stay in Spain between 1831 and 1833. In *Gatherings from Spain* he describes the capture of a gang member and his subsequent execution.

Not all bandits, however, had such a noble reputation. In those days, wooden crosses could be seen at the side of the road marking the sites where unfortunate travellers had been set upon and killed by brigands. Richard Ford came upon such a cross which 'marked the unconsecrated grave of some traveller who has been waylaid there alone, murdered, and sent to his account with all his imperfections on his head'.

It is now reckoned, however, that the number of attacks by highwaymen has been greatly exaggerated and many using the Pass took a perverse delight in expecting some calamity or other, for it added a touch of spice to the trip. Some even felt a sense of disappointment at completing the passage without experiencing some sort of romantic adventure on the way. There is a story that Alexandre Dumas père paid a sum of money to a certain bandit chief, asking him to arrange an authentic-looking attack on his party, but, at the same time, to make sure that nobody suffered any injury.

By the end of the 19th century the danger created by these gangs had started to diminish, although they were ranging the Alpujarra south from Granada when Gerald Brenan lived there in the 1920s. The last known professional villain, Juan Gallardo, was caught and imprisoned in 1932. He managed, however, to escape gaol and die in a more picturesque manner by falling in a shoot-out with the Guardia Civil in 1934. As late as 1961, Penelope Chetwode had an encounter with an amateur bandit-cum-coal merchant who demanded one hundred pesetas from her. She tried to get rid of him by singing three verses of *Die Lorelei* but, as this did not work, ended up handing over twenty-five pesetas!

Earlier still though, in the 18th century, journeying south by way of the Sierra Morena posed added risks. The wild and desolate area to the south of the Pass provided perfect terrain for the bandits. Charles III had the bright idea of making this part of Spain safer by increasing the population in that locality. He pledged free land to any person of Catholic religion who wished to settle there, but stipulated 'foreigners only', because he did not wish to depopulate other parts of the country. People came from all over Europe to take advantage of this offer and, before long, 6000 of them had arrived from Belgium, Germany, France, Switzerland and Greece. The French lot included a group of convicts who were about to be shipped to the French penal colony in the Guyana – the notorious Devil's Island! The Spanish official in charge of all this colonisation was a minister, appointed by the king, named Pablo de Olavide, whose tomb we had seen in the 15th century church of San Pablo back in Baeza. He organised the building of twelve little towns to accommodate these newcomers – the largest of which was back down the road at La Carolina. These towns were constructed in a very non-Spanish manner, with wide avenues and neat little houses, all laid out in a regular grid pattern. A sort of Spanish Surbiton! All went well until, in 1775, Señor Olavide fell foul of the dreaded Spanish Inquisition. They condemned him as a heretic, and sentenced the unfortunate man to eight years locked in a monastery with only religious texts to read. Without his assistance, the colonies soon fell apart and before long half the foreigners had died or gone home to their own countries. The deaths were attributed to the unbearable heat or drinking too much wine and brandy, or perhaps a combination of the two. Most of those who remained married local Spanish women and gradually lost touch with their origins. George Borrow, travelling in this part of Spain in the 1830s, met a family of German descent who had completely forgotten the language and traditions of their forefathers.

As we pushed our way further into this Ciudad Real province we saw with relief from the map that we had now left the most hazardous part of the motorway behind us. It was fortunate indeed, we reckoned, that two new white crosses had not been set in earth. To have met our end in a bandit raid might have been acceptable in a heroic sort of way, I suppose, but being squashed against a wall or in a tunnel offered no glory at all. I'd never attempt that sort of thing again, and certainly cannot recommend motorway walking. Negotiating narrow tunnels and tight corners of a busy highway on foot is definitely asking for trouble.

So goodbye to Andalucía and hello to the next autonomous region of Castilla-La Mancha, also known as South Meseta. The area includes the provinces of Cuenca, Toledo, Guadalajara, Albacete and the one we were currently walking – Ciudad Real. Our map showed that we would soon be entering the sort of country that inspired Cervantes to write his book relating the adventures of the knight-errant Don Quixote and his side-kick, Sancho Panza. It brought to mind the barren, arid parts of inland Australia that I had once experienced, known out there as 'the bush'. This meseta region stretched right across to the mountains of Toledo in the north and held nothing much of interest to attract the tourist. The vast, parched plain, with its dry heat, made it an ideal spot for the development of vineyards, becoming famous for its Valdepeñas wine. As Bob remarked – not much chance of becoming lost in vineyards! The once numerous windmills have all but disappeared from the scene, leaving only a few for sentimental and ornamental reasons, in the northeast corner of the province, near the border with Cuenca. Of the hundreds built in La Mancha during the sixteenth and seventeenth centuries, only a handful are still in existence. Some are situated near the town of Campo de Criptana, a hundred and fifty kilometres east of Urda (where Quixote's encounter is supposed to have taken place) and another, more authentic collection, is near Consuegra, twelve kilometres east of Urda. We came across one splendid example later as we left Los Yébenes on our way to Sonseca, but this area was much farther north. Modern, mechanical methods have since taken over, but it seems they have been too successful in extracting this precious liquid, for their efficiency, as we later learned, has now caused a water shortage.

At that moment, 5 pm on May 5, we were still making our way slowly down towards our next destination, Almuradiel. Running parallel to the road we saw a railway line, along which trains periodically 'whooshed' by at high speed. I caught Bob staring in its direction with a wistful look on his face, and asked,

"Don't tell me that you'd rather be sitting in that noisy thing, instead of being out here on the road enjoying yourself?"

"Man," he replied, shaking his head. "I was just thinking how lucky I am to be standing here on this damned road at all. You know, some of those damned lorries actually brushed my legs coming round those bends! And the tunnels! What a nightmare!" He ranted on for some time in this manner. As a reminder, I threw back at him,

"You can't have it easy all the time."

The road looked as though it continued on for some while in a straight line so, thinking the worst over, I swaggered along, singing a snippet of Harry Lauder, which I considered appropriate to the situation:

'Keep right on to the end of the road, keep right on to the end,
Though the way be long, let your heart be strong,
Keep right on round the bend.'

Spanish 'comida' and siesta time had passed and the amount of traffic increased again. I thanked our lucky stars that we had attempted this stretch on a Wednesday and not at the weekend, when the amount of traffic doubles. People from the cities further north head south to the coast on Friday and return again on Sunday. It is then that complete chaos reigns on the N1V! We would have stood no chance at all. Some of the apartments down in my village of La Herradura are owned by people who live and work in Madrid, and they think nothing of driving the 1000 kilometre round trip at the weekend. Spaniards enjoy fourteen national holidays a year, when everything closes down. The busiest of these is Semana Santa, which falls in March/April, climaxing on Good Friday, and I can assure you that a fail-safe way to commit suicide would be to walk over the Despeñaperros Pass during this Easter period. Of course the summer holidays, July and August, add to the congestion by bringing foreign tourists too. Ah yes, we surmised, it could have been far, far worse!

Now that we had left the really dangerous part of the highway behind, we had more opportunity to look about us. Amongst the craggy rocks stood trees of oak, chestnut and pine and on the high ridges of the sierra, silhouetted against the blue sky, we could see more of the same. These convoluted, irregular mountains are rich in metals and minerals, giving them an interesting greenish tint. The presence of copper has attracted the mining companies of Tharis and Río Tinto to the area.

Diminishing wildlife in these sierras is, at last, starting to get lucky, with seven recently-formed natural parks offering them protection. These sanctuaries run in an unbroken line along the Sierra Morena mountain range. From west to east these are the Sierra de Aracena y Picos de Aroche, Sierra Norte de Sevilla, Sierra Cárdena y Montoro, Sierra de Andújar, Despeñaperros and the Sierras de Cazorla y Segura y Las Villas.

The fact that it is now a safeguarded area makes it a haven for the lynx, which had been hunted almost to extinction. In 1995 it was estimated that only 1300 of these wild cats existed in the entire world, half of them in Spain. By the year 2000 the revised total number was put at 600. Other, smaller, mammals to be found up there include the stone marten, polecat and mongoose. The not-so-lucky wild boar and forest deer are still being hunted, but the ibex is supposed to be out of bounds to the hunter. There are plenty of birds too, including black and white storks, black vulture and red and white kites.

Folk have lived and hunted up in the mountains for quite a while.

Signs of prehistoric habitation have been found in the shape of paintings, discovered high up in the Los Órganos cliffs, daubed on the walls of a cave called Vacas de Ratamoso. Although we kept our eyes peeled, we saw no sign of animal life and supposed that noise and pollution kept them well away from the N1V. We did not blame them.

We carried on, past a railway station, over a slight ridge and there, spread out before us, way down in the distance, lay the landscape I had been expecting. Phew! What a sight! The wide, flat plain stretched far away into the distance like some vast expanse of desert. I felt hot and sweaty just looking at it! The more I looked, the more fascinating it became. Such captivating emptiness, viewed from above, drew me like a magnet. Perhaps my love of the sea explains this attraction to wide, open spaces, or maybe I longed for the promise of a little peace and quiet after the motorway hustle and bustle. Washington Irving must have felt this way. He writes in *Tales of the Alhambra*, 'There is something, too, in the sternly simple features of the Spanish landscape that impresses on the soul a feeling of sublimity. The immense plains of Castilla and of La Mancha, extending as far as the eye can reach, derive an interest from their very nakedness and immensity, and have something of the solemn grandeur of the ocean.' Although I realised that there would probably be more road walking to endure before reaching Madrid, I strode on into Almuradiel with a lighter heart.

It soon became heavier, though, for at the first roadside hostal, a waiter informed us that he had no vacant rooms. The very busy place had a large car park full of lorries and a bar crowded with the usual baggy-trousered, large-bellied, cigarette-smoking lorry drivers. I had made the mistake of asking for accommodation without the customary showing of money and, standing there with packs on our backs, we must have stood out like sore thumbs. The waiter passed our request on to his boss who, on giving us the 'once over', decided that we were not his usual clientele and gave us the thumbs down with a shrug of the shoulders, accompanied by the two words that express so much: "No hay!" he shouted ("There aren't any!"). Customs had not changed much in the last one hundred and fifty years, it seems. Richard Ford found that quite often 'no hay' accompanied by a shoulder-shrug was the answer to a question that had an element of uncertainty.

There was no room at that inn for the likes of us so we trudged on another kilometre down the road to the next establishment, which proved to be a hotel. Now 'hotel' was one step up from hostal, and I could see from the cars parked outside that we would now be entering a much grander realm. So before going inside, we smartened ourselves as best we could by combing our hair, dusting each other down and carrying our packs by hand instead of wearing them. We wanted to make it appear as though we had just parked our car. To be refused admission again meant a further fifteen kilometre walk to the next stop, and we could not be certain that we should find anything there. Inside, with trepidation, I strode as confidently as I could to the reception desk, trying to look as composed as possible. A young woman with thick, black hair and a large bosom looked at us and smiled a welcome.

"We would like two single rooms, if you please," I ordered authoritatively, putting on my best Spanish accent, "away from the noise at the front."

I wished I had been able to dangle some flash-looking car keys in front of her. Luckily the counter hid the bottom half of our bodies, so she could not see our well-worn, scuffed footwear or my dirty shorts. The woman, flicking through the register, seemed to be impressed by my manner. Then, to my dismay, Bob, who had been reading the notices on the wall, pointed to the price list and cried out,

"Hey, man! Have you seen what they charge for rooms here?"

I glared at him and put my finger to my lips, muttering for him to keep quiet. The receptionist looked up from her ledger.

"American?" she asked, in English.

Surprised, Bob looked at her and nodded.

"I spent five years in the States," she said with a noticeable American accent, "working in Manhattan. Which part of the U. S. are you two from?"

I let Bob answer for both of us. He was from Pennsylvania and knew Manhattan well. So did I, as a matter of fact, but I let them chatter away. Bob was laying on the charm in thick slices and I could determine a sparkle in her eyes. Our passports were asked for and Bob handed his over. She raised her

137

eyebrows a little as she wrote the words 'Doctor Robert Smith'. The 'Doctor' had obviously impressed her. It was beginning to look more hopeful. After they had finished flirting, she called to a young man who led us to some clean, comfortable-looking rooms. In order not to appear too eager, I walked slowly around the room in a nonchalant manner, testing the bed, looking out of the window and then going into the 'en-suite' bathroom, where I flushed the toilet and ran the basin taps. Bob stood glaring from the doorway. I then graciously declared to the porter that the room would be all right.

It was not long before I lay back naked in a steaming tub, accompanied by my socks, pants, shorts and shirt, experiencing the delights of soaking and scrubbing away all the dirt and grime that had accumulated from those filthy exhaust pipes. A little later, looking shiny and feeling much better, I met Bob downstairs in an elegant-looking lounge/bar.

"Another fine mess I got you out of – again!" proclaimed a smug, glowing Bob.

"I thought I'd keep quiet and give you a chance with her," I responded.

We sat for a while drinking our beers and eating all the free tapas laid out on the bar top. Then, after sinking down into some very soft, cosy armchairs nearby, we ordered another round. The tariffs were considerably higher than we usually paid but "What the hell!", we declared. "You only live once. And, let's face it," we added, "we're lucky to be alive at all!" We justified our actions and thought up reasons for deserving this unaccustomed luxury. We remembered the recent dangers, the swallowing of all that pollution, the boredom of watching the traffic roar past, the noise, and so on. After a meal in the restaurant, we returned to our seats and sat back with our usual coffee, cognac and cigar, feeling that we had certainly earned all this indulgence.

I felt at ease with the world but noticed that Bob did not appear quite so relaxed. He kept fidgeting and looking around. By now it was quite late – around midnight, I suppose

– and I was drowsily contemplating that comfortable bed waiting for me upstairs when suddenly, the young lady we had met earlier appeared and made her way over to our table. She was much shorter than I had imagined, for I had only seen her seated behind the desk, but there was not much wrong with her rounded figure. Bob, the gallant, asked her if she would care to join us, at the same time asking what she would like to drink. When she was seated he ordered another round of drinks and introduced her to me as Miranda.

We talked for about another half an hour, by which time my aching eyes were starting to droop. The conversation, I noticed, was gradually becoming two-way, with me being the odd one out. Bob did not appear to be tired in the least, and adopting tactics I had seen him use before. His accent now changed into a slow 'James Stewart' type of drawl, and every time he reached across for his glass, he flexed the muscles in his arm, making them ripple. Miranda was looking and listening to him wide-eyed and kept wriggling her buttocks in the chair. Things were starting to stir up inside me and I was glad that I was not wearing my tight shorts. It did not take much working out to see that these two were besotted by each other and I concluded that the decent thing to do would be to retire to my room and leave them to it, so I bade them 'goodnight'. They did not seem too sorry to see me depart but as I was about to go, Bob came across and said quietly to me,

"I was thinking, as we haven't got far to go tomorrow, Roy, that perhaps we could start out a little later. Have a little lie-in, eh? What with the good rooms and all."

Earlier, after a careful study of the map, we had decided that our best plan for the next day would be to head for Santa Cruz de Mudela, fifteen kilometres down the road. From there we could strike out in a north-westerly direction towards Moral de Calatrava, where we had been told there was somewhere to stay. To combine the two would have meant walking forty kilometres in the baking heat of the Calatrava day, so we had opted to cover the distance in two stages.

I looked at Bob, and then over his shoulder to the squirming Miranda, and agreed to the late start.

"Don't wear yourself out too much," I warned. "We've still got a long way to go."

Bob grinned, gave a slow wink and returned to his beloved. Back in my room I tried to comfort myself with *Tess of the D'Urbervilles* but found it hard to concentrate. I kept picturing lucky Bob and Miranda together.

13

Where have all the 'fondas' gone?
Gone to motels, every one.

Although I must have been pretty worn out by the rigours of the N1V, I did not sleep too well. My night had been full of erotic dreams and in the morning I lay there in the dishevelled, tossed-about bed, thinking them over. Perhaps 'nightmares' would be a better description, for, in one, I was making love to a naked Miranda in a long, dark tunnel with a huge lorry, headlights blazing and horn tooting, bearing down upon us. When I awoke I discovered that the sheets were both sweaty and sticky. After taking another hot bath, I lay back feeling utterly exhausted and must have dozed off again, for the next thing I remember was the usual walloping on the door, accompanied by Bob's booming voice,

"Leave it alone, man!" he yelled. "See you downstairs as soon as you can make it."

I found him down in the restaurant tucking into a large plate of fried eggs when I eventually joined him. He did not look half as worn out as I felt. His face had a rather sheepish expression as he turned to me and said, between mouthfuls, "Sorry about last night, man. She might have let you join in, but I did not like to suggest it."

"Suggest it to whom?" I asked, slumping into a chair. - "her or me?"

"Well, er, you know what I mean," he replied.

I knew exactly what he meant and wondered whether I would have taken part in a threesome had the opportunity arisen. After breakfast, as we sat drinking coffee, I asked Bob:

"Have you made your fond farewells to the little barrel of fun yet?"

"I left her sleeping," he answered. "Look here, Roy," he continued, "I'd rather get on the road before she comes down, if you don't mind. I'm all packed."

It was nearly midday and I was in no mood to hang about. Besides which, meeting Miranda was something best avoided. I had seen and had enough of her in my night-time fantasies. She was best left as the girl of my dreams. We paid the bill, shouldered our bags and almost made it to the exit before I noticed Miranda clumping hurriedly down the stairs and making a bee-line for Bob. Her hair was all over the place and she wore a loose-fitting dressing gown.

"Roberto!" she called, "where are you going? You are not leaving without saying goodbye to me, are you? You have not given to me your address in America."

Bob must have had an explanation all lined up, for he answered at once: "Heck, no, sweetheart. I just did not want to disturb you. You were fast asleep so I left my address at the reception desk. Roy, here, was in a hurry to get going."

He was getting his voices all mixed up. The James Stewart of yesterday had changed to Humphrey Bogart. It was especially noticeable in the word 'sweetheart'. Miranda did not seem to notice. She sprang up and wrapped her chubby arms around his neck. I had seen enough and, once more, went outside to leave them to it.

Bob joined me a few minutes later, rubbing the back of his hand across his face. As we strode off down the N1V towards Santa Cruz, I turned towards him, pursed my lips, and said, "Give us a kiss!"

He just growled and kept his gaze fixedly down at the tarmac. Guessing that he wanted to drop the subject of Miranda, but feeling spiteful, I remarked sarcastically,

"Well, Roberto, giving her your home address might prove to be a mistake, you know. She looked a rather fertile young thing to me."

"I gave her an address," he said.

I should not have been so cruel, I know, but just to give him something more to think about, I added, "She's got your passport details, don't forget."

We pushed on. Luckily we had to cover only fifteen kilometres that day for I had felt knackered from the start. The motorway, fortunately, now ran mainly downhill, passing through a sort of valley with high sierras on each side, so we had the benefit of welcome shade for part of the way. We found a treasure-trove of coins by the side if the road. In total, the loose change amounted to five hundred pesetas. We saw no sign of an accident or any other clue which might have helped solve the puzzle of why it was there. A tourist, on his way north, heading out of Spain, might have wanted to get rid of unwanted coins by simply throwing them out of the window of his car. Then again, we debated, perhaps some motorist had felt sick, stopped the car, got out, and as he bent over, the money fell from his pocket. Not quite so elementary, my dear Watson! Sherlock Holmes would have solved it all in a jiffy.

As we neared Santa Cruz de Mudela, three hours later, we passed between two more sierras – the Aljibe on our left and the Acebuche on the right – and it was here that exhaust fumes, being trapped on two sides, really built up. We choked our way through, handkerchiefs tied around our mouths. To the people driving past we must have looked like ghosts of former bandits. When we looked later, the filth churned out by the traffic had left a black, sooty stain on these improvised filters. Having suffered three days of this we wondered how much of this dirt had collected inside our lungs. You can imagine how we felt when, to our delight, the motorway swung off to the left about a kilometre from the town, leaving us to walk the last stretch into town on a traffic-free small road. As we split from the never-to-be-forgotten N1V, we gave it a rude sign with our fingers, coughed some dark, sooty-coloured spit onto the ground, shook each other's hand and, finally, performed a little skip of joy, so pleased were we to be rid of that damned motorway! Good riddance, we declared!

N1V

On our way into the centre of Santa Cruz de Mudela we passed through a large industrial estate where all sorts of things were made, including ceramic tiles, furniture and building accessories. Among them I was interested to see two factories manufacturing knives, and I wondered if they had any connection with the sword-making enterprise set up by a Bavarian army officer in the 19th century. His name was Johann Kaspar von Thürriegel and he was one of the colourful bunch of settlers recruited by Olavide to come and populate the area. Perhaps the skills learned from von Thürriegel enabled the trade to continue. A little way past a football stadium we saw a small bar with the letter 'F' painted over the entrance. This indicated that it was a fonda, or a bar with basic, overnight rooms. The word fonda comes from the Arabic 'funduq', meaning guest-house, and these places, in the hierarchy of hostelry, are one step down the ladder from an hostal. As we had experienced the luxury of a hotel the night before, we reckoned it would balance things out a bit by staying there. I, personally, have always liked fondas and

144

found them to be friendly, clean places which often serve good home-cooked food. They do not usually have water in the room and the toilet is sometimes outside in the yard but, for the price, they are terrific value. Once inside, we shook hands with a tubby, jolly-looking man who introduced himself as Ramón. I gave him our names.

"I am at your service, Roberto and Luis," he declared. The Spanish find "Roy" very difficult to pronounce. When I asked about the rooms, the innkeeper shook his head, sighed and replied,

"No, señores, I am sorry but, unfortunately, since the arrival of the motorway which leads the traffic around Santa Cruz, there is no longer a demand for rooms here or anywhere else in town. Before, when the road ran through, there were two hostales and my fonda, which were all used by the many travellers. Now there are none. The hostales have closed and you will find somewhere to stay only on the motorway itself."

I knew that roadbuilding was big business in Spain. It provided work for the multitude of unemployed and made it

Closed hostal

easier for products grown in the south of the country to be transported to the rest of Europe. The trade in fruit and vegetables, especially, had expanded rapidly. But all this highway construction was bad news for little places that catered for visitors. Unless there was something of particular interest locally, these hostales and fondas had no option but to close, for they had no custom. Not only did foreign tourists remain on these new, straight, fast, smooth-surfaced motorways, but local people also found them more convenient. I feared that we might be seeing the last of these little lodging-houses.

When I first drove through Spain, in the '60s, the journey admittedly took longer, but proved much more interesting than staring at asphalt all day and spending the night in some sterile motel. Once, while driving back to England in my battered old Citroën 2CV, I gave a lift, just outside Granada, to a Norwegian hitch-hiker who was making for Paris. He could speak little English and my Norwegian was non-existent but, somehow or other, we discovered that we both liked playing chess. Neither of us was in any hurry and we played many games together on our journey north. Evenly matched, we would sometimes stop for a coffee in the morning, start a game and end up staying the night, wherever we were. The journey to Paris, some 1300 kilometres, took ten days, but I shall never forget it.

Spain is not a fast country. At least, not in the south, where I have spent many years. It is far better to join the slow pace of life. Trying to beat it will lead only to frustration. If a job of work cannot be finished (or even started) that day – then leave it until 'mañana' and, instead, simply sit down and have a drink. Without doubt, one sure way to reconsider the pace of life is to journey on foot along a stretch of road that has previously been motored. Twenty minutes, or twenty-five kilometres in a car, represents a hard day's walk. The whole perspective of distance changes.

We finished our beers, said goodbye to Ramón and made our way reluctantly back to the by-pass and there, on the edge of Santa Cruz, we booked ourselves into a newly-opened, boring-looking motel, devoid of any character. The angry motorway had not forgotten our earlier, insolent behaviour and was making threatening, growling noises outside our windows so, after completing our duties, we strolled casually back to visit Ramón once again. I was pleased to see that the now busy, bustling bar was doing well, despite the new road. He demonstrated his pleasure at seeing us again by serving us a plate of mixed tapas with our beers. These saucer-sized dishes of food, served with each fresh drink, vary from bar to bar. The word 'tapa' translates as 'lid' and supposedly originated in the 18th century when a piece of bread was placed on top of a glass to deter flies. This developed into serving up a titbit, such as an olive or knob of cheese as well. Salty fish was found to enhance the customer's thirst, so this was added to the list. Examples of tapas are sometimes lined up along the counter – albóndigas (meatballs), pinchitos (little kebabs), gambas (prawns), tortilla española (potato and onion omelette) and many other tasty snacks. In my coastal village of La Herradura, more fish dishes are served: boquerones (anchovies) marinated in vinegar, calamares (squid), mejillones (mussels), sardinas (sardines), and pulpo (octopus) are common tapas. This last dish may sound uninviting, but if sufficiently pounded and properly boiled, served in a tomato and garlic sauce, it can taste splendid. I have had friends come to visit me smack their lips when tucking into a dish of pulpo without knowing what it is.

"Scrumptious!" they exclaim, often mistaking it for chicken.

"I'm glad you like octopus," I respond.

This revelation can stop them in their tracks, and fondness for the platter evaporates. In large towns, and many of the more developed resorts, bars charge for tapas. Where they are served free, a ración (a plateful) can be purchased if the taste proves irresistible.

Delicious tapas like these, cooked by Ramón's wife, were slid through a small hole in the wall which separated the bar from a tiny, adjoining kitchen. From time to time a loud shout was heard, followed by another steaming tray of tasty morsels being pushed through the opening. The only part of this hardworking woman we ever saw was her arm.

One person, we noticed, stood out from the rest. Firstly, he did not wave his arms in the air while loudly discussing the merits of football players and, more noticeably, wore a jacket, shirt and tie. He came over to us and Ramón introduced him as Alfredo, the school teacher. I asked if he could tell me more about Santa Cruz de Mudela. Was the 'Cruz' anything to do with the town being positioned at a crossroads? He seemed only too pleased to display his knowledge. Alfredo said that my reasoning was quite logical and, indeed, could be one explanation, but there were two other theories. One was that it could signify the triumph of the cross-bearing Christians over the Moors, or perhaps a more fanciful story was that the name derived from a tale concerning a person who was about to kill the king, Don Alfonso. This assassin stopped in his tracks on seeing a bright cross appear over the monarch's head. Alfredo then told me an interesting tale about an army of children, 30,000 strong, who came to these parts from France and Germany early in the 13th century to help capture Jerusalem from the Moors. According to the legend, a boy prophet led thousands of children from France and Germany to the Mediterranean, where he promised to part the sea in the manner of Moses. This did not happen and many of the poor, would-be crusaders, trying to find passage home, were sold into slavery by unscrupulous ships' masters responsible for their transport. I learned later that there is a record of such a movement taking place in the year 1212. A boy named Stephen wanted to deliver a letter, reputed to have been written by Jesus Christ, to the French King. He arrived in Paris with a band of 30,000 followers, whereupon the king promptly ordered them to disperse and go home. On the other hand, Alfredo said, the word 'children' could simply have meant innocent people of peasant class. The Pied Piper legend, which sprang up later – in the year 1284 – could well have been founded on these stories.

'Mudéjar' was a name given to a Muslim permitted to live under Christian rule so, he reckoned, Mudela derived from that. He recommended places worth a visit: the famous square bull-ring built in 1614, considered to be the oldest in Spain and, next to it, the shrine of Nuestra Señora de las Virtudes.

I am sure that Alfredo was right but, although we were initially full of good intentions to sightsee, we remained drinking in Ramón's little bar for the rest of the evening. We had walked only 15 kilometres that day, but, thanks to my disturbed night, I felt pretty bushed. With plenty of tapas inside us we did not feel hungry enough for a meal so, later, we thanked our host for his hospitality, said goodbye to the friendly crowd in the bar, and returned to our anonymous motel.

14

Oh, Calatrava, sing to me
Of ages long ago,
When Cross and Crescent, meeting here,
Changed the course of history.

I suffered no sexy dreams that night. Grumblings and rumblings from the angry motorway outside did their best to keep me awake, but to no avail, for I slept soundly and in the morning felt much fresher. At breakfast, 'instant' powdered coffee was served with bread tasting as though it was left over from the day before: standard motorway fare.

After undergoing a few hundred metres more of the already busy road, we finally, once and for all, quit the harrowing N1V by way of a small road off to the left, signposted Moral de Calatrava. As we hurried along it, traffic noise gradually diminished and soon we rejoiced to hear the sound of birds singing once again.

In front of us lay a wide, flat landscape painted in soft, pastel colours of yellows and browns. The scenery appeared quite different from the expanses of dark green we had experienced in the Andalusian olive fields. Our map showed that we were now in Calatrava country. Nearly all the towns and villages hereabout had the word 'Calatrava' affixed to them. Bob started singing 'Calatrava here I come', substituting 'Calatrava' for California. He had a terrible voice and I tried to make him stop by loudly competing with 'It's a long way to Calatrava' but, probably because we felt so good at being, once again, on a clear, empty-looking road, we carried on being silly for quite a while.

Let me tell you what I know about Calatrava. At the beginning of the 11th century times were changing in Spain. The

150

Moors were gradually losing possession of the land and the once-Muslim territories were slowly being re-populated and colonised by Christians. Co-existence was tried but, after a spot of bother in Toledo in 1085, proved not to work. The pioneers of this Christian revivalism were the French Benedictine monks, later replaced by the Cistercians. These robust men were not like the clergy of today for, due to their military training, they knew how to handle themselves in time of conflict. Remember our legendary 14th century Friar Tuck? This territorial changeover from Islam to Christendom was taking place quite smoothly until the Almoravids, the Moors in occupancy at the time, called on the Almohads, a fanatical Berber group from the Atlas Mountains in North Africa, to come over and help them combat this takeover by infidels. The combined strength of these two Islamic armies proved too much for the Crown's forces and the town of Calatrava would have been lost to the Arabs had it not been for the help given by these battling monks.

In 1157 King Alfonso set up the Order of Calatrava. Their headquarters was established in the fortress town of Calatrava but 'Orders' were set up all over this region, including Moral de Calatrava. In the years that followed many other convent-fortresses were established, and the soldier-monks belonging to these Orders held firm for Christendom against Arab attacks. They also encouraged settlers from other parts of Spain to come to their protected areas in order to provide much needed ancillary services. It all sounded a bit like King Charles III's scheme, mentioned earlier. More Orders were established, including those of Santiago, Alcántara, Avis, Cristo and Montesa, all receiving financial assistance from the Church and Crown to help build their fortifications. They experienced squabbles, of course, amongst themselves and between Church and State, but they nevertheless succeeded in combining their strength to defeat the Almohads at the decisive battle in 1212 at Las Navas de Tolosa. This victory then led to the rapid capture of Córdoba in 1236, Valencia in 1238, Murcia in 1243, Seville in 1248, Algarve and the rest of Portugal in 1250 and Cádiz in 1262. Only the kingdom of Granada held out against the Christians until, in 1492, it too fell.

The Calatrava Order grew rapidly in the 12th century, estates being acquired in Navarra in 1163, Aragón in 1179 and, between 1170 and 1218, several more strongholds were built, including a castle at Alcántara. They even managed to establish an Order in the north of Portugal in 1175. By the 14th century the Order had grown large enough to be responsible for 350 towns and 200,000 souls. All this rapid expansion led the king, Alfonso the Wise, to worry about the increasing strength of these Knights of Calatrava and so, to keep them in check, he used some more of his wisdom to install, in their midst, the Royal Burgh of Villa Real, which later became Ciudad Real, or Royal City.

As the reconquest of Spain continued, the purpose of these Orders changed somewhat and, by the late 15th century, they had become a political organisation of nobles. In 1482, they were attached to the crown of Ferdinand and Isabella.

This flat area we were presently crossing may have looked uninteresting but had in fact been very important to the Order. The Arabs, who had learned in their own dry lands how to make the best use of any available water supply, had devised sophisticated irrigation systems enabling them to grow cereals such as wheat, barley and rye. They also continued to cultivate the vineyards left by the Romans. Although the Qur'an forbade them to touch alcohol, the consumption of wine was widespread, honouring the rule of abstinence 'more in the breach than the observance'. The wine from La Mancha today supplies most of Spain with a sound, cheap beverage and of the 1,000,000,000 litres annual output, 75 per cent ends up on the domestic market. The Arabs also bred sheep and horses. In the 12th century, the first windmills appeared on the scene, making it easier to bring water up from underground wells. The turning stone wheel was used for grinding corn for bread. And so, with all this abundant meat, bread and wine, it is no wonder that the land was being constantly fought over!

By ten o'clock we had covered eight of the twenty-five kilometres. Things were beginning to warm up. I pulled my trusty hat well down over the back of my neck and, just to keep the insects happy, applied some Julia cream to my legs. How did the warriors in those far-off days cope with this heat, I wondered? The well-dressed fighter-about-town wore a thick, padded undergarment beneath a coat of chain mail and, in his gloved hands, carried a large, heavy shield and long sword. Sunburn did not worry him for his head was completely encompassed in a large, metal helmet. The poor horses, too, had protective armour in the shape of a head visor and a coat of chain mail covering their bodies to shield them from arrows. All this was bad enough, but when, later, knights encased themselves in full body suits made of heavy, riveted plates, the men inside found that they were being roasted alive and had to spread a surcoat (a vest-like garment) over their shiny armour to deflect the sun's rays. If they sat astride a horse in all this heavy gear and the horse was brought to the ground, they simply fell off and lay there like an upturned turtle, unable to get to their feet.

What a tough lot they must have been! I mentioned all this to Bob, who usually found something to complain about. He had said that he was hot and thirsty.

"Compare yourself with those fellows," I said. "You might have had something to moan about then. Here you are with just a small pack on your back, nobody shooting arrows at you, just taking a pleasant little stroll along a country road." Bob thought for a moment.

"They didn't have to put up with the likes of you, though," he declared. "I think I'd rather have faced the arrows."

So we journeyed on, with the ghosts of the past to keep us company.

A few hours later we reached the River Jabalón, where we sat in the shade of a tree, ate our oranges and discussed the possibility of reaching our destination before 3 p.m., the hottest part of the day. At 1 p.m. we faced another eight kilometres.

"If you stop dragging your feet and hanging behind," I said, "we should make it all right. Your night of fun with the brunette bombshell is starting to hit you now, isn't it?"

Bob was in no mood for this kind of talk. He did look rather exhausted.

153

"If you don't shut up about Miranda, we'll see how fast you can walk with a busted leg!" he exploded.

For the next two hours we walked on in silence, passing through areas of vineyards, olives and open grassland to enter Moral de Calatrava at around 3 p.m. It was a medium sized town of some 5000 inhabitants, built, in the 9th century, on the site of 3rd century Roman ruins. Originally it was called Orreun or 'Curate's House', but acquired its present-day name when given to the Order of Calatrava. It then had the right to display the Calatrava symbol as had all the towns whose citizens participated in the great Christian victory over the Moors. A splendid monument has been erected at the entrance to La Carolina to commemorate this event.

We saw few people on the streets for it was lunchtime but, before long we found a little hostal with a one-star rating, tucked away in the corner of a small square. The bar was busy. The clientele had the appearance of hard-working, weather-beaten men of the land: short, barrel-chested types with thick, muscular forearms sticking out from the rolled-up sleeves of shirts. Every one of them wore the standard

Plaque commemorating battle at Las Navas de Tolosa

154

Monument to Christian victory at Las Navas de Tolosa

155

peaked cap and held a smoking cigarette in his dirt-ingrained, strong-looking, deep-veined hands. They looked a tough bunch and I thought to myself that these were the descendants of the warriors who had fought so well at Las Navas de Tolosa. I reckoned their ancestors must have been infantry rather than cavalry, for I could not imagine any of them astride a horse, dressed in armour. On foot, however, with a shield in one hand and an axe or mace in the other, they would have been a redoubtable foe.

A delicious aroma drifted up from one of the tables and, following the scent with my eyes, I saw a dish of what looked like 'cocido' (a stew made from beans, vegetables, meat, sausage, and just about anything else) being ladled on to plates from a large tureen. It looked very appetising and made me realise how hungry I was. As we neared the bar, the man behind it asked,

"Are you here for the water?"

I was not sure what he meant and thought, at first, that he was asking if we wanted a glass of water to drink. I shook my head.

"Ah!" he exclaimed, "you are not the foreigners who have come about the water."

Bob had heard enough chat. He was thirsty.

"What's he on about?" he asked me.

"The man wants to know if we're here for the water," I answered.

"Tell him that we're here for the beer," growled Bob.

We had no problem with rooms and, after quenching our thirst and tucking into a hearty, tasty meal that lived up to its earlier promise, we sat back, feeling much better. Later on I could see a young boy restlessly busy wiping the table and generally cleaning up the bar, so we went back to our rooms, arranging to meet later. After my usual sock and underwear duties I lay on the bed for a while reading my *Tess of the D'Urbervilles* before dropping off to sleep. For a while I imagined myself beside a cool running stream bordered by shady trees, the scene populated with thatched cottages, mill ponds, overcast skies and delightful blustery showers. Ah! England's green and pleasant land! To any traveller journeying through hot, dusty, dried-up lands I can recommend a dose of Thomas Hardy. He paints a picture of the English countryside so well. I woke and got up after a couple of hours' rest, making sure that there was no repeat of the Linares episode. Nobody in the bar apart from my interrogator who had questioned me about water. His name was Juan and he owned the place.

"What's all this about water?" I asked him, as he poured me a beer.

He looked different from the others I had seen in the bar earlier. His tall, bony body and thin, pale face gave him a rather wasted look. Except for the non-existent beard, he looked like Gustave Doré's illustrations of Don Quixote. With a sigh, he told me the problem. Apparently, the local water supply had started to disappear and everybody was becoming very worried. For centuries, this precious liquid had been pumped up from underground artesian wells and used to irrigate the land, but for the last few years the supply had started to become scarce. Juan seemed to know his facts. The province of Ciudad Real, he said, covered an area of 250,000 square kilometres, a quarter of which was used for growing the famous 'cencibel' grape, which is necessary for making the famous, high quality Valdepeñas wine. The label is well known all over the world, he declared, and if the vineyards suffered in any way from lack of water, then disaster would strike the whole region. He blamed the cumulative result of too many modern farms and agricultural co-operatives for the shortage. He declared angrily that these were draining the more northerly rivers of Guadiana and Cigüela which supplied the local underground water source. The wells were being pumped dry, he complained, and the great wetlands or 'tablas' further north also suffered from lack of water.

"Are you intending to pass through this region?" he asked. I told him that we would be heading towards Daimiel.

"Then you will see for yourselves," he said, "how much it is drying up. All that remains of the great marshlands in that neighbourhood are a few stagnant pools. You will not see many birds. People from all over the world used to come to

157

look at the birds." He leaned forward on his elbows, putting his face close to mine, and whispered in a confidential manner,

"Not to shoot them, you understand, just to watch them."

I tried to appear dumbfounded.

He went on to say that the authorities were also very concerned and were doing their best to find a way to solve the problem. He wondered if perhaps we could be foreign experts coming to help. There had already been some engineers sent from Madrid. I said that I was sorry to hear all this bad news but, sadly, we could be of no assistance.

"Ah!" he bewailed mournfully, "there have always been problems in the dry, hot summers – but now things are becoming desperate."

Bob arrived on the scene and asked me what we had been discussing.

"Bad news," I explained. "It seems that things are drying up around these parts."

"Wow!" he exclaimed. "That does sound like bad news! We'd better get a drink in, quick!"

We sat for a while and I told him what I knew of this Calatrava area we were now passing through.

"What does the 'Moral' signify?" he asked, looking around the room with renewed interest at the descendants of the early warriors.

"One translation is 'mulberry'," I answered, "but it also means the same as it does in English, and if that's the case, it doesn't sound too hopeful for the likes of us, does it? Especially you," I added. "From the way I've seen you treat women, I doubt that you have any at all!"

After a while, we did manage to drag ourselves from our bar-stools and look around town. We found a bull-ring and an attractive plaza, in which stood a bronze statue of Don Quixote, looking like Juan. The excursion was more of a duty than anything else, I must admit, for we felt too tired to be very cultural. We returned to the hostal and waited for the evening meal. Juan continued with his complaining.

"How dare they steal our water!" he grumbled. "And us with the Order!"

He made it seem as though the 'Order' had been awarded to the town yesterday, instead of eight hundred years ago. I understood how he felt, though, for the possession of water has always been an extremely important matter, especially to those in the south of Spain. During the dry summer months, the village where I lived, La Herradura, and its neighbour Almuñécar, constantly ran short of water during the summer, resulting in the supply's being cut off for long periods. Eight kilometres to the west, towards Nerja, a clear, flowing, stream discharged itself into the Mediterranean. The local folk, including myself, took containers to fill with this sweet water. The regional body of Andalucía introduced a scheme to pipe this 'surplus to requirements' liquid to our villages and so ease the shortage. However, it was not that simple. The stream was situated in the Province of Málaga while the two needy villages were in the Province of Granada. With much tunnelling and bridging, all at great expense, the necessary conduits and tubes were laid. Everything was ready for the taps to be turned on when, suddenly, the townsfolk from Nerja and the smaller adjacent village of Maro, decided that the stream belonged to them. They did not want its contents to leave their vicinity, even though it was running away and emptying into the sea. Ugly scenes followed, with the tap-turning water officials being confronted by angry groups of local men wielding large sticks. Police were called in to restore order and it took quite a struggle before they managed to calm things down. Eventually, after much persuasion and reasoning, the supply was connected.

I sympathised with Juan. Without water, folk in these parts would be completely lost. Farming was all they had. There was nothing to attract tourists to the region apart from a few 'Don Quixote' windmills. With our evening meal that night we felt that we should try a bottle of the famous local Valdepeñas wine. It tasted so good that we had another. That went down so easily that, foolishly, we ordered one more. If it was 'for the road', then it certainly was not our road. After that, as we sat back, smoking our cigars, Juan came over to our table and invited us to a glass of some local liquor. This was followed by someone at the bar insisting that we try a shot of something else. We slept well that night!

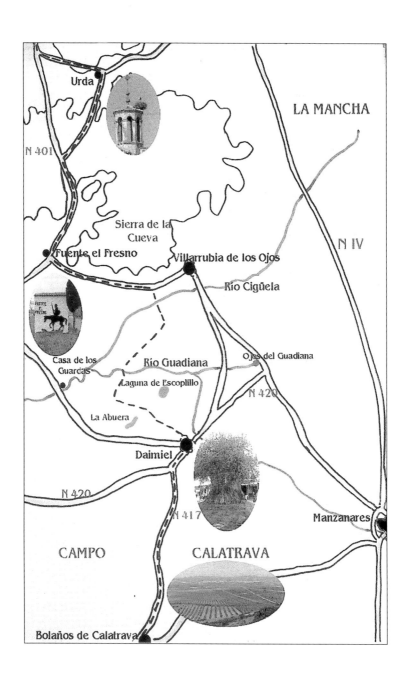

Urda

LA MANCHA

N 401

Sierra de la
Cueva

Fuente el Fresno

Villarrubia de los Ojos

N IV

Río Cigüela

Casa de los
Guardas

Río Guadiana

Ojos del Guadiana

Laguna de Escoplillo

N 420

La Abuera

Daimiel

N 420

N 417

Manzanares

CAMPO

CALATRAVA

Bolaños de Calatrava

15

Of an aching head,
Back to bed
And a bit of 'déjà vu.'

As expected, I woke up with a thick head. Squinting towards the window, I saw that it was not late, for the sun still hung low in the sky and, for a change, I was the one to knock on the door of Bob's room. I heard a groan from within.

Down in the bar, slumped in our chairs, coffee in hand, we tried, through bleary, half-opened eyes, to study the map. Our aim had been to walk to Daimiel, 30 kms away, but it did not take much for us to readily agree that perhaps, under the circumstances, a shorter distance might be advisable. Bolaños de Calatrava, a mere 12 kms distant, would be a better choice for today. After munching our way through the usual tostadas and drinking yet more coffee, we slouched guiltily back to our rooms for a little lie down.

At midday, feeling slightly better, we met up again. Juan could see our sorry state and mixed some sort of fizzy drink which he reckoned would help, suggesting, at the same time, that we might like to stay a further night. It sounded tempting but, somewhat reluctantly, we shook hands with our host, wished him good luck with the water and left the premises.

Outside in the bright sunlight it took quite an effort to get going. I heard Bob breathing heavily. It would only have needed either of us to hint at going back inside, for the day's programme to be called off, but neither of us wanted to be the first to propose it so, unsteadily, we set off for Bolaños de Calatrava. To make matters worse, the way lay uphill. An hour later, I reached the top and stopped to wait for Bob to catch

View across to Bolaños de Calatrava

up. The magnificent view stretched in a northerly direction across the flatlands to the mountains of Toledo. It made me forget my hangover for a moment, but I would have appreciated the panorama more had I been in a fitter state. Bob came alongside.

"Oh why, oh why, did you suggest that second bottle of wine?" I asked, accusingly. It was no good. I could not wind him up. He just plodded on past me, head down. The scenery did not seem to interest him.

"Nothing but water today," I said firmly. "I'm not having your bad habits rubbing off on me."

Two miserable hours later, I started to feel a little better. The uphill stretch had been tough going but had sweated out some of my nastiness. Neat rows of vineyards stretched out in every direction and I could see that this flat, sunny region was perfect for their cultivation – as long as the supply of water held out.

In bygone days the Arabs called this area Al-Mansha, or 'the dry place'. Today it is known as La Mancha.

From our present whereabouts, stretching north to Madrid, we should be crossing a part of Spain that goes by the name of South Meseta. So, just to confuse you further, we were in the autonomous region of Castille/La Mancha, the Province of Ciudad Real, South Meseta or what some call the 'Calatrava' region. It's good to know where you are!

Bolaños de Calatrava soon appeared in front of us, in the middle of nothingness. By the time we reached the outskirts, we felt fitter than when we had departed from our last 'Calatrava'. Though bigger than the last stop, we could see nothing much to excite us as we strolled through its near-empty streets. We found a scruffy-looking little hostal tucked away down a narrow side street and, as we pushed open the door and went inside, I stood rooted to the spot, with a strange feeling of 'déjà vu', for the men lined up at the bar seemed exact replicas of those back at Moral de Calatrava! I could not believe my eyes, for there, behind the bar, was another skinny Don Quixote, looking just like Juan! Could I be suffering hallucination, or mirage, or what? Had the mixture of drink and sun all been too much? Those at the bar turned to stare at us and we just stared right back at them.

Barman looking like Don Quixote

163

For a moment, I imagined that we had been caught up in a sort of time warp and had, somehow, been whisked back to yesterday. The sensation lasted only a moment or two before I soon started to notice little differences, after which the bar soon returned to its usual noisy, bustling state.

The innkeeper's name was not Juan but Pedro, and after serving us two cold beers (so much for the resolution!) and relieving Bob of his passport, he gave us each a key. The rooms were typical of a one star (or sometimes no star) hostal, furnished with a narrow bed (nearly always too short for my six-foot three inches), a small chest of drawers and some sort of provision for hanging clothes. Occasionally, if we were lucky, there would be a bedside cabinet with a reading light perched on top. Fixed to the wall we found a basin with one tap, providing cold water and from the ceiling hung one bare bulb of low wattage. If the room was small enough, we could lie in bed and switch off the overhead light without getting up. We preferred it this way; otherwise it meant crossing the room, operating the switch and then stumbling back in the dark. Under normal circumstances, the beds could be described as uncomfortable, but after a day's walking, we found them cosy enough, and certainly difficult to leave in the early morning. Isn't it strange how beds always seem to be more agreeable when you are forced to leave them? Toilets were usually to be found at the end of the corridor or down in the bar. Quite often they consist of a hole in a metre square ceramic base with two raised platforms on each side on which the squatter places his or her feet. To leave these loos with dry shoes represents quite a challenge. The secret is to be absolutely ready to exit in advance of flushing and then nip nimbly outside the door before the whole floor is awash. Without doubt, most male residents find it more convenient to use the basin during the night. Once, when pissing like this, I ended up with wet feet, for the basin was fixed to the wall, all right, but no further pipe-work had been installed!

Most hostales have plumbing. Fondas, however, are even more basic and sometimes provide only a potty, found under the bed. Meals are shared with the rest of the household and can sometimes be quite memorable and, at other times, completely forgettable. I found that in really cheap lodgings, on occasions, the straw-filled mattress harboured bed-bugs. Next day the resulting red swellings would itch like mad, especially when sweat irritated them.

I once stayed at a fonda which had a shared primitive latrine outside in the courtyard, where they kept a large dog in a sort of cage. This animal would wait until the unwary, half-asleep prospective user came within range, then make his move, pouncing with ferocious, bloodthirsty cries. I fear that reaching the lavatory might well have been too late for some.

After our usual thirst-quenching session, Bob and I sat down at a table and worked our way through the 'menu of the day', while discussing the remarkable resemblance these local folk bore to those of Bolaños de Calatrava. It fascinated Bob. By the end of the meal we concluded that perhaps it was not so strange, for most of them were probably related. The distance between the two places was, after all, only twelve kilometres. Until fairly recently, the general public did not travel very far and, as with the mountain folk, wedlock with near relatives was quite common. This led to quite a few physical and mental defects in their progeny. We had noticed instances of this inbreeding in the villages we had passed through. In most cases these unfortunate children, and later adults, were cared for by the locals, or, if they were not too severely handicapped, some sort of work would be found for them. Most sellers of lottery tickets in Spain are disabled.

A good friend of mine, born deaf and dumb, was known as the 'Mudo', with a sister suffering the same misfortune, known as the 'Muda'. Not being able to speak or hear did not prevent the 'Mudo' from communicating, however, and, with his simple sign language he was able to speak with people of any nationality. The 'Mudo' was one of the most talkative men in the village. Very clever with his hands, he became among other things an accomplished carpenter, shoe-repairer and fisherman. He showed me the choice places to find fish and the best methods to catch them. His knowledge of the surrounding countryside was outstanding and he knew the medicinal uses for many of the local plants. The village folk respected him for his skills and they constantly called upon him to help in some matter or other. Physically, he was very strong and woe betide any person he caught making fun of him. I sat in a bar with him once when someone, behind his back, started to mimic the little grunts he made while talking with his hands. The 'Mudo' became aware of what was going on and walked over to his impersonator. The bar fell silent. To everyone's amusement, my 'mudo' friend pointed down towards the offender's private parts with one hand, while wriggling his little finger in front of him with the other. The inference was obvious and the embarrassed man did not make the same mistake again. The 'Mudo' liked to show off a medal, presented to him during the Civil War for an act of bravery. It seems that, when a plane crashed into the bay, he swam out, dived down and rescued the pilot. What a character! His affliction did not stop him from living life to the full.

At the time of this walk, however, the way of life was changing rapidly. A new breed of car-owners travelled further afield to court the young ladies and this brought new blood into the families.

In the '60s, when I first came to Spain, vehicles on the ancient, pot-holed roads were few and far between, and consisted mainly of four-wheel-drive Land Rovers, used by the police, Guardia Civil or important government officials. I used to drive my battered old car into Almuñécar each week to visit the newly-built post office and open my 'apartado' – a private box set in the wall into which mail was deposited. On one occasion, when I returned to my car, I noticed that six little yellow tickets had been placed under the windscreen wipers, each stamped with a five peseta marker. What did all this mean, I wondered? Watching me, on the other side of the road, stood a jolly-looking, chubby individual dressed in a tight-fitting, blue uniform. This local bobby, Fernando, waddled across and gave me a smart salute.

"I see that you have found the tickets, Señor Roy," he said.
"What do they mean, Fernando?" I asked.
"Aha!" he replied, "I myself put them there!"
"Why?" I again asked. "Have I won a prize, or something?"
"No, no!" he cried excitedly. "Let me explain. It means that you must give me thirty pesetas. You see,"- and he pointed to a poster stuck on the wall above my car – "You see that sign, Señor Roy. It says that you must not park your car here." The poster read, 'No Parking'.

"But, Fernando," I protested, "that notice was not there when I arrived. You stuck it to the wall while I was at the post office, didn't you?"

He looked down at his shoes.

"Well, yes, I did," he admitted. "Yours was the only car I could find."

"You don't really expect me to hand over thirty pesetas, do you?" I exclaimed, handing him back the yellow slips. He held them in his fat hands for a while, frowning. Then he beamed a smile and returned three to me.

"Fifteen then?" he suggested.

I paid fifteen pesetas to a delighted Fernando.

By 8 pm, the bar in the hostal at Bolaños de Calatrava had started to fill with Moral lookalikes and their conversation seemed to be, once again, mainly concerned with the prospect of water shortage. It worried them, too. The television blared out news of the Falklands War but did not seem to interest these people. Only when some mutilated body appeared on the screen did they take notice. Then, for a short while, the chatter would die down and heads would be shaken amid loud cries of indignation. British bullies! What they would like to do to that Señora Thatcher! The Spanish have a long list of defamatory adjectives that can be directed at women. Bob had handed over his American passport to Pedro, so we sympathised with the others at the way the poor Argentinian soldiers were being treated by those British nasties. I spoke to Pedro about the resemblance he bore to the hostal keeper back in Moral and it turned out that Juan was his cousin.

"Yes," he declared, "we both have the same fine features, I know."

He leaned forward and whispered, confidentially, "My father knew Juan's mother very well."

The place filled with noise and cigarette smoke. It takes only two vociferous customers to create quite a din in a Spanish bar. With tiled floors and walls and no soft furnishings to absorb sound, they provide very good acoustics. Picture a dozen or more hearties arguing matters, with the television holding forth at full blast and a group of children warming up their vocal chords for use later in life. To an Englishman, used to the comparative peace of an English pub, the tumult can all be a bit overpowering at first, but after a while, regular users of Spanish bars become used to it all and ignore the hubbub. If you want the cheap drinks and the delicious tapas served in these places, the commotion has to be tolerated. By this time Bob and I had become immune to it all and took no notice. The combination of television and noisy conversation made eavesdropping impossible, for there was just too much sound coming from every direction. In quieter establishments, like those in England, with everybody whispering to each other, it is almost impossible not to listen-in to other people's chat.

We sat happily amid this blanket of sound sipping our beers and munching away at the tapas. If we needed to communicate we simply had to shout very loudly, try to lip read or simply wait until later. Our drinking that night stayed disciplined, for we determined not to over-indulge again. Bolaños de Calatrava was twice the size of Moral de Calatrava, with a population of 10,000, but we felt in no mood to sightsee. After a miserable, wineless meal at the hostal we bade 'buenas noches' to the bar and retired to our rooms. Once there I made an effort to involve myself with *Tess* but, even with the racket coming from the still-boisterous bar, I soon fell asleep.

16

Of water, witches and windmill inventions,
Very old trees and good new intentions.

I felt quite pleased with myself the next morning for having stayed so resolutely 'on the wagon' the night before and determined to continue with this healthy habit. Why not start as bright and cheerful as this every day?

"The consumption of alcohol and walking in hot sunshine is not such a good combination," I declared firmly. "I know we get thirsty but there are other refreshing drinks besides beer, you know, Bob."

Bob said nothing, just sipped his coffee.

"What's wrong with fruit juice or lemonade?" I suggested. "We always seem to ask for beer when we arrive somewhere, don't we?"

Bob looked at me. "Which drink is in your mind after seven damned hours of being scorched on the road?" he asked sarcastically. "Fruit juice or lemonade?"

He had a point.

"All right, then," I agreed. "But we go over the top, don't we? One beer is all right, I suppose, but we don't stop at one, do we? Next time, let's just start out with something non-alcoholic, just to quench our thirst, and then see how we feel about beers, O.K?"

"I'll just follow your example, man," promised Bob.

The straight N417 to Daimiel, our next objective, stretched out in front of us across a flat, arid landscape. We encountered little traffic, with just an occasional tractor rumbling past, churning up a cloud of red dust. In every direction, far into the distance, stretched row upon row of vines standing in neat lines amid chestnut-coloured soil, broken up by an occasional huge wheatfield. The grape harvested in these parts produces a wine with a rich, earthy taste and is reckoned to be the best, although the nearby vintners of Toledo, Albacete and Cuenca may not agree.

Whoever reigned in this part of Spain controlled the strategic Meseta region which led to our old friend, the Despeñaperros Pass – gateway to Andalucía. The outposts established hereabouts would have been able to feed the inhabitants with a supply of essential foodstuffs in the shape of bread, wine and meat. To take a town by force of arms is one thing, but to hold on to it is a different matter. In the barren mountainous regions, where supplies to a garrison had to be delivered, besiegers could cut lines of communication and starve the besieged into surrender.

Around here, however, with good, rich soil, plenty of sunshine and, most importantly, water from the underground artesian wells, the strongholds had everything nearby to render them self-sustaining, and consequently could hold out indefinitely.

This part of Spain seemed to have little in the way of historical or architectural treasures to attract sightseers, so most travellers passed straight through, keeping to the N1V. The absence of tourists made the area most agreeable to us both: we knew that we'd have our share later on in places like Toledo. We found the walking easy; feeling in a good mood, I slackened my pace to let my partner catch up. We had, by now, passed the halfway mark and I asked him what he thought of the trip so far. Bob, never the most talkative of companions, gave me little apart from a few grunts. He did not seem at all pleased that I had waited for him and appeared to slow down even more so that I could get ahead again. He preferred to keep his own company: I quite understood the way he felt. A week or so before, with our minds focused on painful blisters and aching muscles, we had had little room in our heads for day-dreaming. Now, though, with our bodies untroubled by niggling distractions, we drifted into a sort of trance where the body moves of its own accord as kilometres and hours passed by unnoticed.

During the monotonous, unchanging twenty kilometre stretch to Daimiel I conjured up all sorts of images. There, across that field, Christian, cross-bearing soldiers advance, followed by a mass of frightened-looking peasants scurrying along with their simple weapons of pitchfork, axe and scythe. I hear screams as a flight of arrows rains down on them. Then, suddenly, galloping through their ranks, a group of heavily armoured knights appear astride large, snorting horses. These mounts are powerfully built, and chosen for their size, strength and endurance rather than speed. I imagined them similar to the huge, gentle drum-horses we rode in the Horse Guards. (I recall their names as being Hadrian and Hannibal.) These great, charging beasts, with metal-encased riders on their backs, must have been an awesome sight to the poor infantrymen. In mediaeval terms, they must have looked like tanks! Crusaders, armed with swords shaped like the cross, were fighting at close quarter with turbaned Arabs who wielded curved scimitars, symbolising the crescent moon. Amid all the cutting and thrusting, a sudden surge by a massed group of yelling men might well have decided the battle and I realised how important the assistance of local peasants must have been. They well deserved the Calatrava distinction awarded them. In this robot-like manner, oblivious to everything, I carried on down the road for the next four or five hours when, abruptly, my line of thought was broken by a sudden increase in traffic. We had arrived at a junction where our little road joined another, busier one leading to Ciudad Real. Consequently, for the last few kilometres, I was brought back to the 20th century. A short distance into Daimiel found us standing in an oblong-shaped plaza which had a pretty, circular, flower-edged enclosure with a fountain in the middle at one end, and a very ancient-looking, gnarled and knobbly olive tree at the other. "Funny place to grow olives," Bob remarked. I learned later that this time-honoured growth had been planted by the Moors over one thousand years before. A bronze plaque announced the fact. It read,

Olive tree in Daimiel

'Olivo milenario que en esta plaza de Daimiel reposas al fin tus brazos: ya no quiero más aceite, ni tu leña, ni tu bálsamos, ni tus sabios consejos de viejo árbol. Nos has dado tanto!

Dame esa ramita verde, aquella tan alta, la de la esperanza, la del amor, para entregársela al pueblo: al que ríe, al que llora ... al que siente el corazón.

(Thousand year old olive-tree who, at last, can rest your branches in this square of Daimiel: I no longer want your oil, nor your wood, nor your balm, nor the wise counsel of an old tree. You have given us so much!

Give me this green twig, that one so high, that one of hope, that one of love, to offer to the town: to whoever laughs, whoever weeps ... whoever feels the heart's emotion.)

Around this Plaza de España we found shops and bars set in the shade of the overhanging, galleried accommodation

Bronze plaque beneath olive tree in Daimiel

above, and it did not take long for us to plonk ourselves down at one of the tables. It reminded me a bit of Baeza. A young man came out from a bar and asked what it was we wanted.

"Well," questioned Bob, "what's it to be, Roy? Fruit juice or lemonade?"

He'd been waiting to ask me this all day.

The camarero stood there patiently waiting while I sat there tongue-tied.

"Well, I'll have whatever you are having," I announced at last. "Er, you see, I know I said that we—"

Bob had heard enough.

"Dos cervezas," he ordered.

After limiting ourselves to a couple of beers apiece we booked into a small hotel just around the corner. The rates were a little higher than those at our customary hostal but, to our delight, the rooms each had an en-suite bathroom. I lost no time in running a tubful of hot water into which I deposited all my dirty laundry and then created a few soap-suds by washing my hands in their midst. Tucked away down a little side street, we found a bustling little bar with a come-dor at the back. Here, we sat ourselves down and ordered the menú del día. This set menu (in more 'touristy' places known as 'menú turístico') is usually good value. By law, all restau-rants should provide them but sometimes they have to be requested. Our meals consisted of a starter of paella (a saucer-sized plate of saffron rice mixed with peas and a few pieces of meat), followed by a deep dish ladled to the brim with cazuela de conejo (rabbit casserole), and finally, a postre of helado (ice cream). All this, along with a bottle of wine and pieces of bread, cost 500 pesetas apiece (£2.50p). With a full stomach and feeling pleasantly relaxed, I went back to join my soaking clothes in the tub, then took a late siesta.

Later that evening Bob and I set off to look around Daimiel. We found a tourist office back in the square and acquired a little town-guide, which included a map marked with places of interest. There did not appear to be too many and those shown were grouped quite close together, so we

174

decided to pay them a visit. We inspected the Casa de Cultura, which had some local paintings on display, a theatre, a really ugly bull-ring and a couple of churches. We learned that signs of prehistoric habitation lay nearby, and that a Roman bridge survived to the north of the town. In the 8th century the Moors, realising the strategic importance of Daimiel, had built a castle here and, using it as a base, ruled the neighbourhood until deposed by the Christians. Defeat in battle did not prevent the Arabs from staying on and communities of Jews and Moors still lived in the vicinity until the late 15th century when, after the fall of Granada in 1492, the Jewish population was given the choice of becoming Christian or leaving Spain – which meant virtual expulsion. It was then that the dreaded Inquisition started their persecutions, accusing local women of practising the art of witchcraft. Daimiel became known as 'the village of witches'. George Borrow met a man, a smuggler, who wore a band of rosemary around his hat in the belief that it would discourage witches and ward off misfortune that might be encountered on the road.

When he lived in Yegen, Gerald Brenan discovered that villagers in the Alpujarra sincerely believed in witches. Certain persons, such as the ninth male child, were thought to possess magical powers and were called upon to perform acts of sorcery which included casting spells and mixing love potions. People's faith in these incantations had the effect that they sometimes worked.

The parish church of Santa María La Mayor was built in the 14th century and was followed, two centuries later, by La Iglesia de San Pedro, which was constructed in the mid 16th century on the orders of Charles V.

In 1887, Queen Regent, Doña María Cristina, upgraded the village to town status and during the Spanish Civil War an up-to-date hospital and airfield were built. Bob was intrigued by the stories of witchcraft and associated executions which took place in the town square. Being burned at the stake seemed to be the common punishment for sorcery.

"Wow! I bet that tree could tell a tale or two," he declared.

Our sightseeing soon built up quite a thirst so, before much longer, we ended up in our usual spot. Every time Bob asked for two beers I gave a 'tut-tut' and he reciprocated disapproval when I came to order. During this 'tutting', the others in the bar must have wondered what we were playing at. Perhaps they thought we were practising our bird sounds in preparation for a forthcoming visit to the Tablas wetlands.

The little guide had plenty of information about this wildlife reserve, which lay ten kilometres to the north, an area we would have to pass through the next day. It was known as Las Tablas de Daimiel and had been declared a National Reserve in 1966, and then a National Park in 1973. These marshes centre around the rivers Guadiana and Cigüela and an impressive description of birds and other wildlife was listed. The park attracts bird-watchers from all over the world. I found no mention of the water being extracted for commercial reasons or how these wetlands were slowly becoming drylands. I mentioned the subject to a weather-beaten-looking individual standing next to me in a bar.

"Ah!" he sighed, "the river will soon be blind."

I could not make this out. Perhaps he had misunderstood. I tried again.

"The eyes are slowly closing," he said.

I considered that he must be some sort of loony but later discovered that the boggy land near to the river Guadiana is made up of a series of small islands with some of the pools of water formed between them being known as 'ojos', or eyes. Although I can find no such translation in the dictionary, Gerald Brenan, in *South from Granada,* quotes Dr Américo Castro who claims that the word 'ojo' can also mean 'spring'. Philip Ward has informed me that the Arabic word for 'eye', 'ain, also means 'spring'. In fact, a town nearby is called Villarrubia de los Ojos. This explained the mystery. The pools of water were disappearing and so were the 'eyes'. Apart from bird fanciers not many visitors came to Daimiel. Bob and I liked the place, a very Spanish, neat little town. We found another restaurant for our evening meal, which turned out expensive but not a patch on the cheaper one we had eaten at earlier. There was no fixed price menu so we ended up ordering à la carte. My bistec (beefsteak) was so tough that I could hardly cut it and Bob's pollo (chicken) must have lived to a ripe old age and had plenty of exercise. He reckoned that it was like chewing a parcel of rubber bands. You don't always get what you pay for. During the meal we discussed plans for the following day.

"I wish I knew more about goddam birds," Bob said. "We seem to be constantly passing through these swamplands full of feathered friends. Wasn't that bloody hot Guadalquivir area a bird sanctuary or something?"

I told him of the problems faced by the locals concerning the water, which, if it returns, will attract back the army of birds that used to breed in these parts. Among these are mallards, red-crested pollards, gadwalls, pochards and the rare ferruginous duck. The reed-beds were famous for their herons, coots, moorhens, water rails and great-crested grebes. This was apart from the wintering birds that included pintails, shovellers, black-tailed godwit, snipe, black kites and imperial eagles. The mammals were headed by wild boar, red foxes and large families of otters. But marshland was the habitat for most of this long list of animals and without sufficient water, this sort of terrain necessary to their survival, would cease to exist

"That's capitalism for you!" he retorted. "If they need water for their damned factories, they won't spare a thought for anyone else!"

Nevertheless, we agreed that the day had been good to us and so, after coffee and cognac, we went back to the hotel to join our damp laundry.

17

Where the eyes are slowly closing
We discover that right is sometimes wrong

As I sat at a table the next morning, trying work out the best
route to Fuente el Fresno, two of the customers, wearing
identical corduroy caps, came across from the bar to investi-
gate. For a while they stood quietly behind us, puffing away
on cigarettes, then one of them asked if he could be of any
assistance. When they learned of our intended destination,
their advice was that we should take the bus, but when I told
them we wanted to walk, they could not believe their ears.
Walk? Did I not realise that Fuente lay at least twenty-five
kilometres away? One man pointed down at the Tablas de
Daimiel area.

"The birds are all to the south of Fuente," he declared
advisedly, and added with a sigh, "– the few birds remaining,
that is."

When I said that we were not bird-watchers, his brow
wrinkled.

"You are not bird-watchers but you are intending to cross
the Tablas on foot?" he asked. "Why do you choose to go to
Fuente el Fresno, anyway? There is nothing there of interest."
He chuckled. "Even the ash trees have gone." ('Fresno' means
'ash tree'). I gave the old explanation of wanting to see more
of Spain's beautiful countryside.

"The americanos wish to see more of our beautiful countryside by walking across it!" the man shouted across to the
others. He then returned to join his friends at the bar. I could
hear muttering and the word 'locos' (mad) seemed to crop
up quite often. This was not the first time I had overheard
this word used by villagers when they learned of our trip.

178

Richard Ford was taken on a visit to a lunatic asylum where 'locos' were hospitalised and discovered that Englishmen, because of their eccentric ways, were imagined to be at home there!

"Now then, Bob," I said, pointing to the outspread map, "it looks as though we can cut right across country here, and avoid the roads for most of the way."

Bob followed the path traced by my finger, which led in a north-westerly direction.

"Look," I continued, "between these two lakes, turn east a little, cross this river and then join up with this little yellow road that runs straight to Fuente. No problem."

If I had left it at that, things would probably have been all right, but my next few words had an immediate effect on him.

"And there's no need to worry," I added, digging into my pack and pulling out an object tied to a piece of string. "Look! Don't forget that I have my trusty compass!"

It took quite an effort to placate Bob and convince him that my idea would be so much better than simply sticking to the roads.

"We can't possibly go astray," I assured him. "We just head for those mountains in the north."

We headed out from Daimiel in a northerly direction along a little downhill path and, before long, did indeed pass between two lakes – La Albuera on our left and, a few kilometres over to the right, the Laguna de Escoplillo. The landscape, at first, was like the day before, with vineyards everywhere. In the distance we could see the Sierra de la Cueva and today's destination lay at its base, some thirty kilometres away. After an hour of easy walking we came to a point where our track joined three others and I realised later that we should have continued straight on here and joined up with a road that crossed the river Guadiana at a place called Casa de los Guardas. This followed westward to Malagón and northeastward to Fuente el Fresno. Instead, we made the mistake of turning to the east. I say 'we' but I must admit that Bob merely followed my compass readings, so I suppose it could be considered my fault. I told him that we should soon join the road that would take us across the river, but an hour later we still found no sign of road or bridge. A few more kilometres further on we came to a stream which had a rickety-looking wooden plank laid across it. Bob regarded this structure with suspicion.

"I thought you said a road," he said, pointing at the primitive footbridge. "That thing was not built for cars."

To his dismay, I held my compass this way and that against the map.

"Sometimes these maps are not to scale," I announced, trying to sound confident. "The road for vehicles must be further on."

The land stretched out in front of us was dead flat and my friend peered ahead with doubt written all over his face.

"I can see for miles," he claimed, "and I can't make out any damned road."

"Well, it must be there somewhere," I maintained. "Maps don't lie. Just follow me. Don't worry."

"I think I remember hearing that somewhere before," groaned Bob. "Remember Torres?"

Four or five kilometres later we met up with an ancient-looking van which came rattling towards us out of a cloud of dust. It seemed to be held together with bits of wire. I waved it down and asked the driver, who looked very much like his vehicle, where we were headed. He seemed a little worried at being stopped by two weird-looking characters and kept his engine running while he shouted that he had come from Villarrubia de los Ojos. I hoped that Bob had not heard or understood this exchange of words but he had picked out the name of the village and was hopping mad. He snatched the map from my hands and stared down at it.

"Villarrubia!" he exploded, angrily. "You and your damned map reading!"

The van driver had seen enough. He put his foot down hard on the accelerator and sped off. When Bob eventually quietened down we looked again and saw where we had gone wrong. The choices were whether we should re-trace our steps for ten kilometres and go back to the crossroads, or turn left from where we were standing and head across country with the hope of finding another route to Fuente el Fresno. We chose the latter. Going back over old ground had no appeal. A little later the vineyards had all but disappeared and we came to a dried-up area of low scrubland, the earth badly cracked with sorry-looking reed beds sprouting up here and there, looking as though they were waiting pathetically at a bus stop for the water to arrive. When, eventually, we came to the River Cigüela we found it shallow enough, but too deep to allow crossing on foot. I looked in both directions for some sign of a bridge, trying not to catch Bob's eye. I saw nothing but more marshland and the long, snaking river stretching away far into the distance. I could almost feel the heat coming from my walking partner. He was boiling. I tried to lighten things up a little.

"Not much in the way of bird-life around here, is there Bob?" I asked brightly, looking about me.

"Bird-life!" he raged. "I don't care about bloody bird-life! How are we going to cross this damned river?"

"We could always chop down some trees and build a raft," I dangerously suggested. "Like they do in films. You know, like Robert Mitchum did in *River of No Return*" – and I started to hum the theme tune.

"Change 'river' to 'Roy' and it might just apply to you if you don't shut up," snapped Bob.

We sat and ate our oranges in silence, then tossed a coin to decide which way to travel. It did not matter much because the map showed that, unless we could find a crossing, it would mean a fifteen kilometre walk in either direction before reaching a ford. After a miserable hour of tramping to the left and finding nothing, we turned around and tried the other way. A few kilometres to the right of our original starting point I spotted a man crouched down among the reeds on the other side. He appeared to be fishing but, as we got nearer, I saw that what I thought was a fishing rod in his hands was, in fact, a long barrelled rifle, a 'fowling piece'. We stood looking at each other from opposite banks for a

Playing his part to diminish wild life – Juan

moment or two and then he pointed to a ladder-like piece of wood, half hidden in the tall grass, spanning the river. Without his help we should never have spotted it, for it lay where the reeds grew at their thickest. As we approached, we noticed a piece of rope strung out above it, offering some kind of hand support. By taking advantage of this dodgy-looking apparatus we shakily managed to get across to the other side and, once there, breathed a sigh of relief. Our saviour was there to greet us – without his weapon. I reckoned that he must have hidden it somewhere. He himself had installed the rustic bridge, he informed us, for he acted as guide to those who came to see the wildlife. Would we care to visit his house, just a short distance away and try some home-made wine? The day had not gone too well so far and the thought of something alcoholic appealed to us very much, so we readily accepted his kind offer.

He led us through the long grass to a large, single-storey building set by the side of a road and there we knocked back some of his hooch. Soon we started to feel in much better shape to continue the last stretch towards Fuente el Fresno. I noticed that, hanging in a rack on the wall above the fireplace, were two more lethal-looking guns, and wondered how much they had contributed to the diminishing animal life – especially the edible variety. The young, fit-looking man seemed to be living all alone for I saw no sign of anyone else around and his untidy rooms lacked any feminine touch.

As we sat drinking, our host introduced himself as Juan. He explained that the scarcity of wildlife meant that he was no longer kept busy guiding visitors. The land through which we had journeyed that day had once been much deeper in water and it would have been impossible, a few years ago, to cross it as we had done. We felt a strong temptation to remain a while longer and keep Juan and his wine company but we knew that we still had a three hour hike ahead before reaching our destination. Juan offered us a lift in his car for these last ten kilometres and looked astonished when I refused. I needed a quick explanation. My brain clicked into gear.

"My friend here is afraid to travel in motor vehicles," I said, sadly.

It was not enough. Juan wanted more.

"You see, he suffered a terrible tragedy as a child."

I began to warm to my tale and carried on: "Both his parents and sister were killed in a car accident. It was all very sad. He travels only on foot now, and I am accompanying him on his journey through Spain because he does not understand the language."

"But why should he wish to walk through Spain?" asked a stunned-looking Juan.

He had me stumped. I could think of no reasonable justification.

"I am sworn to secrecy," I offered, sadly.

Bob could see that he was the topic of conversation by the way that Juan was gazing sympathetically at him.

"What are you saying about me?" he asked.

"I'll tell you later," I replied.

Farther down the road Bob insisted that I tell him more, so I obliged.

"The man was clearly upset at our refusing his offer of a ride into town," I told him. "I had to tell him something, didn't I?"

"Well, next time, you be the one to have had the accident," he snarled. "I'm tired of being the fall guy!"

"It was just the first thing that came into my head," I explained. "What does it matter, anyway?"

"It matters to me!" declared Bob. "He probably thinks I am some sort of nutcase now." I shrugged my shoulders.

"It seems to me that everybody we've met so far thinks we're crazy to be walking everywhere anyway," I informed him. He thought for a moment and grunted,

"Yeah – and maybe they're right at that."

At eight-thirty in the evening we finally wandered past yet another reminder of Don Quixote and on into Fuente el Fresno. It had been a long day. We had reckoned on twenty-five kilometres' walking, but thanks to our taking the wrong path and stumbling about in the dried-out marshes, we must have added at least another ten.

The town nestles at a crossroads on the N401. From the eastern edge, the Sierra de la Cueva sweeps up to a height of 1200 metres and to the north is the Sierra de la Calderina, which acts as boundary between the provinces of Ciudad Real and Toledo. The inhabitants were mainly employed in viniculture and I knew that they must share the same concern about the water problem as those back in the other places we had passed through. The name 'fuente' suggested that there must have been plenty of water in the old days along with the 'fresnos'. An aqueduct dated back to the Roman occupation, a 13th century church called Santa Quiteria that had been built on the site of an old castle. This mediaeval building remains intact but the other church – the Iglesia de Nuestra Señora del Carmen – was constructed in the year 1898 and, fifty years later, had to be demolished because the steeple had become unsafe! It proves that they knew how to build in the old days. We strolled wearily through the streets and, before long, arrived at a large plaza with a plain concrete fountain at one end and a children's playground at the other. I noticed building work going on all around.

Because of its position on the main Toledo road, the town boasted an hostal. Small and scruffy though it looked, we booked in, deposited our packs and then went straight out

Entrance to Fuente El Fresno

again to find somewhere to eat – for we felt very hungry. At a restaurant back in the square we greedily scoffed a plate each of chuletas (chops) and chips, all the while being ogled by the locals. After the meal we left our table and, to the consternation of those at the bar, went across and joined them. I noticed that whenever we approached, customers would fall silent, quickly make room for us and sometimes even offer up their seats. The usual questions came thick and fast. Why did we choose to visit their village? Our nationality? Were we married? If not, why not? Children, occupation, age, etc. As we had come to expect by now, the thing that baffled them most was our reason for walking. It was simply beyond comprehension why any sane person should choose to travel on foot when he could afford the bus or train. I found that the best way to stop this constant grilling was to make a few enquiries myself. Did the prospect of water shortage worry them? Of course it did. It was sometimes difficult to buy anything during all this interrogation, because we would find that our glasses had been refilled and our drinks bought by someone else. But if we returned this generous act of hospitality by buying a round, we ran the risk of having to accept another measure from each person in the bar – and this could amount to quite a few. The other thing that concerned them was the disappearing people problem. In 1950 Fuente el Fresno had 5000 residents but, by now, 1982, this figure had shrunk to 3500. Many of the young people wanted to move to the more exciting cities of Toledo or Madrid; those that remained were producing few children. Contraception had become acceptable: the extended families of yesterday had become a thing of the past. Why then, I asked, was all the building work going on? It seemed that the remaining villagers wanted to live in up-to-date, well-lit, well-plumbed abodes with modern kitchens full of formica and stainless steel. The lovely old traditional furniture, often hand-made by their parents or grandparents, they considered old-fashioned, and they could not wait to replace it with modern rubbish, which could be cleaned with a damp cloth instead of polish and elbow grease. Their antique furniture attracted dealers from the larger towns, and fetched a tidy profit. Years ago, in the '60s, I remember an enterprising gentleman from Madrid arriving in Almuñécar with a van-load of aluminium-legged, laminated-topped tables and exchanging them, by calling from house to house, Aladdin-style, for the exquisite, almond or olive-wood pieces of furniture that had been in the family for generations. He demonstrated to the gawking onlookers how food could be cut on the surface of the modern table without leaving a scratch and how easy it was to lift from the ground. They all thought him mad to want to exchange a marvel like that for an old, cumbersome piece like theirs. He had soon swapped all his wares for a van-load of treasures. On the bar wall I noticed faded photographs of the old plaza. One, dated 1954, showed at its centre a beautiful, ornate bronze column with shiny taps sticking out from its side. Underneath, a caption referred to this primitive fountain, and the fact that a new one had since been built to replace it. This must have been the modern, ugly concrete excrescence we had seen earlier. Ah, well! The only thing to be said for this new square was that several ash trees had been planted around the edge along with elm and carob.

Even with all its terrible modifications, Fuente el Fresno turned out to be a likeable little place. It made me wonder what would become of those living there if ever the shrinking water supply caused a serious problem to the vineyards.

18

*When we and the ants
Have something in common,
And a village that rhymes
With 'murder'.*

"I can't see any way over these hills," I said the next morning, between mouthfuls of tostada. "It looks as though we may have to stick to the road for the first part. Look here, Bob." He bent down and peered at the range of sierras shown on the map as the Montes de Toledo. They stood between us and Toledo.

"Stick to the road, eh?" he asked, mockingly. "Does that mean we won't need any of your damned compass reading and the consequent pleasure of getting lost again? Phew! That's a relief!"

He had touched on a sore point. I still felt peeved at being responsible for the previous day's mistakes. Besides, it was a bit too early in the morning for me to take all this sarcasm. I snapped back at him,

"That's it! I've had enough of map reading and putting up with your bloody swearing! I do my best! Let's see if you can do any better!"

I folded the map and slammed it down on the table in front of him, then reached down into my pack, drew out all the others, and slammed those down as well.

"I leave it all to you now!" I said, angrily.

This idea did not please him at all. He realised that he would have to carry these heavy items in his pack and refer to them from time to time. I remembered having watched him try this once before. It became quite a performance. He had removed his horn-rimmed spectacles and, with his head almost touching the paper, tried to study the map with perspiration running down his forehead, onto his nose and, finally, into his eyes. After cursing and dancing around for a while, he had given up. However, at that moment, he saw my chagrin and stuffed the pile of charts into his bag without saying another word.

So we started out on the uphill road from Fuente el Fresno in silence. Before long, as usual, I had stridden out way ahead. Annoyed at his outburst that morning, I wondered when I should have the chance to ask him directions. It did not look very likely, though, because this N 401 appeared to continue on in a straight line, slashing its way through the landscape like a taut piece of elastic, without any turn-offs to left or right. After two hours of steady uphill walking, with the Sierra de la Cueva on our right, I saw a sign planted by the side of the road, informing us that we were now leaving the province of Ciudad Real and entering that of Toledo. Here, at the summit of the Sierra Calderina, I stopped and looked back. There, spread out immediately below, lay the reed-sprouting, marshy area we had struggled over the day before, known as Las Tablas de Daimiel and, beyond this, I could see a vast expanse of flat, rust-coloured land broken up here and there by the dark greens of vineyards. In amongst all this were scarlet stretches of ploughed soil, punctuated here and there by patches of yellow broom. I thought back on the four never-to-be-forgotten days we had spent down there. Did the amount of blood spilled across this land account for the earth's colour, I wondered? How many poor souls, in days long gone, had entered this Calatrava region, never to leave alive?

The name suggested the sort of place where battles were destined to take place. 'Calatrava' had a nice ring to it. 'The Battle of Calatrava,' or 'He fell at Calatrava' – or maybe I was just confusing it with 'Balaclava'.

Some fifteen kilometres out of Fuente el Fresno, I found a little road turning off to the right. This was the moment I had been waiting for. I quickly hung my pack over the road sign, then stood in front, completely hiding it from view. As Bob approached I asked innocently,

"Which way, Bob? Straight on, or off to the right?"

I looked on gleefully as he removed the bag from his shoulders, put it down on the ground, unzipped a side pocket and removed the maps. He then searched through them all until he found the right one, opened it and pushed his glasses to the top of his head. With a pained, screwed-up expression he held the map a few inches from his face. After a few minutes of searching he held it towards me, jabbed his finger at a certain mark and asked,

"We're about here, aren't we, Roy?"

I pushed the dagger home.

"Don't ask me!" I retorted. "You're the bloody map-reader!"

Again, he held the paper close and studied it as best he could.

I looked up at the sky and started to whistle the melody to the song,'Why are we Waiting'. That was the last straw.

"It's straight on!" he proclaimed, angrily.

Revenge is sweet.

"Really?" I said, raising my eyebrows. "That's not what it says here," then stepped aside to reveal the sign pointing off to the right which read,'URDA 10 kms'. Bob stood staring at it, open-mouthed. I was preparing to move on rather quickly when, thankfully, his face broke into a grin.

"Come on, man," he said. "Let's forget this morning. You know what I'm like before my first coffee. I guess anyone is better at map-reading than I am, considering the state of my eyes."

And so, with the air clearer and both of us feeling much better, we set off on the next stretch of the day's walk, downhill all the way. Urda lay in a little trough surrounded by various sierras and running through its centre we could see the shiny streak of the river Amarguillo. Down below to the east, lay La Mancha – the immense, level area that stretches from the Montes de Toledo right across to our old friend, the Sierra Morena.

Hardly any traffic disturbed our passage so far, and none at all on this last stretch. I eased my pace a little and waited for Bob to catch up.

"How's young *Tess of the d'Urbervilles?*" he surprised me by asking. It was quite chatty for him. I was normally the one to initiate a conversation.

"Oh, I've nearly finished it," I replied. "Have you got anything I can read?"

"Nothing that would interest you, I don't suppose," he answered. "Except maybe one about Machiavelli."

I thought for a moment.

"Who was he?" I queried. "Didn't he make violins?"

Bob looked exasperated.

"No, he didn't make violins," he said, tersely. "He was a philosopher – but I'm sure you could teach him a thing or two!"

I later read *The Prince* and realised what he'd been getting at.

Up in the heights the air had been pleasantly cool but, as we had come quite a way down the long, straight undulating, road across open vega, things began to heat up again by two in the afternoon. Once again, the day was fine and sunny with not a cloud to be seen in the clear, blue sky. Walking together did not last for long and we soon fell back into our normal stride-patterns, spaced apart.

With La Mancha ahead, my thoughts naturally turned to the one and only Don Quixote. I could easily understand how his imagination had conjured up all those images. Around here, the heat and visual monotony produce a soporific state and it would have been so easy to mistake windmills for giants. At the same time I had also begun to understand his battle against progress and why he had been considered a Luddite of an earlier century.

Our opinion of machines, especially the combustion-engine type, had changed too. The final straw had been the three-day nightmare over the Despeñaperros Pass. After days of easy, unhurried walking along little tracks, a hiker develops a different conception of journeying and asks why the world must be in such a rush. Does it really matter about the cubic capacity of a car engine relative to fuel consumption? Is it so important to save a few minutes on a voyage from A to B by tearing along at breakneck speed? That occasional white trail marked out overhead by some passing jet seemed so alien to our present mode of travel. Those four days it had taken us to complete the 90 kms from the motorway at Santa Cruz de Mudela to the Montes de Toledo could have been covered in an hour or two by car, but what would the driver have gained by peering through the windscreen? By contrast, our days had been rewarded by sharing little adventures and experiencing a deep sense of satisfaction. We felt more in tune with the long lines of ants we had constantly to step over. There they were, painstakingly carrying some heavy load to their nests and here we were, slowly nibbling away the kilometres, metre by metre, pace by pace. This sense of proportion and gradual achievement can be understood only in wide, flat areas like La Mancha. Those forested and mountainous areas had been exciting enough, but we sensed no timelessness there.

Perhaps we too appeared to be tilting at windmills by trekking 500 kms across Spain. We raised fingers in mockery at machines and modernity. To hell with the motor car! Look what it did to Mr. Toad! It was even harder for Bob to condemn the automobile. In America, he said, everybody drives everywhere. Fuel is inexpensive, cars are large and, besides, he pointed out, it can be dangerous to walk, with too many hot-heads on the streets. He made me laugh when he told me how folk would drive to a gymnasium in order to exercise themselves by using a walking machine!

Later that day I told Bob what had been going through my mind. He was interested in the Don Quixote analogy.

"I see," he said, "and I suppose that I shape up to be Quixote's side-kick, Sancho. The stupid one!"

"Oh, no," I explained. "Sancho was, in fact, the wiser of the two. Cervantes portrayed Don Quixote as the aristocratic, distinguished one."

Bob looked me up and down.

"That figures," he said.

From Urda, a road ran east to the larger town of Consuegra and north-west, through a pass in the mountains, on to our next port of call, Los Yébenes. The reason for not heading straight there from Fuente el Fresno was that, even for fine, fit fellows like us, a distance of forty-five kilometres in one go we considered too much, especially as it would include a lot of uphill walking. So, although Urda was a little off to the side of our straight line, we had agreed to split the journey by taking this detour. "And what difference does it make if I do go out of my way a little, if I go out of my way at all? After all, what does it matter?" writes the traveller Camilo José Cela in *Journey to the Alcarria*. He seems to have been a pretty fast walker for he says later, "Twenty or twenty-five kilometres is a good day's march; it means spending the whole morning on the road." He must have started out earlier than we.

Bob did not like the name of the village. "What an ugly name!" he said. "Urda sounds a bit like 'murder.'"

In Roman times, an aqueduct twenty-four kilometres long started at a natural spring source in Los Yébenes and ran through Urda on its way to supply water to the town of Consuegra. As Los Yébenes lay at 808 metres altitude, Urda at 763 and Consuegra 705, the water would have flowed by gravitational force. But twenty-four kilometres! What a feat of engineering! The aqueduct fell out of use in the 17th century. At Segovia, in the province of Castilla and León, one of the great tourist attractions is the 728-metre, 20,400 granite-block aqueduct with its 163 arches, built by the Romans in the 1st century A.D. without using a drop of mortar to hold it together. It is still in use today.

When the Romans moved out, the Visigoths moved in and the remains of one of their temples can be seen, acting as foundations to an 18th century sanctuary, La Ermita de Nuestro Padre Jesús Nazareno.

In mediaeval times, those living hereabouts must have been a warlike lot, always at the ready for a punch-up, for they not only helped to drive the Moors from Toledo in 1085, but then again sent a company of fighters to assist in the famous set-to at Las Navas de Tolosa. For this they received 'recognition' by the Archbishop of Toledo and, soon

193

afterwards, in 1286, the parish church of San Juan Bautista was built.

As we made our way into Urda we could identify it at once as 'our' sort of place, for it lacked every hint of tourism. The locals stared a little more intensely than usual, but seemed friendly enough. Everyone we passed greeted us in some way, giving an air of 'old Spain'. The crumbling, white-washed walls of the single-storied houses, some of which had grass and flowers growing from their red, pantiled roofs, were packed closely together in a ramshackle way. All this, and the fact that the narrow, cobbled streets had not yet been paved over, suggested that the customary desire to modernise had, fortunately, not yet been adopted here.

As we entered the Plaza de la Iglesia and looked about us, a grizzled, bent old man, leaning on a stick and dressed in clothes that looked two or three sizes too large for him, stood staring in our direction with unabashed interest. A tiny, wide-eyed young girl held his hand. After a moment, they came towards us, he advancing with effort while the child skipped along by his side like a newly-born spring lamb. Silently, he pointed upwards with his cane towards the top of the church, lurching sideways as he did so and nearly collapsing on top of his little companion. There, built high up in the steeple, we could see a large stork's nest with a stork in residence, sitting amongst the jumble of large twigs.

"For how long have the storks been building their nests up there?" I asked.

He gave a sigh of pleasure. The child looked up at him.

"Forever," he said, wonderingly.

I had heard that these great birds do, indeed, return each year to the same place. As we stood there, all four of us gazing silently upwards, another huge stork, with something in its mouth, glided clumsily in to join its mate, knocking a few sticks from the nest as it did so, for there was hardly room for them both. The old man could scarcely contain his excitement.

"Look, look!" he cried.

Stork's nest in Urda

We found a small fonda in the centre of town near the Casa de la Cultura and once again discovered nobody else in residence. The owner, called Gerónimo, informed me that we were the first people to stay that year and he found it difficult to remain open. Although the fonda was part of his own house he still had to pay taxes on the lettable rooms and was losing money. I asked whether the village had seen many foreigners.

"You may be the first and last to stay here," he said sadly.

Twenty years before, the fonda had been used regularly by horse dealers and mule drivers journeying between Consuegra, Ciudad Real and Los Yébenes. But, he continued, a distance that used to take two or three days could now be covered in a few hours by motorised transport and Urda had nothing to attract the tourist. So, he lamented, nobody stayed in Urda overnight. I sympathised with him and told him that we had found that to be the case in other places we had passed through on our way north. I then told him more about our trip, but the more I rambled on about our walk from Granada, the more worried he seemed to become. I don't think he believed a word I said, and to shut me up, offered us both a cold beer, helping himself to a large whisky at the same time. After two weeks on the road Bob and I must have looked like a couple of unkempt, disreputable tramps and I could see that poor Gerónimo did not know what to make of us. He looked relieved when I offered to pay for the rooms there and then instead of waiting until morning. To show his gratitude he poured out two more drinks for us and another double whisky for himself, then led us to a little room behind the bar where we all sat down.

I asked him if he would tell us what he knew about Urda and he seemed only too willing. In the 19th and early 20th century, it seems that the village had been renowned for gangs of highwaymen who set up home here and ranged the nearby sierras, committing all sorts of foul deeds. Situated in the middle of nowhere, far away from the capital, this place proved an ideal hideout for these desperadoes. His story reminded me a bit of the tales about the Despeñaperros

Pass, where the setting is much the same. In both places escape into the mountains would have been easy if any imminent danger of capture had threatened. When I interrupted him to say that we had heard similar accounts of bandits in the Sierra Morena and went on to mention the name José Cabacho or 'El Tempranillo,' he became quite animated.

"El Tempranillo!" he cried. "That baby! That amateur! What did he know of banditry? Here in Urda we had the likes of 'Castralos', 'Los Longinos', 'El Cleofe', and, of course, the most terrible of all – 'Juanillones' or 'Gabino Serrano'. Their names are legendary throughout the world!"

He sounded so proud and protective of his villains that I guessed they must have been local folk heroes like our Robin Hood or Dick Turpin. It's strange how 'baddies' are usually remembered more than 'good guys.' Our host, now on his fourth whisky, began to regard us thoughtfully. Perhaps, because of the way we looked, he was thinking that outlaws were about to make a comeback.

There was still time to look around more of the town before eating and, as Gerónimo had fallen asleep in his chair and the supply of beers seemed to have dried up, we visited the museum, which had on display paintings and sculpture by an artist called ' Guerro Malagón'. Also on show was a local 'treasure', which consisted of the figure of Christ carrying a cross, standing in a very elaborate, golden, wheeled boat. All this cultural activity seemed to renew our thirst, so we decided to do something about it at a nearby bar. With each swallow our imagination became more fanciful. Bob was fascinated by the stories I passed on to him about the bandits. He looked about him and speculated on the possibility of any particular dwelling having been the home of some brigand or other.

"You know, Roy," he said ponderingly, "this little town may not have much to offer a tourist at the moment, but, wow! – it was a gangsters' hideout!"

He went on to say that, in the U.S.A., anywhere having a connection with famous outlaws like Jesse James, Billy the Kid or Wyatt Earp had swarms of sightseers. Blockbuster

197

films had been made about their lives, numerous books published and many folk-songs composed. Why couldn't Urda be exploited in the same way? We took the topic with us to a restaurant where we continued making extravagant plans for this sleepy little village.

"It needs some clever impresario to come out here and take charge," said an enthusiastic Bob. "Plaques on the walls, a Museum of Banditry, postcards, photographs of the children and grandchildren. Why! Gerónimo would have to expand his business rather than close down."

We agreed that these run-down, one-horse villages needed changes: they needed visionaries like us to recognise their potential and exploit it.

"And their names!" Bob started up again. "Castralos! Juanillones! They have just the right ring to them. An American tourist would go crazy. A bit like Bonnie and Clyde. Just imagine the sign reading 'Castralos lived here'. Of course, more information would be needed – like how many people they had murdered – you know, all the gory details,

Possible bandit house

including how they eventually met their sad end. That sort of thing."

He thought for a moment.

"If their end wasn't tragic – if they'd died in their beds –well then, a little artistic licence would have to be used. Colourful people like that must die with their boots on to be of any great interest. You know what I mean, Roy. Boy! What a chance going to waste!"

So we continued with our monumental plans for an unaware Urda until we had finished our cigar and coffee, then we sleepily returned to the fonda – and bed.

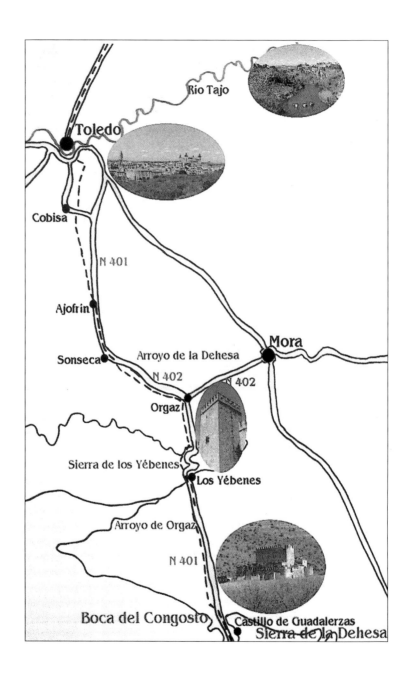

Río Tajo

Toledo

Cobisa

N 401

Ajofrin

Sonseca

Arroyo de la Dehesa

Mora

N 402

N 402

Orgaz

Sierra de los Yébenes

Los Yébenes

Arroyo de Orgaz

N 401

Boca del Congosto

Castillo de Guadalerzas

Sierra de la Dehesa

19

Merrily and muddier on our way,
Ruttish and randier every day ...

"I hope our old friend Don Quixote was not listening in last night," Bob said the next morning. "If he'd heard the plans we're making for Urda, he'd have run us through with his lance, for sure!" Yesterday's topic had not been forgotten.

"Look over there," he instructed, "at that guy by the bar. You can see the bandit strain in him, can't you? He sure has a mean streak. Just look at his eyes." He nodded towards a tall, wiry-looking individual dressed in tight trousers, white open-neck shirt and leather boots and jacket, innocently drinking his early-morning brandy. He could well have been on his way to a stable.

"It's a good job we don't look wealthy, Roy," he whispered. "This is the sort of place where we could disappear without trace."

We finished our breakfast, said goodbye to Gerónimo and all the other descendants of desperadoes, and set off on the road to Los Yébenes.

Our first eight kilometres were slightly uphill, running to the left of the Sierra de la Dehesa. At a crossroads we turned on to the N401 again and continued north along another very straight, unswerving road. It looked to me as if we might well be following the path of the Roman aqueduct. A little further on we spotted a large, turreted castle standing all on its own about half a kilometre over to our right. This Castillo de Guadalerzas seemed to be in such a good state of repair that I felt it could have been built yesterday and half-expected to see Charlton Heston come galloping through

Castillo de Guadalerzas

the arched doorway waving his sword in the air to the cries of 'El Cid'. Bob was most impressed.

"Just look at that!" he gasped. "If we had something like that where I come from there would be sightseers all over the place. Hot-dog stalls, souvenirs and all that. McDonalds would have staked their claim immediately."

"I think I prefer it the way it is," I said.

"Oh, me too," agreed Bob. "But you've got so much of this sort of thing over here in Europe. In the States, we haven't."

At times like this Bob reminded me how lucky I was to live where I did.

As we passed through the mountainous bit he was constantly pointing out some craggy jumble of rocks that, he judged, would have been a good spot for robbers to lie in wait.

At the summit, before beginning our descent, I turned to look back down to the jumble of red roofs pierced through the middle by the stork-nested steeple. Urda lay there, sprawled out like some lonely, marmalade cat waiting for a tickle under the chin. I found the sight most endearing. It brought to mind a sort of H. Rider Haggard 'lost world' except that, instead of being at the top of some plateau in the middle of a jungle, this cut-off cluster of dwellings nestled at the base of towering sierras.

Before long the road joined a railway line on its left-hand side and then, later, flowing merrily along on the right, appeared the river Algodor. Railway and river stayed with us until we all squeezed through a narrow gap in a mountain known as the 'Boca del Congosto' or 'mouth of the canyon'. At this point Bob became really animated.

"Definitely the number one spot for an ambush!" he exclaimed, and explained how any traveller crossing the flat areas on each side of the sierra could be watched by those up here in the heights.

"And this is the only way through," he added. "The perfect place for it! Oh, I wonder what savagery has been committed here?"

On the other side of this pass the road, railway and river meandered their separate ways and we followed a small path running off in a north-westerly direction. The views down and over the land ahead were again fantastic. We could see our destination, Los Yébenes, seventeen horizontal kilometres ahead, nestling at the bottom of yet another range of high sierras called what else but the Sierra de los Yébenes. It was then down and down until we found ourselves, once more, on the flatlands. We had dropped a thousand metres and knew that we had to endure a hot, sticky three hours. But what did we hardened travellers care? Had we not conquered the steaming Tablas de Daimiel and the fiery Calatrava? By now, we felt so full of confidence that the Kalahari Desert would have been a piece of cake. The only hitch to our steady progress appeared when we reached a little tributary to the River Algodor (shown on the map as the Arroyo de Orgaz). We found it running with water. Off to our right we could see the road-bridge but it looked to be about three or four kilometres distant. Too far, we decided. We would try

Arroyo de Orgaz

wading this time. To our relief, the stream proved to be shallow and, apart from nearly becoming stuck in the sludge, which came up above our knees, we managed to labour our way across and reach the other side in two muddy pieces. Then we noticed a line of stepping-stones a little way downstream. Ah, well!

As I sat drying my feet, I looked about me and realised what a really beautiful part of Spain this was. In the distance, and all around, were the differently named sierras which combined to form the Montes de Toledo. Arroyos and ríos watered this countryside, making it relatively lush. Any monotony in the landscape was broken up by clusters of trees made up of oak, ash, willow and maple.

In fact, the last few days had been ideal. We had been playing leap-frog with the sierras by performing a series of 'up and overs', without knowing what to expect on the other side. The weather and scenery had been delightful and the sweet-scented, rosemary-sided roads, with little or no traffic, a pleasure to tread.

Just before entering Los Yébenes we left our footpath, rejoined the road and strolled merrily into town, passing a cemetery and new-looking sports centre on the way. It would be only another forty kilometres, or two days, before we reached the big city of Toledo where we intended to rest for a day. Bob informed me that he wanted to rub shoulders with a few tourists and chat with someone who spoke English. I looked at him quizzically.

"Someone else who speaks English," he elaborated, with an emphasis on the 'else', and continued,

"Just plonk myself down in some shady spot and play it all by ear. If a couple of ladies happen to sit at the next table and we happen to strike up conversation, well ... who knows? One thing might lead to another."

The thought of a couple of ladies coming our way sounded fine to me as well. All this outdoor exercise (apart from the really exhausting bits) had left us very fit and feeling pretty randy. There were many times during the day when our thoughts were not exactly of a cultural or historical nature, I must admit. Bob had been lucky with Miranda back at the roadhouse but I think that we were both feeling somewhat sex-starved. There had been plenty of attractive women in the towns and villages we had passed through but these temptresses were, we knew, completely out of bounds. The fact that they were so untouchable made them more desirable, and often, at the end of the day, lounging back in our chairs, we would share our fantasies. If any person, sitting nearby, had understood English, they would certainly have been shocked by our revelations. It was like a late confessional.

Los Yébenes has quite a history. The Arabic name 'jabal', meaning 'mountain', is apt enough, for high peaks tower directly behind the town. Points of interest include remains of a bronze-age settlement, Roman villas, mines and the aforementioned aqueduct. Existing fortifications, both Arab and Christian, demonstrate the town's historic importance. A good water supply and the control of passage through these Toledo mountains made it strategically crucial. The

Christians finally took the town from the Arabs early in the 13th century, when they started building castles and churches, such as the parochial church of Santa María.

After the battle of Las Navas de Tolosa, the Christian victors haggled as to who would control this terrain. After much debate it was shared between the city of Toledo and the Knights of St. John. The boundary between the two factions would be the main road running through the centre of Los Yébenes and on to Seville. This division lasted until 1835, the time of unification.

After quenching our thirst and sampling some delicious tapas, we booked into an hostal at the edge of a modern-looking, newly tiled square. Later I realised that we should have searched further before taking rooms there for a petrol-station on the other side of the road seemed to attract all the motor-cycles in the neighbourhood. For some reason it was – and still is – trendy to remove silencers from these under 50 c.c. machines, resulting in a terrible roar as they rev up.

In the centre of the plaza I noticed another, recently-installed, concrete fountain looking very much like the one we had seen back in Fuente el Fresno. Was a fast talking sales-man travelling around selling these ugly new monstrosities to the local villages, I wondered?

As we ambled through the narrow streets we could see that Los Yébenes was a much smarter and more sophisti-cated place than Urda, with houses in good repair and the local folk quite smartly dressed. The fact that it saw plenty of visitors was confirmed by the lack of notice taken of my shorts!

After a while we found ourselves in another, older looking square – the Plaza San Juan – which had just about every-thing in it: a tourist office, town hall, cultural centre, health centre, two churches and a games room full of pin-ball machines. Plenty of people were strolling about and Bob lost no time in wishing "buenas tardes" to any young lady who happened to pass him by. If any of them had stopped and spoken to him I don't know what he would have done, but they mostly just smiled shyly and tossed their heads. Real beauties with thick, abundant, jet-black hair, flashing brown eyes, rather haughty carriage and fine figures, they left us with our tongues hanging out.

"Roy," asked Bob, by now desperate, "can't you just ask one of these señoritas if they would care to join a couple of lonely strangers for a drink? They might like to improve their English. I could give them a couple of free lessons."

"Yes, I bet," I replied. "In what? Besides, they might be señoras and have a señor around who might like to give you a lesson or two."

He kept on and on, but I shook my head and eventually he gave up.

"Huh!" he grumbled. "Where's your sense of adventure now, then?"

"Kept firmly in my pants," I answered.

"Firm is the right word," he moaned.

The square continued to bustle with activity until well past midnight. We just sat there watching the action, slowly working our way through a bottle of the red stuff while doing justice to a ración of albóndigas con patatas bravas (meatballs with spicy fried potatoes). It wasn't until a tired-looking waiter started piling up chairs and tables around us that we took the hint and made our way back to the hostal.

20

Of being led astray by following our noses,
And on into marzipan town.

I didn't manage to sleep soundly. The busy hostal had thin
walls along with noisy plumbing and I soon discovered that
I had been given a room next to the frequently-used bathroom. The racket created by motor bikes outside my window
did not help either. Bob had been luckier. His room at the
back suffered less of a racket.

"Keep your hands by your sides at night," he advised the
next morning, as he noticed the bags under my eyes. "You'll
wear yourself out."

I felt too tired to think up some witty reply. Sonseca,
twenty kilometres away, would be our target for that day.

We searched in vain for some alternative passage over the
Sierra de Los Yébenes rather than staying on the N401, and I
cast my eye around the room, looking for some likely-look-
ing person to ask. The others all appeared to be the types
that would rather drive than walk, but I took the map over
to one of them anyway, asking if he knew of any footpaths.
He replied that he did not and then put the question to his
neighbour, who shook his head. The man on the other side
of him stretched across and, before long, I had a little group
of coffee-slurpers peering over my shoulder at the map,
offering guidance. One of them, a hale and hearty-looking
young man, said that he knew of a track used by goatherds
which could be found a short way out of town, starting at
the Ermita San Blas. He had followed it himself as far as
Orgaz. I folded the map, packed it away, thanked them all for
their help and off we strode.

Climbing the hill out of Los Yébenes, I passed the news on to Bob, who stopped in his tracks.

"You're having me on!" he exclaimed. "The path leads to where?"

"Orgaz," I replied. "A town we have to pass through on the way to Sonseca."

"Orgaz – mm!" he mused, and we both laughed.

"That must have been your problem last night," he said. "That's why you look so shattered."

A little farther on we found the hermitage, the Ermita de San Blas, and saw the goat track beside it. I pulled out my compass to check the direction, and heard Bob groan.

"If that damned compass of yours says it's down there," he cried, pointing to the footpath, "then we'd better stick to the road!"

"Do you want the map again?" I asked, threateningly. It shut him up.

We turned off the road and started to follow a little trail of goat droppings. A short while later we reached the summit of our present sierra and looked down across the other side towards Sonseca. Wow! Although the others had been good enough, this stood out as the most splendid panorama of the trip so far. A veritable patchwork quilt! To the Moors, coming north from their hot, dry countries, such a view must have represented the garden of paradise.

Zig-zagging down the hillside, the main road cut through all this splendour and led into an assembly of white houses which we took to be Orgaz. Beyond that, through the distant haze, we could just about identify the town of Sonseca.

Suddenly, as we rounded a hill, we came face to face with a large, recently-renovated, white windmill standing there calmly contemplating the wonderful view. This majestic, pointed-topped building appeared to be very pleased with itself to be in such a privileged position and gave the impression that it was waiting for someone important to arrive. (Maybe the return of Don Quixote!)

"Take care, your worship," said Squire Sancho, "those things over there are not giants but windmills, and what

Windmill above Los Yébenes

seem to be arms are sails, which are whirled round in the wind and make them turn."

After two difficult hours we covered the four kilometres down the rough track and eventually reached the base of the Sierra de Los Yébenes. Going down a steep hillside with loose stones underfoot can be treacherous. My cowboy boots with their smooth bottoms had hardly any grip and were certainly the wrong footwear. Goatherds wore canvas sandals with soles made from old car tyres called 'abarcas' and, in these, they seemed to be able to frolic about these mountain paths like the goats they tended. Bob reckoned that Michelin X soles would have been favourite! Gerald Brenan advises prospective hikers to wear rope-soled shoes because they are less likely to slip and are light.

As we moved downwards, treading very carefully, Bob came up with a name for this sort of terrain, describing it as 'Broken Leg Country'. We took very small paces, feeling our way with outstretched toe before putting our full weight forward, for I had learned the hard way that this is the best method on this sort of surface. However tempting the alluring view ahead, it is wiser to keep eyes fixed firmly on the ground.

It would have been faster and safer to have stayed on the road.

"Let's leave all that scrambling about to the 'cloven foot brigade' in future," commanded Bob. "Goats we ain't!"

Four level kilometres further on found us in Orgaz, positioned at a crossroads where the N401 meets the N402.

We had intended to pass straight through and carry on to Sonseca, ten kilometres away. I say 'intended' because, as we ambled along we suddenly became aware of a delicious aroma wafting out from behind a bar's curtained doorway. Under normal circumstances we never stopped at this time of day. Out on the road, we just looked for somewhere shady to sit and eat whatever we happened to have with us, usually an orange or some other fruit. But on this occasion, we stopped, sniffed the air, looked at each other for a moment, then pulled aside the curtain and went inside. The appetising, savoury smell came from a dish being eaten by six, short, stocky men seated at a large wooden table. The sight of us brought about the usual stunned silence. It was as well that none of them understood English for, as we pulled up two chairs to sit and join them, Bob came out with one his polite observations.

"It only wants one more of those little guys," he said, "and I'd guess they were waiting for Snow White."

"You could make up the number," I responded, "– as Grumpy!" They continued to stare at us for a moment or two longer, then, without a word, pushed two empty glasses our way and filled them with red wine. Next, they called for two more deep dishes and, from a gigantic tureen, one of these kind gentlemen filled our plates to the brim with a steaming 'potaje', full of chick-peas, different sorts of vegetables and some kind of fish (usually cod).

Bob broke the silence. "Don't they have a menu or something?" he asked me. "Isn't there a choice?"

I knew, from experience, that this sort of place was family-run, serving only one dish of the day.

Castle at Orgaz

"There's a choice, all right," I answered. "You can take it or leave it."

The meal lived up to its promise and was stupendous (stewpendous?). The others at the table watched us finish the first plateful, then ladled in some more. Our empty glasses were refilled, then came the questions. Travelling on foot? To Madrid? Not even bicycles? They gazed in disbelief. A fat man started chatting away to Bob, who kept nodding in agreement to everything being said without understanding a word. The others let it be known that they were lorry-drivers and offered us lifts to Toledo or even all the way to Madrid, if we liked. Our refusal left them shaking their heads.

Later, with many fond farewells and wishes of 'buena suerte' and 'buen viaje' the friendly hauliers departed. We stayed a while longer, finished off the last of the wine, then asked for the bill – only to be told that it had already been settled. The table, I was informed, had been reserved by those sitting there and it was they who had ordered the 'estufado' in advance. We had unknowingly shared their meal. Was it because of our ragged, poverty-stricken looks that these kind, hospitable gentlemen decided to give us a 'hand out', we wondered? No: they were impelled by natural goodwill to men. Whatever the reason, their generosity was much appreciated.

With full stomachs we sat drowsily, knowing that we had over-eaten and drunk too much wine. If there had been somewhere in Orgaz to spend the night we might well have been tempted to forget Sonseca. But in the absence of a fonda, we shouldered our packs and continued unsteadily on our way.

During the ten-kilometre slog to Sonseca, my head throbbed, my body ached and after an hour of painful walking, I developed a raging thirst which I managed to satisfy a little by making a hole in an orange and sucking out the juice. Five hard kilometres later we came to a stream – the Arroyo de la Dehesa de Villaverde – which we crossed, once again, by removing our boots and socks and wading. At the half-way mark I saw that Bob had bent over and adopted the 'ostrich position' which showed him with his head submerged under the water. I followed his example and held my hot, sore head under the cool, flowing stream. It felt good!

By the time we reached the outskirts of Sonseca the effects of our over-indulgence had started to wear off a little. Sweating and exercise had helped, but I still felt very thirsty. At a football field we turned off and made our way towards the town centre where we had been told there was a residencia in the Plaza de la Constitución. (This was similar to a hostal but consisted of lettable rooms in someone's apartment.) There, in the square, we saw it advertised by a sign poking out from the third floor of a block of flats. Carefully, we put away all our washing, tidied ourselves up as best we could, climbed up the three flights of stairs and knocked at the door. It was opened by a frumpish-looking old lady who eyed us up and down disapprovingly and then, somewhat reluctantly, took our money and handed over some keys. Once inside the room, I lost no time in holding my mouth under the basin tap and drinking my fill. Along the corridor I discovered a bare, towelless, soapless bathroom, furnished with a small, chipped bath over which a rusting shower-head dangled. Bob and I took turns to stand under it and wait for the trickle of cold water to slowly dampen us all over. This 'water torture' was worth suffering, however, for afterwards we both felt much fresher and decided to go and search out the delights of Sonseca.

As we sat at a table outside a bar in the centre of town, nibbling at a thick slice of tortilla, watching the folk moving about in a determined, business-like manner, we came to the conclusion that things had begun to change as we moved northwards to the bigger cities. The open agricultural parts of Spain farther south, with endless expanses of olive trees and extensive vineyards, were disappearing and so was the easy-going, relaxed style of living in favour of a harder commercialism.

On our way into town we had noticed fields of almond trees and these, we learned, were harvested to make the delicious marzipan for which Sonseca is famous throughout

Spain. As well as this, it had thriving, centuries-old furniture making and textile industries.

The effect of our lunchtime episode meant that an early night might be our best plan. After all, we wanted to be in good shape for Toledo, so we paid the spruce, white-coated, tie-wearing waiter and retired early.

21

A day to remember
Of rabbits, rifles and mines!

I had a scary dream that night, probably brought about by over-indulgence back in Orgaz. With a large crowd of dwarves looking on, I was being lowered into a deep, dark pit. The pale face of Snow White stood out above the others and I was crying pitifully to her for help. Nothing happened, so, in a frenzy, I started banging furiously on the lid of the coffin. With a start, I sat up in bed to find that the thudding sound was coming from the door to my room.

Apparently, Bob had been banging away for some time and, in doing so, had woken up all the others in the apartment, including the old lady. By the time I was fully awake Bob's loud voice had been joined by hers and several others from the neighbouring rooms, shouting, rather rudely, for him to be quiet. I made ready as quickly as I could, then went out into the hallway, where I found a desperate-looking Bob cornered by our wrinkled hostess, who was waving a finger under his nose and admonishing him severely. He looked distinctly uncomfortable and was trying his best to squeeze past her and make for the front door. He could not, of course, understand what she was saying but could see her obvious ire. As I approached them I said, in my best Oliver Hardy voice,

"Another fine mess I've got you into, Stanley!"

She turned and started on me.

"Tell the old girl that I'm sorry," pleaded Bob, "and add that it's all your fault."

We got out as soon as we could. As we hurriedly clambered down the stairs I could hear the old girl's voice shrieking after us,

"And don't come back here again!"

We had reckoned the distance to be covered that day to be about thirty kilometres and our intention had been to leave Sonseca early in order to arrive at Toledo early enough to find somewhere decent to stay.

"You'll have to get a move on today," I said to Bob. "No lagging behind."

As I had been responsible for our late start, you can guess his answer.

For the first five kilometres, as far as Ajofrín, we stayed on the road which, all of a sudden, seemed to be full of vehicles. On the other side of the village we came across a track which looked as though it was heading in our direction, but, as there was nothing shown on the map, I asked at a filling station. Yes, I was told, the path did lead towards Toledo but first it passed through a small place called Cobisa, twelve kilometres away. In order to get off the busy N401 we decided to give it a try.

I loved the pleasant walking: the weather was perfect and we both felt in tip-top form. Bob seemed to have got over his encounter with the old woman and, for a change, had tried to keep up with my guardsman's pace. All around, the land was becoming more barren, with uneven, rough ground broken up by large expanses of smooth rock. Farmers had no chance of ploughing and planting in this soil: it looked suitable only for cattle to graze and, with this in mind, we kept our eyes peeled for bulls. I had been warned, by a reliable source, that on open, unfenced terrain like this, bulls might pose a problem. In the company of cows they were no danger, it seemed, but on their own they were best avoided. So for the next three hours we stayed together and kept a close lookout for anything with four legs. With few trees about, we knew that if we came across bulls we had the choice of turning around and retracing our steps, skirting around them, or simply putting on a brave face and trying to march straight past. The last choice did not go down well with either of us. Which of us would be the one with the 'brave face' to go first? When it came to facing up to bulls, we both admitted to being cowards. We had lately been watching television showing bullfighters being tossed all over the place, and knew the fate of poor old Manolete back in Linares – and he was an expert! So, with this in mind, we trundled uneasily along until we reached a deserted minor road which, our map showed, led to Cobisa. We breathed a sigh of relief for we knew that there would not be cattle left loose near a highway. Our worries were over, we reckoned. (Little did we know!) The only creatures we had seen since leaving Sonseca were green lizards, lying on the rocks to bask in the sun. As we came towards them they stayed stock still, contemplating us with their beady, glinting eyes but, if we stepped too close, they would, at the very last moment, zip away.

Before long we saw a cluster of white houses in the distance, which we guessed to be Cobisa. On our way towards it I noticed another track leading off to the right. It was not shown on the map, but, according to my compass, looked to be the most direct route to Toledo. To stay on our present course and pass through the village would mean a longer, more roundabout route. As we were already behind schedule, I managed to persuade Bob that, by taking this footpath, we could cut off a few kilometres and make up some lost time. Though not easily convinced, he agreed to give it a try.

"What the hell!" he said. "At least we got as far as here in one piece without getting into a hassle with bulls. Anyway, Toledo can't be that far away and it's so big we can hardly miss it."

It looked about five more kilometres to go. The first two were no different from the last ten but, after that, the path became less distinct and the scrub denser with trees and bushes. We plunged onwards. At first we saw just one or two rabbits sitting nearby, watching our progress, but gradually their numbers increased. During the whole of our journey from Granada we had seen no more than a dozen or so but now, suddenly, hundreds of them sprang around all over our feet.

218

"Why doesn't someone come out here and shoot some of these damned rabbits?" asked a perplexed Bob.

I could offer no explanation. It was a mystery. Their usual scarcity was the result of avid hunting, for the meat was a delicacy. Why had this lot escaped the pot? We kept steadily to the path and, a short while later, were delighted to see the black turrets of the Alcázar fortress poking out over a distant ridge. This huge building, we knew, represented the highest point in Toledo. Not far to go now.

He saw them first. I must have been looking down at the rabbits. There was a mumbled curse from behind and I turned around to see Bob, standing motionless with his arms raised, staring straight ahead.

"Don't argue with those guys, Roy," he said, quietly. "They've cocked their rifles and their fingers are on the trigger."

I looked back towards Toledo and, to my astonishment, beheld three young soldiers, dressed in camouflaged combat outfits, pointing guns at us. Two of them held rifles and the

View of Toledo, showing the Alcázar fortress

third one, who seemed to be an officer, had a pistol in his hand. This one barked at me.

"Hands up!"

I did as I was told.

"What's going on?" I asked.

With all the rabbits around I should have asked, "What's up, Doc?" I suppose, but I didn't want to complicate matters. I could see that the soldiers were very much on edge. One of those pointing a rifle was visibly shaking and I hoped that he still had the safety-catch on. We all stood very still with little bunnies jumping merrily around us and over our feet. The soldier with the pistol commanded sternly: "Come with me. Remain strictly on the path and keep your hands raised."

With him leading and the other two walking behind we were accompanied slowly down a narrow, twisting path to arrive at a high, wire-meshed gate, topped by rolls of barbed wire. On the way I noticed that the officer in front had been treading carefully and I guessed that this was to avoid stepping on the rabbits. (There was another reason, I learned later!) Once inside the compound we were marched past a group of gawking, open-mouthed army personnel, and up some stairs leading to a green, wooden hut, which had the Spanish flag flying outside. The soldier in front opened the door and went inside. The next few moments were pure Keystone Cops. With my hands still raised above my head I was unable to follow, so I stopped still where I was. Bob stumbled into my back and the two armed men coming up the steps behind him almost fell over each other. The problem was solved when a voice from inside the hut instructed us to lower our arms and enter.

Once my eyes had become used to the darkened interior I made out six officer-looking types standing around a desk and another seated behind. Without further ado, our packs were taken from us and the contents tipped on to the floor. The maps were unfolded and carefully scrutinised while we were thoroughly searched. Bob's little camera was placed on the desk and our passports taken from us and their details copied into an impressive-looking ledger. The discovery that

220

I was British seemed to cause concern and they all started talking at once. The officer sitting behind the desk stood up and came over to me. His height and fair hair made him stand out from the others and from the mass of gold bands around his shirt collar I knew him to be a military big-shot. He had a no-nonsense manner about him.

"What are you doing in this area?" he asked me curtly, in English.

"We are walking to Madrid," I answered.

He turned to the others and translated into Spanish,

"He says they are walking to Madrid!"

This answer was greeted by unbelieving smiles and shakes of the head all round. Some story!

He repeated the question and I gave the same reply. Is this where he punches me in the stomach, I wondered? I asked if I might be permitted to show him the route we had walked so far, but he did not seem to be interested and continued with his questioning.

"Did you not see the signs on the fence stating that this a military area and strictly forbidden to the public?"

I told him that we had seen no such signs.

"They are clearly visible all along the perimeter fence," he said.

Once again, I told him that we had come across no signs and no fence.

"Look," I said, taking a chance and pointing to the map lying on the desk. "We came this way across open country and that's probably why we saw no fence."

He followed the dots drawn on the map as far as Sonseca and then asked which way we had come from there. I took a pencil and traced the route.

"Impossible!" he declared. "That area is mined!" He looked angry.

I stood there open-mouthed. Had I heard correctly? Mines? Did he mean the explosive sort? It was hardly likely that he meant coal mines. Had we walked across a minefield? It slowly dawned on me that we had done precisely that. It explained all those rabbits. Other thoughts were racing through my mind. Here we were, two fit-looking foreigners, one of whom was British, moving around in a prohibited military area. Our ridiculous story of walking to Madrid from Granada must seem very feeble and ridiculous to those in the room. What were we doing there then?

I knew from the television news that an Argentinian cruiser, the *General Belgrano*, had been sunk by a British submarine on 2 May and that the H.M.S. *Sheffield* had been bombed and destroyed by an air-to-surface missile. There had been a few other incidents as well. What I did not know was that on this very day, 14 May, the British Special Forces had landed on Pebble Island, with 11 enemy aircraft being destroyed on the ground and three of their 'Skyhawks' shot down. What was worse, Margaret Thatcher had stated that a peaceful settlement to the conflict might not be possible. I was aware that Spanish sympathies lay completely with the Argentinians and the British were considered to be the wrongdoers. For all I knew, the Spanish had joined hands with their oppressed brothers across the Atlantic and we were suspected of espionage. While I considered all this, our belongings were being thoroughly searched. They held books by their covers so that pages flew open, my diary was being scanned by a man wearing glasses and our clothing had been turned inside out. Bob's camera had disappeared from the desk-top.

To my surprise, they then ordered us to sit down and, as we sat there wondering what would happen next, the officer who had been reading my diary came over and asked if we were thirsty and would we care for a cold beer! Was this the soft approach, I wondered, before the firing squad? All the while, the two young soldiers were still pointing their rifles at us. Our beers were brought in and we drank them in silence, making no sudden movement, for I guessed that these gun-pointers were bored, reluctant conscripts doing their military service, and might well pull the trigger just to break the monotony of army life. The crowd around us seemed to have relaxed a little by now and sounded to be busy discussing the merits of various football teams. The

222

atmosphere had changed. The door flew open and a full crate of beers was brought in to be shared by all in the room. Our two young guards had to lean their weapons against the wall in order to prise the tops from the bottles. If the guns were still cocked and had fallen over I imagine they would have gone off. With beers in hands everyone became friendlier. The man who had been leafing through Bob's scientific manuals, was asking him which branch of medicine he practised and my former, fair-haired interrogator asked me if I had a place to stay in Toledo. When he learned that we had yet to find somewhere he wrote down the name of a hostal which, he said, was owned by his sister-in-law.

Questions came thick and fast. Had we visited Toledo before? What did we think of their country? What of the Iron Lady, Señora Thatcher? (Although they held her responsible for the problems in the Malvinas they still seemed to hold her in high regard.) In a short space of time the scene had changed from seeming hostile and unfavourable to becoming amicable and favourable. There was more to-ing and fro-ing in and out of the hut and soon we were handed back our passports. They returned Bob's camera (minus the film, we discovered later) and then they all came over and shook hands. The tall officer said that we had wandered unknowingly into a secret, out-of-bounds military establishment and in doing so had somehow, miraculously, crossed a minefield. The word 'unknowingly' led me to think that they must have believed our story and considered us to be innocent of any intentional mischief.

"How were we to know?" I asked. "There's nothing on the map to say that there's a secret military camp here."

"No," he replied with a little sigh. "That's because it's secret. We do not mark secret camps on maps."

A waiting camouflaged jeep drove us a few kilometres in the opposite direction to Toledo and we were let out through another high, padlocked gate set in a long 'keep-out' type fence. From the road we could see the signs, complete with skull and crossbones, warning of mines and forbidding entry.

Military camp near Toledo

It was an hour before we saw the outskirts of Toledo again – an hour of walking and talking. How did we manage to end up in a minefield without encountering any obstacles? We learned later that the small road to Cobisa had signs at each end prohibiting entry to the public, and was used only by military personnel. By cutting across instead of travelling along it we had completely missed these warnings. Was the land really mined or were they just saying that? We never knew but rejoiced to be unharmed and looking down on Toledo at last.

"Lucky we're still in one piece, eh, Bob?" I put to him.

"Two pieces," he answered, dryly. He always managed to come up with some smart-alec answer.

What with a late start and the unexpected delay at the military camp, it was getting quite late in the day and we had yet to find somewhere to stay for the night. Amid all the earlier hustle and bustle I had somehow managed to lose the address of the officer's sister-in-law but we imagined that it would be easy enough just to continue on down, cross the river Tagus, enter the city and find an hostal. A short while later, however, we were looking over this wide expanse of water but could see no obvious way of reaching the other side.

"Where are all the damned bridges?" asked an exasperated Bob.

With cars whizzing past us on the busy road behind, we stood on a paved path and searched in vain for someone to ask directions. Our escapade with the soldiers, along with a thirty kilometre walk, had taken a lot out of us. We just wanted, at that moment, to find rooms, remove our packs, and relax, and felt frustrated to see this magnificent, enticing city just a short distance away and not be able to reach it. It stood there like some beautiful siren, calling to us from an inaccessible position to come over and sample her delights. Under normal circumstances we would have found the imposing sight charming but, at that moment, we were in no mood to be charmed. To find a crossing, should we follow the river round to the right or to the left? It was like arriving at the river Cigüela in Las Tablas all over again.

I thought, for the moment, that Bob had left the choice to me.

"What do you think?" he asked.

"As the saying goes," I answered, "right's always right."

"In that case, let's go left," he said.

I am not sure whether we found the quickest way, but half an hour later we saw our pavement curve down to a bridge crossing the Tagus and continuing on to an arched gate in the great wall. This proved to be the Puente de San Martín and just before reaching it we came across an ice-cream stall, where we greedily swallowed two delicious ice-creams apiece. Feeling a little more refreshed, we passed through the archway and found ourselves in a busy plaza which had little narrow streets running out from it in all directions. A few questions and a hundred yards later we booked into one of the many hostales dotted about. Though excited to be in the big city at last, we felt pretty exhausted so, after eating, we overcame the urge to explore and decided instead on a good night's sleep. We wanted to be fit and refreshed the next day to enjoy this great city and be ready for anything or anyone that came our way.

22

Down and out in Toledo
With lesbians all over the place.

It felt good to just lie in bed the next morning and contemplate the day ahead. I had heard many good things about Toledo and hoped that it would live up to my expectations. Today, I thought to myself, I must try to smarten up a bit, so I sorted through my belongings looking for something fairly clean and not too crumpled to wear. My one and only shirt had been dumped on the floor of the military hut the day before and then stuffed hurriedly back into my bag, so it was not in very good shape. Still, I had nothing else so I put that on, along with my shorts. My cowboy boots looked rather the worse for wear so I tried to give them a face-lift by wiping them with a piece of damp cloth but the result left them so besmirched that I soon gave up. They gazed up at me so pitifully, covered in muddy streaks.

"What's all this about?" they seemed to ask. "We haven't let you down yet, have we?"

They were happy the way they were.

I did the best I could and then went down to meet Bob who, I could see, had likewise made an effort to spruce himself up. Just for today, we agreed, pesetas were not important and we resolved to splash out on a special sort of breakfast in one of Toledo's best plazas. So, a few narrow passages later found us sitting like lords in the main square – the Plaza Mayor – tucking into platefuls of bacon and eggs. Many other people milled about, mostly tourists by the look and sound of them, chattering away in every language under the sun, with cameras hanging round their necks and guidebooks at the ready.

It did not take long for Bob to strike up conversation with two chic-looking German ladies sitting at the next table. He deliberately kept the chat going in their language although I am sure they spoke English perfectly well. I let him get on with it. He had suffered from being left out in the cold, as far as communicating with the locals was concerned, all the way up from Granada. Now was his chance to get his own back. These middle-aged Fräuleins were, I could see, eyeing us up and down rather apprehensively and, as soon as they had finished their coffees, they got to their feet and walked off without so much as an "Auf Wiedersehen".

Bob looked hurt.

"A couple of lesbians, I reckon," he announced, with a dismissive sort of wave of his hand. What other reason could there be for their resistance to his irresistible charm, he wondered? I gave him a reason.

"It could be the egg-yolk you've got running down your chin," I said.

We sat there in the lively, sunlit plaza for over an hour, soaking up the atmosphere, and would probably have stayed longer if it had not been for the frequent table-wiping by a waiter, who asked each time if we wanted anything else. When his actions became too annoying we settled the bill and left. Our breakfast cost more than we should normally have spent in three days.

The fabulous cathedral, built on the site of the Great Mosque, stood majestically on the other side of the square. When the Moors surrendered the city to the Christian King, Alfonso VI, in 1085, it was agreed that this mosque could remain intact as a place of worship for the Arabs. However, having entered Toledo, the king broke his promise and knocked the building down to erect the cathedral in its place.

This Gothic edifice was started in 1227 and finished two hundred and fifty years later. The outside was difficult to examine due to all the shops and houses squashed up against it so we crossed the square and went in through a cloister at the side. For a short while we just stood very still. Out of the corner of my eye I could see Bob gazing about, open-mouthed, as he took in the fairy-tale world of gold-leaf glitter and shadowy sculpted shapes, illuminated by electric candles and spotlights. I reflected on how different it must have been with only shafts of coloured light shining in through the stained-glass windows. But it was the size of the place that staggered me. I had not imagined the interior to be so spacious. Two massive, richly decorated structures at the centre housed the choir and altar and, as we slowly walked past, I noticed that the backs of the wooden stalls were intricately carved with battle scenes depicting the conquest of Granada. Each of the fifty-four panels showed the Moors to be on the receiving end, notwithstanding the fact that they had beaten off all-comers for the last six hundred years. Ah, well! What else could you expect in a Christian church! Continuing along the sweeping aisle towards the Capilla de Santiago, we glanced over to our right and saw, up above, a large hole, seven metres across, which had saints, prophets, angels and cardinals peering down from it, looking as though they might topple out at any moment. The effect was stunning! This marvel is known as the Transparente, put there in the 18th century by Narciso Tomé and his four talented sons. But it was the paintings here in the Cathedral that we really wanted see and it was not long before our wishes were granted. Passing through the anteroom, itself hung with great works of art, we entered the Sacristy. It was difficult to know where to look first. The vaulted ceiling was covered with a glorious fresco by Luca Giordano while the walls were lined with masterpieces by Titian, Bellini, Van Dyck and Goya. At the far end, dominating the room, was El Greco's 'Spoliation of Christ', which showed Jesus being stripped by soldiers before the Crucifixion. That was not all. The adjoining chamber, the vestry, had paintings by Velázquez and Rubens. It was all a bit overwhelming. Gerald Brenan's friend, Roger Fry (the chess player) put it like this in *A Sampler of Castile*: 'The architecture, the sculpture and painting in a Spanish church are all accessory to the purely dramatic art – the religious dance, if you like – of the Mass. By the very superfluity and confusion of so much gold and glitter, guessed at through the dim atmosphere, the mind is exalted and spellbound. The spectator is not invited to look and understand, he is asked to be passive and receptive: he is reduced to a hypnoidal condition.'

How different it must have been when the Moors were in residence, I pondered. Here, inside the former Mosque, no works of art would have been on display for the Qur'an forbids the representation of the human figure. Instead, the walls would have been decorated with artistry just as masterful in the shape of intricate, geometrical calligraphy. I had seen wonderful examples of this in the Alhambra Palace in Granada.

It would have been so easy to pass the whole day inside this fabulous cathedral but, as our time was limited and we wanted to see more of the city, we headed west to the Iglesia de Santo Tomé. Our taste-buds had been whetted for more El Greco. And there it was, 'El Entierro del Conde de Orgaz' (The Burial of the Count of Orgaz). This Count, a citizen of Toledo and lord of the town, died in 1323 and, as he was being lowered into the grave, two saints, St. Stephen and St. Augustine, descended from heaven to do the job themselves. While George Borrow was in Spain selling Bibles, he visited Toledo in 1837 and much admired this masterpiece, hanging where it does today. "Could it be purchased?" he writes. "I should say it would be cheap at £5000". As we stood there studying the painting, I asked Bob what he was thinking.

"I was thinking about that terrific meal we had back there in that little town," he laughed, then added, "No, man, seriously – that Greek certainly knew how to use a paint brush, didn't he?"

"Actually he was from Crete," I corrected him smugly.

"Then why was he called El Greco?" questioned Bob.

"Probably because the Spanish thought he was Greek," I replied. We continued to discuss his works for a while longer, and both wondered why all his figures had such elongated shapes. I learned later that he suffered from an astigmatism which distorted his vision.

El Greco lived in Toledo from 1577 to 1616 and certainly left his mark on the city. We found many more examples of his work in other churches and museums. In *The Face of Spain*, Gerald Brenan deems him a 'newly canonized saint who brings the tourist pilgrim to the doors and fills the pockets of tradesmen and hotelkeepers.'

After its capture by the Christians in 1085, Toledo became the centre for Arabic and Jewish studies, and I expected to see more signs of synagogues. To the south-west of the city, not far from our hostal, I found two, close to each other, the older being the Santa María la Blanca, built at the end of the 12th century. Inside, there was a very definite Moorish feel to the place. Twenty-four octagonal columns, each topped by a capital of Arabic pattern, supported arches of Moorish design. It was from here, in 1405, that an angry mob dragged worshippers to the promenade, slit their throats and hurled them onto the rocks below. The hurlers had been inflamed by the preaching of an eloquent Dominican orator, Vicente Ferrer, who had delivered a sermon against the Jews. The other, smaller synagogue is the Tránsito, built by Pedro the Cruel in 1366. It was a simple, box-like affair with small, high windows that gave light to elaborate ivory and mother-of-pearl ceilings. After all the ornamental, fussy and, sometimes, I thought, somewhat ostentatious decoration we had seen in some of the other places, the restrained simplicity of this building was most appealing.

Walking around Toledo would have been agreeable but for the cars and delivery vans driving through the narrow lanes, forcing pedestrians to give passage by jumping into doorways.

"We just can't escape these damn machines, can we?" complained Bob.

The perimeter of the city is defined by external walls which run alongside the river Tagus, so it feels a bit like being on an island. Once we started our tour of this living museum we found it hard to stop, for around every corner we found something of interest. Gerald Brenan, who returned to Spain with his wife thirteen years after his departure from Yegen, advises, ' The best way to see Toledo is to forget about directions and town plans and take any street that takes one's fancy.' And this is precisely how we went about things. For most of the day we strolled this way and that without any real objective in mind, often finding ourselves back where we had started. It did not really matter. We simply set off again in a different direction. At times we became hopelessly lost, but, once again, did not care.

Narrow streets of Toledo

Everything seemed pretty much intact, in all its glory, from Roman times up to the present day. Toledo had not suffered the pillage and plunder experienced by other great cities in Spain and its peaceful surrender to the Christians in 1085 allowed the inhabitants – Jews, Visigoths, Arabs and Christians – to continue practising their own religions and live amicably together. Inside the safe walls civilisation flourished and Toledo became the cultural centre of Spain as well as the country's capital. It was not until 1492, when the Jews were expelled, that its importance started to diminish and soon afterwards, the royal court moved to Madrid, which then became the capital.

For 127 years, from the date of this surrender in 1085 until the final defeat of the Moors in 1212, Toledo remained a safe haven from the ravages between Christians, Almoravids and Almohads taking place elsewhere in Spain. El Cid and his army of mercenaries came to prominence, offering their help to whomever offered most plunder. No wonder the smart ones kept out of all this trouble and strife by remaining safely inside the city.

All this plodding about made us thirsty, and compelled us (unwillingly, of course!) to make frequent stops at many of the little bars we came across on our way. By the end of the day the muscles in my legs seemed to ache even more than usual and I calculated that, with all this sightseeing, we had covered as many kilometres, if not more, than we would normally have covered on the road. It could be, though, that the unfamiliar hard cobbled surfaces we trod that day accounted for our fresh aches and pains.

The sights were so fabulous that sometimes even eyeing up the ladies had to take second place, although, on occasion during our meandering, I became a little confused when I heard Bob shout out, "Wow, man! Just look at that!"

I was not sure whether he was referring to some shapely female who had caught his eye or some building he had noticed. We tried 'chatting up' a number of women during our travels, for it was quite easy to strike up conversation with someone looking at the same church. Later in the evening our persistence paid off. We met a couple of Swedish girls, Helga and Olga, who agreed to join us for a drink.

'My one', Olga, (for Bob had decided how we should be paired off), asked me, "Do you stay long in Toledo?"

"Just two nights," I answered.

"Aha!" she cried, "You are touring, yes?"

"Well, sort of," I replied.

"By car?" she asked again. I shook my head. This was becoming a guessing game. The young lady studied me carefully.

"Aha!" she proclaimed, triumphantly, "Of course! You are bicycle-men. I look at your legs! So healthy and strong!"

I explained all. As Olga slowly began to take in the fact that we were both journeying across country from Granada to Madrid on foot, she started to look quite worried and leaned across to speak rapid Swedish to her companion. My revelation had unsettled them and their attitude towards us changed. Perhaps they thought us to be a couple of nutcases. Whatever the reason, neither Bob's flexing muscles nor my English magnetism seemed to be getting us anywhere so we didn't mind too much when, before long, they paid for their own drinks and left, saying they had something to do.

"Lesbians all over the place!" declared Bob.

After this disappointing episode we decided to call it a day, but neither of us could remember the name of our hostal or its exact location. I thought this way and Bob, of course, reckoned another. After searching about trying to find some familiar spot that would trigger our memory, we fortunately came across a plan of the city fixed to the wall. With this to help us, we managed to determine by which bridge we had crossed the river when first entering Toledo. This Puente de San Martín, we found, lay in the south of the city, while we at that moment, of course, were standing close to the Museo de Santa Cruz, in the north. Out came my compass and to Bob's (and my) surprise, by twisting this way and that through a myriad passageways, continuously heading southward, we eventually arrived in a part of town we recognised and thereby found the hostal. I proudly put away my compass and then, feeling pleasantly worn out, wearily headed for bed.

Helga and Olga did not escape quite so easily. They featured prominently in my dreams that night, proving to me that they were not lesbians after all.

233

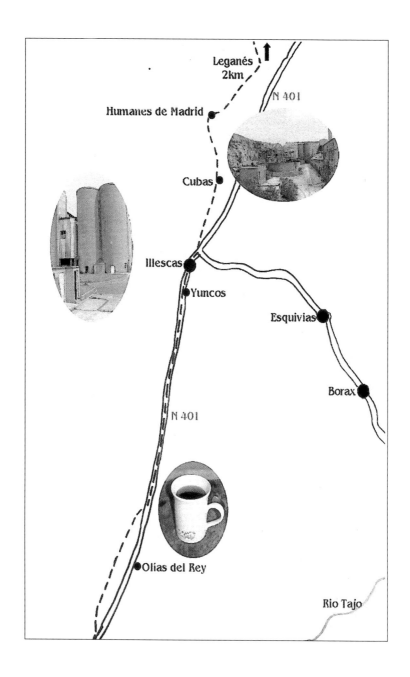

Leganés
2km

N 401

Humanes de Madrid

Cubas

Illescas

Yuncos

Esquivias

Borax

N 401

Olias del Rey

Rio Tajo

23

*An Art Deco oasis
saves the day ...*

We regretted leaving Toledo. The city had stolen our hearts away and we both had to admit that one day had not been nearly enough. Bob reckoned that our stay there resembled falling in love with a beautiful maiden and then having to leave her without experiencing true intimacy. The city seemed to have brought out the romantic in him and, as we headed north along our old pal the N401, he continued to wax poetic. There was no way he could have been drinking that early in the morning, I thought to myself. Neither could he have got hold of anything else - as far as I knew.

"It's there like a casket of jewels waiting to be opened," he carried on dreamily.

"So you managed to tear your eyes away from the ladies for a moment or two, did you?" I laughed. "Toledo must have impressed you more than somewhat."

"Man!" he announced. "What a place! I'm serious, I'm going back there some day and maybe buy myself a little apartment or something. Just live there for a while."

"What about all those lesbians?" I asked him with a grin.

"Who cares!" he retorted. "There are other things in life besides sex, you know!"

"Yes, I know," I answered, still smiling. "But for how long?"

This sort of banter continued as we threaded our way, assisted by my trusty compass, through Toledo's labyrinth of narrow streets and alleyways once again. We kept to a northerly direction and, by some fluke, emerged at an exit called Puerta Nueva de Bisagra where, directly in front of us, we were delighted to see a sign that read - 'Madrid 69 kms.'

I gave the compass a little kiss, looked triumphantly at Bob and returned it to my pack. Here in Toledo it had redeemed itself for all its past mistakes.

So back to the hard slog of walking the hard shoulder on the main road to Madrid. On Sundays, fortunately, although there are plenty of private cars, heavy lorries are absent. We had been so intent on finding our way out of Toledo without becoming lost that we had not stopped for breakfast. The map showed that, ten kilometres down the road, was a village named Olías del Rey and it was there that we hoped to find somewhere open that served coffee and food.

As we marched along I could see Bob becoming more and more irritable. He had not yet had his 'fix' of caffeine and his earlier quixotic behaviour had disappeared. With a hard edge to his voice, he said, almost accusingly,

"This time yesterday, Roy, we were sitting in that square eating bacon and eggs and drinking coffee," he said, emphasising the last two words, "and look at us now! I sometimes wonder what on earth we're doing!"

"It was you that reckoned man needs a challenge," I declared, and jokingly threw a few lines from *Tristram Shandy* at him. 'As we jog along, either laugh with me, or at me, or, in short do anything – only keep your temper,' and then continued with a bit of W.C. Fields: 'Start the day with a smile, Bob, – and get it over with.'

My little snippets had not helped matters.

"Walking along this highway without any coffee inside me is challenge enough," he retorted, "without your second-hand comments!"

About half-way to Olías del Rey we saw a little path turning off the road which seemed to run in a parallel direction to ours, so we walked along it. As long as we could either see or hear the sounds of traffic, we calculated, we must be all right. I rapidly strode on ahead for I knew that my cantankerous, coffee-less companion would not exactly be perfect company. Soon, our little trail started to veer farther and farther away from the N401 but I knew that, as I could still just about determine the faint sound of vehicles in the distance,

I had no worries. Besides which, with the sun still at our backs, I knew that we must still be heading in a northerly direction.

In a lacklustre landscape, just a few thirsty-looking trees stood here and there. According to the map's contours, it would be pretty flat all the way between here and Madrid and I thought back with some nostalgia about the good old days spent crossing the sierras further south. All we had to look forward to from now on were the ugly, industrial parts of Spain.

An hour later we were comforted to notice that our foot-path was gradually bending towards the road sounds again and before long we had regained the N 401. Once there, I looked ahead for some sign of a village but the highway continued straight on with no buildings in sight. Bob had been looking the other way.

"What's that?" he asked, pointing.

I turned the other way and saw a cluster of white houses. By keeping to the path we had somehow bypassed Olías del Rey and would have to walk back a kilometre or two if we wanted to visit the place. This we did, with the hot sun shining on our faces and filthy exhaust fumes wafting up our noses. Bob grumbled and uttered curses at nearly every step. At the junction where the road turned off towards the village we came upon an old-fashioned-looking petrol station consisting of two 'art deco' style fuel pumps and a small shop-cum-office. Sitting outside in the shade was a short, elderly man flicking through a 'girlie' magazine. I walked over to him and asked if he knew of anywhere nearby that might serve coffee.

"Yes," he replied, with a smile. Bob understood the 'yes' and looked on expectantly. "Yes, there is a bar in Olías", the man continued, "but, today being Sunday, it is closed till evening."

I relayed the bad news to my friend. His shoulders sagged even more and he looked as though he was about to collapse to the ground. After asking a few more questions I learned that the next bar likely to be open would be at a place called Villaluenga, twelve kilometres on towards Madrid.

"But," the man added, "I do have cold drinks and magdalenas here in the shop."

He had seen our disappointment and was doing his best to be helpful. Cold drinks sounded all right to me but I knew that another twelve, coffee-less kilometres would be hard for Bob. 'Magdalenas' I knew to be small, sweet cakes.

"Thanks," I answered, "but we were thinking more about a hot drink – like coffee."

"Well, I do not sell it, but I could make some for you, if you wish," he offered.

We wished, and so, thanks to his kindness, we were soon sitting with him, drinking coffee and eating cakes, watching the traffic speed past. The coffee was fine, but the magdalenas took some swallowing: they were very stale. When I told Bob later that the petrol pumps had been put there in the '30s, he replied, "Yeah, along with those little cakes."

His transition amazed me. As he sipped his coffee, his glowering looks gradually faded away to be replaced by one of catlike contentment. If he had been able, I think he would have purred.

I noticed that our breakfast session had not been interrupted by anyone stopping to buy petrol, and I asked why.

"Ah, well," the little man explained. "During the last decade there have been two new filling stations built on this road. One is at Cabañas, seven kilometres to the north, and the other at La Dehesa, five kilometres the other way, towards Toledo. They are very modern with many pumps and other accessories."

He had been there, as I had guessed from the look of his antiquated machines, since the '30s. Initially, his had been the only place for many miles around that supplied fuel but, with road improvements and more vehicles, competition had moved in.

"The little man stands no chance against these giants," he sighed sadly.

We both felt sorry for our kind host and, as we left, thanked him for his hospitality and wished him good luck, although the future for his business did not appear all that rosy to me.

Back on the road we found that traffic had increased and figured that the Madrid folk were on their way home after a weekend away. The cars whooshed past and we looked desperately for some alternative to staying on this busy highway. The only escape, as far as I could see, was to try walking the railway line that ran to Villaluenga, but when we reached it we found no space at the side for pedestrians and we'd be forced to tread the wooden sleepers which snaked off into the distance like some elongated caterpillar. Bob spoke against the idea. I remembered his reluctance once before as we were leaving Baeza. He seemed to have something against walking rails.

"Why take chances?" he argued. "We're nearly there now."

I stood by the side of the hectic, dirty road and looked longingly at the empty, beckoning track.

"You do what you think best, Roy," said Bob, who could see that I was considering the option. "I'm sticking to the road." And off he went.

With a shrug of the shoulders, I followed him. He was probably right.

At Villaluenga we found an open bar/restaurant and broke free of the traffic for a while by going inside and tucking into a selection of tapas, accompanied by a drink or two. As we sat there, we saw the restaurant section slowly fill with people and I realised, as it was two-thirty in the afternoon, that most Spanish motorists would be stopping for their 'comida'.

So, back out again onto the near-deserted road, we continued on our way in comparative peace for the next hour or so and had almost reached our destination before the smell of burning tyres started up again.

Yuncos seemed quite a large town with 100,000 inhabitants. Its name derives from 'juncos' (reeds) and it was originally known as 'Las Ventas de Juncos' (The Field of Reeds). The flat, fertile land was ideal for cereal growing. The Romans called it 'Via Sacra' (Sacred Way) and the Arabs knew it as 'Bab Shara' (Door to the Field). Documents dated 1181 mention a farmhouse, transferred from Cobisa, being installed here and inhabited by one Martín Raimundo who started a vineyard. The local museum has on display a large number of artefacts that were discovered in the large, Bronze Age cemetery and these items signify that Yuncos was occupied by Romans, Visigoths and Moors.

Surprisingly in such a large town, we could find nowhere to stay. There may have been a hotel or motel out on the main road but here in town our only hope, we were informed, was to seek out a woman named Brígida who had rooms to let in her house. She was not easy to find and we had to track her down by asking directions in many different bars. Our quarry turned out to be a wrinkled old dear, sporting a fine growth of moustache. At first she eyed us suspiciously and insisted on taking a hefty deposit along with our passports before showing us to our rooms.

Later, I asked her where we might find somewhere to eat in Yuncos. She ordered us to sit down and then handed us a bottle of wine and some glasses. Next, she lit a gas ring, placed on it the biggest pan I have ever seen and proceeded to fry up eggs, tomatoes and onions. The effect of the wine on an empty stomach made me quite talkative, and I started to relate our adventures.

Brígida's interest in our travels seemed genuine and she listened to my tales attentively. Just as we were about to start eating, the door opened and three other men came in, stared at us for a moment or two, shook us by the hand and then sat down with us at the table. These, we learned, were the other guests staying at the house. She started up the frying pan again and they devoured the same fare. With the drink flowing and the food continuing (she brought cheese and fruit later), we stayed there talking and making merry until quite late. One of the men talking with Bob said that he intended crossing the Atlantic to look for work in America. I acted as interpreter and, many glasses of wine later, Bob shakily wrote his address on a piece of paper, insisting that the Spaniard come to visit him when he arrived in the U.S.A. The old lady sat with us and just laughed along with everything and everyone, although Bob said to me later that he did not like the way she had been 'giving him the eye'.

"You'd better make sure that you lock the door then," I advised, "and put a chair against the handle. She will have a spare key!"

24

Oh, what a night it was,
It really was
Such a night!

This would be our last full day of walking. The distance from Yuncos to Madrid was thirty-seven more kilometres and I suppose if we had wanted to make the effort, we could have polished that off in one go. Instead, we opted to complete the trip in two stages, for we intended to arrive early at my friend's house in good shape. Tonight, we should stay somewhere just outside the city and, next day, take our time in covering the last short stretch. After all, we were in no hurry.

As I descended the stairs I was greeted by the delicious aroma of coffee being brewed and, there, in the living-cum-dining-room, was a busy Brígida doing things with pots and pans. The other gentlemen, she informed me, had left very early for they worked at the 'diggings'. Grave diggings? Archaeological digging? It was a bit too early in the morning for questions so I left it at that.

I sat at the table and waited for Bob, who came to join me half-an-hour later, looking a little harassed.

"Sorry I'm a bit behind, man," he apologised. "I couldn't get my door key to work. There's something wrong with the damned catch."

Brígida served our breakfasts and then left us. She returned a few moments later and returned our passports and deposits. I reckoned that she had been checking the rooms to see if anything was missing.

"Why did your friend lock the door to his room?" she asked me coldly, on her return. Whatever Bob had done to get it open, she must have spotted it.

"She wants to know why you locked yourself in your room last night," I told him. "What do you want me to tell her? That you were frightened she might burst in and jump on you?"

Poor Bob squirmed visibly and kept his eyes fixed on the table-top.

"Er, tell her that I sometimes sleepwalk in the night," he blurted out, "and that I always fasten the door, just in case."

I relayed this explanation to Brígida but I could see that she did not believe a word of it.

"Tell him," she said, jabbing her finger in Bob's direction, "tell the doctor that we do not have thieves in this house!" She must have seen the title from his passport and seemed most upset that anyone of his standing should find it necessary to lock his door, for she finished off with, "And him a man of medicine!"

However, it looked as though all was soon forgiven because as we left she gave us both a bristly, moustache-tickling kiss on each cheek and bade us to ' Go with God'. (I noticed that the older Spanish folk still used the full 'Vaya con Dios!' rather than the shorter, more common 'Adios!')

So we started on the last stage of our journey. I had mixed feelings about the imminent end to it all. I felt a deep sense of satisfaction at having overcome all the obstacles we had encountered on our way, including, at times, the strong temptation to call the whole thing off but, at the same time, I felt sad to think that it would soon all be over. Perhaps my analyst friend was right in claiming that there is a masochist in all of us and that we have to suffer a little sometimes in order to cherish certain everyday things. The first, unforgettable sip of cold beer at the end of a baking-hot hard day, for example, or the exquisite pleasure of simply stretching out on a bed, taking the weight off sore blisters and allowing aching muscles some respite. These, and other never-to-be-forgotten sensations, could never have been fully appreciated had it not been for this walk.

Illescas, four kilometres down the road, was famous for having five paintings by El Greco hanging in its Hospital de la Caridad, and we felt we could not pass through without taking a look at them. We found his paintings addictive. As well as those back in Toledo, we had both seen a wonderful example of his work, 'The Opening of the Fifth Seal', at the Metropolitan Museum of Art in New York, and, by comparison, these sombre paintings here in Illescas were, I must admit, a little disappointing.

The circular 'Anunciación' and 'Natividad', the curved-topped 'Virgen de la Caridad' and 'San Ildefonso' and the larger oval 'Coronación de la Virgen' are all masterpieces, of course, full of colour and brilliant light alongside the dark shadows. Perhaps I was just not in the mood to fully appreciate them. El Greco lived, after his marriage in 1548, in the nearby small town of Esquivias.

At this point the map showed a small road running off from the N 401 that cut across country to Humanes de Madrid and then followed the N404 to our next destination, Leganés. There was nothing 'country' about the area though. Soon after leaving Esquivias we quit Toledo province and entered that of Madrid.

From here on, everything gradually became much more built-up, with industrial buildings dotted about all over the place in various stages of completion, most of them sorry-looking affairs, built of corrugated sheeting. Some seemed active, some half-finished and others looked as though they had been abandoned, with older structures already starting to rust. Many were separated from the road by high wire-meshed fences behind which large dogs ran up and down, barking dementedly at the sight of us. These animals looked as though they meant business, so we carried a stick in one hand and a brick in the other – just in case they managed to escape from their enclosures.

Our surroundings became more and more desolate as we continued on our way, with litter all over the place, building rubble dumped by the side of the road and vehicles left, it seemed, where they had broken down.

By the time we reached Humanes de Madrid we wanted to escape from the god-forsaken neighbourhood for a while and decided to look for somewhere to eat. This would at

Abandoned industrial building near Madrid

least get us off the road and away from the nerve-racking hassle from the dogs. We struck lucky. I noticed a concrete, warehouse-like structure with numerous lorries parked outside. In the past we had always found this to be a sign of good, cheap food. My reckoning proved correct for we enjoyed probably the best meal of the whole trip. It consisted of a splendid cocido, followed by a thick slice of juicy pez espada (swordfish) accompanied by crispy patatas fritas, and finished off with a delicious home-made 'flan' (crème caramel). Bob made a note of the address in his little diary.

"If I'm ever out this way again," he declared, "I'll make a point of coming back here to eat."

As we stood outside amid all the out-and-out wretchedness, I asked myself why anyone in their right mind would ever choose to be out this way again!

Feeling much better in stomach and spirit, we pressed on through another estate and soon arrived at a town called Fuenlabrada. It looked pretty hideous but we nevertheless considered staying the night. The ones nearer to Madrid might be even worse!

A little way along the main street we came to a point where the road crossed a slimy-looking stream, which smelled so vile that we had to hold our breath and wave our hands in the air to get rid of the swarm of flies. It seemed to me that all the factories in the vicinity must use this green stretch of liquid for getting rid of their waste products. That decided the issue for us and we carried on to our original destination – Leganés.

Once there, we booked into a cheap little hostal, dumped our bags in the room, and then went out to refresh ourselves. We both felt, and probably looked, pretty grimy and certainly in need of a drink. The nearby buildings looked modern and the bars we came across, with fluorescent lighting on the outside and loud pop music blaring forth from inside, hoped to attract a younger clientele than us. After looking around unsuccessfully for something more to our taste, our growing thirst drove us into the next place we came to. It was called Bar Venus. On the wall above the bar

I noticed a picture of a flamenco dancer sandwiched between photographs of Mick Jagger on one side and Elvis Presley on the other. Bob had once said that, if the opportunity ever came our way, he would dearly like to sample some flamenco and, as I considered us to be near enough to Madrid for there to be a chance, I asked the bored-looking young man behind the bar if he knew of any such music in the area.

He looked up from his newspaper and answered, "No."

If I had been asking for an ounce of hash or where I might find a shot of coke, I think this surly youth might have been of more use, but I could see that we were not his sort of customer. As we stood there sipping our beers, a man standing by himself a short distance away turned towards us and spoke.

"Excuse me, señores," he said, "but you will not find that sort of thing around here, I'm afraid." He let out a puff of cigarette smoke and smiled.

"No," he continued. "The young people do not understand their own culture and prefer to listen to the 'pop' music, you know."

He approached holding out his hand saying, "My name is Fernando."

We shook the proffered hand and then introduced ourselves to him. He was quite a tall man with longer hair than was usual. From his very dark skin and flamboyant clothing, complete with a thick gold chain showing at the open neck of his flowery shirt, I took him to be of Romany stock, and thought that he should know a thing or two about flamenco. He then went on to tell us of a club, not too far away, where they played the sort of music we preferred.

"Just a short drive of eight kilometres," he said, and proceeded to draw a map. I held up my hand to stop him and explained our position.

When he learned that we had no transport, he stood looking us up and down for a moment, shrugged, and then offered to take us there in his car. I translated for Bob. Neither of us was too sure about this colourful character.

"Your offer is very kind, señor," I said, "but it would mean that you would have to return us here for we have taken rooms in a hostal nearby."

No problem. He would be pleased to give us a lift back. Bob thought that we should give it a go. Why not, he asked? What had we got to lose? If the worst came to the worst we could always take a taxi back, couldn't we? He finished off with, "And look at us, Roy! I don't think anyone would consider us worth robbing."

I knew that if we did not go he would never let the matter drop about having missed an opportunity to hear real flamenco and would have held me responsible, so I thanked Fernando and accepted his offer.

As we sped through the streets in his beaten-up old car, our new friend told us that he was from Madrid, unemployed and living with his sister, who ran a bar a short distance away. We would meet her soon, he promised. After what seemed to be a little more than a 'short distance' the car screeched to a halt outside a noisy, brightly-lit bar, wherein he introduced us to his skinny, hollow-eyed sister. She did not appear to be at all pleased to see her brother or us. We sat there being deafened by the blaring juke-box while Fernando knocked back three or four large whiskies in quick succession, treating us to the same. His sister, I saw, raised her eyebrows and muttered something under her breath each time he helped himself to the drinks. There was no hurry, said our guide, for the other place did not start until quite late. It was 11 p.m. When we eventually left (without paying, I noticed) his next bout of skidding scared us so much that I shall never know how we arrived in two pieces. Bob muttered that he would not be letting this mad guy drive him anywhere again.

Once inside this flamenco bar we stood and looked about us. There appeared to be plenty of customers. In the dimly lit interior I saw couples dancing in the small space between tables, with others sitting at a crowded bar. As my eyes became accustomed to the murkiness I suddenly realised that everyone there was male! Nearly all were dressed in women's clothes! Where were we? A transvestite bar!

I could only assume that Fernando, who had disappeared, had taken us for a couple of gays and had brought us here to join in the fun. Bob wanted to clear off at once, but it was not that easy. We had no idea of our present whereabouts or, as usual, the name of our hostal or its address. If we had been able to find a taxi, what could we tell the driver? No, all we could do was accept things and wait for a later joy-ride back with Fernando. The next three or four hours proved quite an experience. The clientele found us interesting and laughed when I told them our story. An apologetic Fernando who, by then, had realised his mistake, was found and brought before us, but he just carried on with his joking and laughed along with the others. By this time he had drunk too much to care anyway.

"Drink up my friends," he cried. "We all make mistakes!"

Later, we saw a show of sorts, but instead of flamenco it turned out to be a transvestite strip show. Ah, well!

As the night wore on and drinks went down, we became more relaxed and agreed that, at least, the evening had not turned out to be boring! By 4 a.m. the crowd had started to break up and leave the building and we soon found ourselves bustled with others through an exit, out into a dark street. Suddenly, over by the front door we saw people shouting and swearing at each other and then, all at once, a fully-fledged fight started. In the centre of it all we spotted our Fernando throwing punches and kicking out for all he was worth. Others rushed over to join the fracas and Bob was all for getting stuck in, to 'give our mate a hand' as he put it. I was not too keen to get involved but, if it had not been for the voice coming out of the darkness, might well have signed up myself. I could not believe my ears.

Someone very near had said, in accented English, "If I were you, I would leave this place at once. The police will soon be here." I looked about me and, at first, could see no one, but then, suddenly, was startled to see a dark, round face looking up at me. Whoever it was sounded female – but then so did most of those we had met in the club.

"Who the hell are you?" the ever-polite Bob demanded of the apparition.

The owner of the face said that she (for she it was) was simply trying to help us. It would be better if we got away from this scene as quickly as possible. Get away? I explained that we had no car and had left our belongings in Leganés.

"Then you can spend the night at my home and take the bus to Leganés tomorrow," she advised.

I thought I had the picture. She was a prostitute.

"Look," I said to her, "we haven't any money, if that's what you're after."

From what I could see of her face in the darkness, she looked offended and certainly sounded it.

"Do as you wish!" she exclaimed angrily. "I am only trying to help you!"

By now, I felt too tired to work things out. The whole evening had been one where events had taken us over and I decided just to drift with the tide.

"Thanks," I said, and we followed her back to an apartment around the corner where she made us coffee and told us more about herself.

It seemed that the poor girl, whose name was Anna, had met up with a Spaniard in her home town of San Fernando, Trinidad. (That was the accent!) The man had popped across to her island from neighbouring Venezuela, seduced her with promises of marriage, made her pregnant, brought her back to Madrid and then cleared off. Since then she had struggled to provide for herself and the baby by doing a bit of 'this and that'. Now, she desperately wanted to get away – preferably to America. Her chatter went on but I was so utterly exhausted that I could hardly keep my eyes open. After handing me a blanket, Anna took Bob by the hand and led him away, while I lay down on the floor and fell fast asleep to the sounds of creaking bed springs. Some time later I emerged from a deep, muddled slumber to the sound of a baby crying somewhere nearby. A light-bulb lit up above my head and a stark naked Anna, with large buttocks and breasts wobbling from side to side, came in and made her way to the other side of the room. I dropped off again until roused later by a clatter of dishes. The smell of coffee suggested that breakfast could be on its way so I sat up to find myself in a tiny area that acted as living, dining, kitchen and, it seems, nursery as well. In came a yawning, stretching Bob who winked at me and then sat at the table. Anna served us coffee and toast, nattering all the time, while a chocolate-coloured infant made little gurgling noises over in the corner.

We left soon afterwards and took a bus back to Leganés where, in the hostal room, I could hardly recognise the haggard, hollow-eyed face that stared back at me from the mirror above the wash basin. So much for our good intentions to end our walk in a bright and cheerful state! The whole affair that evening remains a bit of a mystery. What was Anna doing outside the transvestite club at that hour in the morning? How did she support herself and the baby? Bob would never reveal whether he had paid a donation for her services. He claimed that she had hopes that he might be able to help her get to America.

"Oh, yes!" I retorted. "And what if, instead, she suddenly finds that she has two little mouths to feed!"

25

Parting is such sweet sorrow

It was nearly midday before we arrived back at Leganés to collect our belongings and continue into Madrid.

We sat slumped in our chairs for a while, trying to summon up some energy. The combination of a hectic, near-sleepless night, along with too much booze, had left us dead on our feet. Although our intention had been to walk right across town to reach my friend Anne's house, we changed our minds and decided that Madrid started where the Metro began. Leganés itself, in fact, had become a city suburb and it would not have been too difficult to convince ourselves that we had already completed our journey but, stout fellows that we were, we managed to struggle a few kilometres more to the Metro at Carbanchel. It was a job to stay awake on the comfortable, gently rocking train that took us to our stop in the north of Madrid. From the underground station I telephoned Anne to let her know that we were almost at her door, then we sought out a nearby bar, ordered yet more coffee and sat ourselves wearily down. We needed a little while to ourselves. It would be our last chance.

"Well, man," Bob toasted, raising his cup. "Congratulations. We made it, you old pain in the ass!"

He then reached down into his pack, pulled out two long, Cuban cigars encased in metal tubes, and handed one across the table to me. I realised that he had carried these all the way from America and somehow kept them hidden. His gesture touched me. What could I give him?

"Just a minute," I said, pulling out my little compass. "Here's something for you to remember me by, you miserable old bugger! You can smash it up if you like."

He held it in the palm of his hand and gave it a long look, then gently buttoned it away in his pocket.

Neither of us spoke for a while. We just studied our coffee cups. I broke the silence. How could we possibly smoke these fine cigars without our customary cognacs, I asked?

So there we sat, deep in thought, sipping our drinks and smoking cigars with the realisation that our journey had finished. The cognacs seemed to revive us a little and I understood why the sleepy, early morning drinkers we had seen on our travels had needed their shot of alcohol to get them started. It acted like a squirt of 'easy-start' to boost their engines!

I had been sending postcards to Anne during our trek north so she had been half-expecting us. When we arrived at her house we found a little welcoming party and soon, sitting in soft, comfortable armchairs, we faced a barrage of questions from those assembled. One military-looking type, known as 'the Major', told us how lucky we had been to survive crossing the minefield area north of Toledo. He knew the mines to be a fact!

We stayed in Madrid for a few days more, then Bob flew off to Berlin while I took the train back to Granada and made my way to La Herradura. For quite a while I felt a great sense of loneliness without the company of my walking pal and learned later that he had felt the same way. The shared adventures had made our bond very close. We had learned a lot about each other and about ourselves. Both of us started our walk as grumpy, self-centred, intolerant middle-aged men forced to put up with each other's company in difficult circumstances over a long distance. If nothing else, we must have acquired a degree of tolerance. But more than that. How does the saying go? "A friend in need is a friend indeed"? We certainly came to need each other.

The episode must have ignited some desire to repeat the experience, for the following year we set off again to walk from San Sebastián in the north of Spain, down to Madrid. Then, another year, from Lisbon in the west, across Portugal, to end up once again in Madrid – and finally, from Valencia in the east across to Spain's capital once more. Each time, kind Anne offered us the hospitality of her home. The journeys all more or less covered about five hundred kilometres and our chosen path would be determined by the customary straight line drawn on the map. One thing I had learned from this first trip was that the right equipment made life a bit easier, so I bought myself a decent pair of walking boots for subsequent expeditions.

Although, since then, I have walked many other parts of Spain, including the 700-kilometre stretch along the Pilgrims' Way up in the north, it is the memory of this first hike that sticks in my heart and mind. I imagine that many of the little towns and villages we passed through have changed completely. With new motorways criss-crossing Spain and more people owning cars, the little fondas and hostales we stayed at have probably gone forever.

Tourists with hairy legs will have become commonplace by now and sounds of a snigger are no longer heard. 'Old Spain' is getting harder to find, but I am sure that up in the high sierras there are still little villages with no roads running to them, where people rely on their mules as a means of transport. There the old way of life will not have altered too much and local folk are likely to be as friendly and hospitable as we remember them. Who knows? Perhaps, one day, Bob and I will go and, as he would say, 'check it out'.

"Look up and down that lonesome road,
Hang down your head and cry.
The best of friends is bound to part,
So why not you and I?"
(from 'George Collins', traditional folk song)

The End: Cigars and cognacs